MASCOT — Street cop of 1890s has long symbolized CPP's grass roots approach to protection services. This statuette commemorated firm's 20th Anniversary in 1984. Subsequently, in 1988, CPP acquired Pinkerton's Inc. —the world's oldest private security firm. The combined firms are now called Pinkerton's Inc.

Security Subjects

A Primer For Protection Officers

Security Subjects

A Primer For Protection Officers

By THOMAS W. WATHEN
Chairman
Pinkerton's, Inc.

GUARDIAN SECURITY PUBLICATIONS
Van Nuys, California • USA

Published by GUARDIAN SECURITY PUBLICATIONS
16514 Arminta Street
Van Nuys, California 91406 U.S.A.

Printed in the United States of America

———————————————————

Library of Congress Cataloging in Publication Data

Wathen, Thomas W.
  Security subjects.

  Includes bibliographical references and index.
  1. Police, Private—Handbooks, manuals, etc.
  2. Private security services—Handbooks, manuals, etc.
  3. Industry—Security measures—Handbooks, manuals, etc.
  I . Title.

HV8290.W34   1989   363.2'89   87-14839

ISBN 0-9618588-0-X
ISBN 0-9618588-1-8 (pbk.)

DEDICATION

This book is dedicated with a great feeling of gratitude, respect and sadness to Max Larsen. Max was the editor of the first edition of this book in 1972 and also for this expanded revision. His patience, talent and perseverance were all endearing traits and I am grateful to have called him friend in every sense of the word. Max passed away as this book went to print. I know he would have been proud of its completion.

CONTENTS

PREFACE

The title of this book was derived from a training program the author inaugurated in early 1967. "Security Subjects" was the name given to a numbered series of short transcribed telephone messages used to train and otherwise inform our security officers.

The "Subjects" proved to be an extremely valuable educational tool since all officers, regardless of their locations or shift, could hear instructions in very concise form from the company president personally. Security officers liked this medium, supervisors benefitted and clients were most encouraging. We have continued the program to this date and intend to keep up the service.

In this volume we have bridged together the many "Security Subjects" to create a comprehensive guide for uniformed security officers who truly want to attain proficiency and professionalism in their jobs. The absence of such a guide for our own officers prompted the writing.

My initial thanks go to the officers, staff and clients of California Plant Protection, Inc., CPP Security Service and now CPP/Pinkerton for their loyalty, encouragement, support and their many good ideas. My sincere thanks also to my dear friend, the late Max Larsen, without whose editorial assistance this revision would have taken years to compile. To my many colleagues throughout the world in the American Society for Industrial Security, the Research Security Administrators and the Council of Industrial Security Executives, I express my appreciation of their work and worth and hope this guide will be of some assistance to them.

As this book was being completed, California Plant Protection, Inc., which operated nearly 130 offices throughout the United States and Canada, acquired the venerable Pinkerton's Inc. This occurred on January 19, 1988. We adopted the Pinkerton Corporation and did business as CPP/Pinkerton, throughout 1988. Subsequently, the firm became simply Pinkerton's Inc.

THOMAS W. WATHEN

ACKNOWLEDGEMENTS

First, thanks to Rhoda Boris, my assistant and good friend for 18 years, for her tireless aid on myriad details. My appreciation to Minot Dodson, Gordon Mills and Dick Mayo of CPP for their valuable suggestions on overall contents.

I'm indebted to many experts inside and outside of CPP & Pinkerton's for specialized addenda. Contributors included Bruce Menzies (bank security); Ron Hunt (labor strikes); Dick Dewar (Olympic Games); Ron Schumann (first aid); Jerry Brown (theft terms); Maurice Dispennett (firearms); Carla Gedman, Larry Marshall and Brian Westphal (hospital security); Curtis Moore (airport security); John O'Neill (nuclear security); Gary Stuart, Damon Zumwalt and Peter Kranske (spectator events): Dr. Daniel Blake, California State University (economic crime); Ron Warren (protecting retail stores), and Richard Webster (shopping center security).

Finally, I want to acknowledge key participants in the graphics and production of this textbook. Photo setups were arranged by Lou O'Neal, Norm Laird, George Goddard, Ken Coolidge, Dan Hoyt, Ed Tracy, Dave Hetzel and Art Simmons. I also commend the professionalism of Tony Santoro (art direction); John Forsman and Ernie Cowan (photography); Sheri Masser (typography), and Chuck Colburn of Delta Lithograph Company (printing).

Special thanks to Editor Max Larsen for helping me put it all together.

THOMAS W. WATHEN

CHAPTER 1

PRIDE IN PROFESSIONALISM

PROLOGUE

Society is changing faster now than ever before. Awesome technical advances since World War II have dramatically reshaped the way people live and work.

While this socio-economic change has spawned many benefits, it also has made life more complex. One unwelcome side effect has been an increase in the volume and sophistication of crime. Hence, *security* assumes added importance.

Following are excerpts from a report titled "The Growing Role of Private Security"* released by the National Institute of Justice in July 1984. This abstract summarized a 30-month study conducted for the U.S. Department of Justice by Hallcrest Systems, Inc.

"Today, private security plays a major protective role in the nation's life. Total expenditures for private security products and services were estimated at $22 billion for 1980. In 1979, federal, state and local law enforcement expenditures were only $14 billion.

"Private security personnel outnumber sworn law enforcement personnel and nonmilitary government guards nearly 2 to 1. Total private security employment in 1982 was conservatively estimated at 1.1 million persons—449,000 in proprietary security and 641,000 in contract security.

"The Bureau of Labor Statistics forecasts that about 215,000 new operating personnel will join private security employment by 1990."

---

* The term "private security" includes both proprietary (in-house) and contract security officers and services.

Major findings of this research included:

- "Private security is an often-overlooked resource available to complement police efforts.

- "Potential areas in which the private security industry may play a bigger role are burglar alarm responses, prosecution policies in cases of internal theft, moving hazardous materials, helping to counter terrorism, and security for public events.

- "There is limited interaction and cooperation thus far between the public police and the private security industry in crime prevention and public safety.

- "The quality of security personnel is a major concern to the police, who favor (as does most of the security industry) state legislation to license and upgrade the quality of security personnel. Fewer than half of the states have provisions for licensing and training security officers, despite the existence of standards and model statutes produced in earlier national research.

- "Two major problems hamper police-security relationships— off-duty police moonlighting in private security jobs and the excessive number of false burglary alarms to which police must respond."

Top management recognizes that adequate security—protection of assets—is vital to business success.

Modern security expertise is a distinct discipline. Today corporations are hiring executives specifically schooled and experienced in private security management, rather than ex-law enforcement officers or federal agents. Major American universities grant advanced degrees in security studies.

The old-time night watchman has been replaced by a new breed of uniformed security officers with more education, training, motivation and pride. They have much broader responsibilities, requiring superior proficiency.

Their work is enhanced by better physical security measures, including reliable electronic systems to detect fire and intrusion.

This book is addressed to those officers—protectors of industry and business—proud men and women performing a valuable service in a professional manner.

Unlike 1972, when the first edition of this book was published, a mass of security training literature is available from governmental, academic and corporate sources. Many firms issue manuals to their security officers, tailored to each company's needs. But a modern universal primer, a basic training manual covering the entire private uniformed security sector, is still difficult to find. This book is an attempt to fill that void.

Here is a training compendium learned in the "school of hard knocks" by California Plant Protection, Inc. and Pinkerton's Inc. Instructions are honed to bare essentials to help officers protect people, property and information efficiently.

Hopefully, lessons presented will improve work satisfaction, performance and advancement for security officers everywhere.

BASICS

Take Pride

Edgar A. Guest, the famous Michigan writer of homespun poems, said, "You can do whatever you think you can; it's all in the way you view it."*

Cultivating self-improvement requires an important catalyst: self-esteem. Learning more about security work will help to improve your performance. Then the better you do your job, the more satisfaction you'll get out of it. That's why this book was written—for people like you.

Pinkerton's adopted this principle as the firm's official policy, philosophy and purpose, summarized in the words, "TAKE PRIDE." The following is quoted from our Officer's Manual:

TAKE PRIDE in your position and responsibilities as a security officer; they are important and respectable.

TAKE PRIDE in your company and your fellow officers; they are well qualified and have an unequaled reputation in the business protection field.

TAKE PRIDE in your personal appearance, uniform and equipment; they reflect much credit on you and your company.

TAKE PRIDE in our customers, their employees and their products and services—reflecting your interest and concern for

---

* From "How Do You Tackle Your Work?" *Collected Verse By Edgar A. Guest*, quoted by permission of Henry Regnery Company Publishers, Chicago, Illinois.

some of the finest organizations worldwide.

WE TAKE PRIDE in having you as an employee of Pinkerton. We welcome you to our organization and ask you to remember our basic requirement...TAKE PRIDE.

Main Role

The main reason you are a security officer, whether you work days or nights, on a fixed post or roving, is to *protect the assets assigned to your safekeeping.*

You don't enforce law and order. You *prevent* security breaches within your assigned area. While you're on the job, the business interests under your protection must be your interests.

What Do You Protect?

You protect assets—mainly *people, property* and *information.*

Facilities and assets vary. They're different for a bank, factory, hospital, an office building, airport, a construction site or even a herd of livestock. Classified and/or proprietary information also may be entrusted to your care. But the business owner values employees and patrons (human life) more than money, information, equipment or supplies—more than anything else!

Protecting assets involves controlling losses. You protect profits which enable the company to grow, to hire more people, to buy more equipment, to produce more goods or increase services, and to pay higher wages. You must ensure, in large measure, that this chain of progress is not broken. Losses due to pilferage, fire, work accidents, vandalism or even falsifying timecards shrink profits. Any and all losses diminish job security for employees.

Business management recognizes the necessity to minimize losses. Your presence on the property serves notice that the firm has taken precautions to protect its personnel, property, secrets and profits. You should be extra curious, observant and quick to report anything and everything that might represent a loss or potential loss.

The greatest source of corporate losses is internal stealing. This widespread abuse, called economic crime, costs the nation an estimated $67 billion annually. Everyone picks up the tab: business owners, employees and the general public. This subject is discussed at length in sections headed "Pilferage," "High Cost of Employee Theft," and "Preventing Employee Theft" in Chapter 9.

No Popularity Contest

Doing your job right may not always make you popular. That's one of the minor irritations of your occupation. You cease to be an effective security officer if you permit violations of such rules as "no smoking," "no horseplay" or "no drinking." You must not permit "Good Old Joe" to ignore his company's policies just because you know him. Neither can you overlook mistreatment of equipment without reporting it. You are not being a "fink." You're doing the job you're paid to do—protecting the firm's interests.

Reliability

The single most important quality you must have to be a security officer is *reliability*. If you don't report for duty or don't call to report that you will be absent or late, no one is protecting your post.

If you're not on the job, you can't protect anything there. Your appearance, your physical fitness, alertness, ability to communicate and knowledge of security instructions all go to waste if you fail to show up when scheduled (or even if you're late or leave your post unattended).

All the other directions, reminders and tips in this book are important, but *no rule is more important than being on the job* or reporting early that you will be absent or late.

Attention to Duty

Reliability also consists of attention to significant details.

Firms that have protection services expect security officers to be on duty at all times.

Your duty does not begin and end with your clock patrol. You are required to be alert and sensitive to all possible threats against company assets throughout the entire time you are on duty.

You can't see outside movement or hear unusual noises if you're watching television. You can't hear irregular sounds with a radio on. A personal visitor at your post distracts you from your duties. When reading on post, you cannot be alert to movements within the full range of your vision.

Experience has taught that attention to duty pays off handsomely.

Good Security Habits

Good security habits are truly good friends. They expand your smile and add bounce to your walk. Daily practice of the following pointers is guaranteed to heighten your stature as a security officer:

- **Reliability and promptness**—keys to success for a person or company.
- **Curiosity**—a prime attribute for one in your position.
- **Neatness**—a "must" for anyone in uniform.
- **Courtesy and tact**—your best tools for dealing with other people.
- **Inventiveness**—solving problems through your application of good sense and initiative.
- **Discretion**—keeping a "tight lip" about your business and those who employ you.
- **Loyalty**—knowing you work for an organization that is loyal to you and appreciates your efforts.
- **Tolerance and patience**—coping smoothly with people, things and events during duty hours.
- **Communicating**—reporting unusual things you see or hear in writing.

CHAPTER 2

POLICY GUIDELINES

Rules guide the conduct and action of every security force. These are set forth as performance standards and methods of procedure. They tell the security officer how to behave and how to do his/her work. They present a clear statement of the organization's security policies and practices. The employer's control system educates the security officer and tells him/her how to get help fast to resolve problems.

Facility protection directives are not issued as punitive measures, but as guidelines for tight security. Good directions ensure consistency of practice.

The most common guidelines include an officer's manual (handbook), training aids, post orders, U.S. Department of Defense (DOD) Industrial Security Manual for Safeguarding Classified Information,* and special instructions such as those protecting proprietary information (trade secrets).

When an officer has a question, he/she should be able to get a prompt, reliable answer from a supervisor.

The following sections typify policies for protection officers. These instructions are basic, but not all-inclusive. Historically, government regulations are wordy, hence they are merely mentioned rather than reprinted verbatim. Rules governing firearms, fire prevention and control, protection of information and first aid are only outlined here, since they will be detailed in later chapters.

STATE REGISTRATION

California Plant Protection, Inc., sponsored legislation requiring

---

*The author was privileged as a young Air Force officer to serve on the committee which drafted and coordinated the first DOD Industrial Security Manual in 1954.

state registration of contract security officers. California passed such a bill in 1973. That is believed to be the first state law of its kind. In 1974, California went a step further by establishing firearms training standards for security officers. When this book was published, less than half of the states had statutes for the licensing and training of security officers.

The California law ensures that a private security officer has no significant criminal record at the local, state or federal level (even FBI records are checked). Registration information on file with the state includes a person's name, address, Social Security number, physical description and a full set of fingerprints.

Each officer pays for and keeps a registration slip. It is his or her ticket to work.

PRACTICAL GENERAL POLICIES

If unable to report for duty, officers should phone the security office to which they report in plenty of time for supervision to get a replacement. Acceptable excuses for an absence include an accident or debilitating illness on the part of the officer, or the death or severe illness of a family member.

Security officers assigned to work alone (unsupervised by another officer or other employees of the organization being protected) should be required to call in at least once per hour at times designated by the dispatcher. The dispatcher should be notified by the officer as soon as he or she reports for duty and when ready to go off duty or is relieved. This procedure is for the officer's own protection in case of illness, injury or foul play.

If an officer sustains an injury while on duty, he or she should know where first aid is available. Any injury or accident should be reported by telephone to the home office immediately and, as soon as possible, in writing.

Officers should not have personal visitors while on duty. Relatives or friends who deliver lunch should not remain longer than a few minutes—certainly not more than five minutes.

Officers should not leave the premises of the property or facility to which they are assigned without being properly relieved or at the end of a designated shift.

All officers on all jobs should report regularly to their supervision. When a supervisor is assigned over several persons at the same location, only the supervisor needs to report to management. Daily reports should be required from all facilities, regardless of location and unless otherwise stipulated by management. Report schedules are usually assigned by management.

Keys entrusted to security officers should be promptly attached to a large ring, stick or other device which makes it difficult for the officer to misplace the keys. This will also prevent taking the keys off the job and will make them easier to find if lost.

Any officer who changes his/her address or telephone number should report the change immediately to supervision.

No officer should be accompanied by a dog or other animal of any kind or size while on duty. Insurance restrictions usually limit the use of animals in protection work.

OFFICER'S MANUAL

General Orders

Following are typical general orders stated in a security officer's manual:

1. My first responsibility is the protection of life and property surrounding the post or patrol to which I am assigned.

2. I will maintain a neat appearance at all times in keeping with my position of responsibility.

3. I will maintain a military bearing and a courteous attitude at all times while on duty.

4. I recognize that I am the first person with whom a visitor comes in contact at the facility to which I'm assigned.

5. I will follow all written and verbal orders given by my supervising officers. I will, daily, review all such orders to prevent misunderstanding.

6. I will pass on to my relief any and all orders pertaining to my post. I will not permit anyone to relieve me who is not "fit for duty" but will notify my immediate supervisor and remain on duty until properly relieved.

7. I will not leave my post without authorized relief under penalty of immediate dismissal and may not perform or engage in personal work or activities while on duty without the specific permission of my supervisor.

8. I will not use foul, abusive or blasphemous language at any time, regardless of provocation.

9. I will not wear or carry any firearm or other weapon except with written permission from my employer. In addition, I will comply with all state laws and requirements before wearing any firearm. When required to wear such a weapon, I will keep it in serviceable condition at all times and maintain proficiency in its use.

10. I will report any and all unusual incidents to my immediate supervisor and make a written report of such incidents no later than the end of my current watch (shift).

11. I may not, under penalty of immediate dismissal, sleep, drink intoxicating beverages, engage in horseplay or fight while on duty or while in uniform. (See footnote)

12. Familiarity or unnecessary conversation with employees or other persons on the premises is prohibited.

13. I will familiarize myself with the functions and operations of any emergency communication system, fire hydrants, first aid facilities and use of firefighting equipment. I will know how to reach the police/sheriff and fire departments.

14. Smoking on duty is prohibited except within the confines of the guard house or station when on a fixed post, and then only when not engaged in business. This also applies to eating of lunches and snacks.

15. I will avoid an easy-going or careless attitude.

16. I will refrain from conversation, on or off duty, concerning any official or company problem with anyone not authorized to receive the information.

17. I will never issue a statement to a newspaper, radio or television reporter relative to any activities of the company. Such inquiries will be referred to the public relations department or the security manager.

18. I will not permit vending, soliciting, collecting contributions for any purpose whatsoever or distribution of handbills on the premises I'm protecting without authority of management.

Uniform and Appearance Regulations

1. Unless otherwise specified, all officers will wear the prescribed uniform. No fancy buckles are permitted on regular or "Sam Browne" belts while in uniform.

Neither will I report for duty or be in uniform when I am drinking or taking drugs or medication which could affect my judgement or abilities—even if prescribed.

2. All uniforms must be maintained in a clean and pressed condition.

3. All leather goods including cap visor, belt holster, "Sam Browne" belts and shoes will be shined at all times.

4. Officers will appear on duty clean-shaven and with a neat haircut.

5. Officers are responsible for maintaining in good condition all equipment issued to them or located at their duty post.

6. The uniform shoulder patch will be located three-fourths of an inch from the top shoulder seam. The name tag will be centered above and touching the right breast pocket.

7. When jackets are worn, the breast badge must be on the outer garment and visible to everyone with whom you come in contact.

8. Caps must be worn at all times when not inside an automobile, except on occasions when special headgear is issued.

9. Uniforms may not be worn when off duty except in travel between your home and assigned post.

10. Your employer's regulation shoulder patches are the only kind permitted to be worn.

11. Sweaters and odd jackets are not permitted to be worn over uniforms. Appropriate rain or cold weather coats to be worn over the uniform will be stipulated.

12. Unless on official business, officers may not enter bars, cocktail lounges, taverns or other places where alcoholic beverages are served while in uniform.

PROTECTION OF DATA

Regulations for handling classified data are spelled out by the U.S. Department of Defense.

In addition, most organizations want to keep proprietary data (trade secrets) out of the hands of competitors.

All officers must make sure that sensitive data, either classified or proprietary, are not left out of locked containers or discarded as trash. Restricted areas in which such data are located will be considered "out of bounds" to unauthorized persons. Any negligence or suspicious activity surrounding these areas should be reported, verbally and in writing, to your supervisor.

Protection of information is covered fully in Chapter 10.

CITIZEN'S ARREST

A security officer has no authority under law beyond that of any private citizen. You are, in fact, subject to civil suit for false arrest or imprisonment if you detain someone illegally.

Take no chances. If in doubt, ask your supervisor. Your principal duty is to prevent, rather than to apprehend.

As in all rules, there are extraordinary circumstances under which a citizen's arrest would be proper, as well as helpful to constituted authorities. For example, if you are a direct witness to a felony such as homicide, arson, burglary, robbery or rape, and there is no policeman, sheriff or highway patrolman present or immediately available, a citizen's arrest would be justifiable.

However, this is not to be interpreted that any protection officer would be obligated or required to do so if such action would be in foolish disregard for your own personal safety or that of other innocent parties in the vicinity.

In such a case, look over the situation as calmly as possible and carefully note any information or description for use in the eventual capture, trial and conviction of the criminal.

To make a citizen's arrest, the security officer must have reasonable cause to believe that the person to be arrested is actually committing or attempting to commit a felony, or has just committed a felony and is fleeing.

Information concerning the crime given to you by a third party is *not reasonable cause* to make an arrest of any kind. You must witness the act personally to have any justification for an arrest.

Under no circumstances should you ever "play policeman" either while on or off duty. Evidence of this tendency should result in disciplinary action or dismissal.

SEARCHES

Except in those few instances where an actual arrest is made (for felonies committed in the officer's presence), the right to search is very limited. See your state's Penal Code for exact rules on arrest and search.

If the company to which you are assigned has such rules *in writing*, you may do the following:

1. Require employees to open lunch buckets or bags.

2. Require employees to open briefcases, purses or other hand-

carried containers or packages.

3. Search employees' lockers (only in the presence of a company supervisor and preferably also a union representative).

You may *not:*

1. Search anyone's automobile or other vehicle without their specific permission, which must be witnessed or be in writing.

2. Search anyone's person or clothing without their permission (witnessed or in writing).

3. Search anyone's house, apartment, garage or other dwelling structure without their written permission *and* without a witness (must have both).

For examples of legal precedents, see Search and Seizure section in Chapter 19, Airport Security.

CARE AND USE OF VEHICLES

Company-owned vehicles of any kind are the responsibility of employees operating them. This equipment should be kept clean, neat and operable by the employee to whom it is assigned. Office personnel may arrange for washing exteriors of these vehicles, but the employee operating the vehicle should hose off excessive mud or dirt daily at the end of his/her work period. Autos assigned to protection officers also should be kept clean and neat at all times.

Only the supervisor on duty should sign for gas, oil and maintenance. Repairs of vehicles must be approved by appropriate authority and a purchase order issued.

Usually, only company employees are permitted to ride in that firm's vehicles. A security officer who operates a vehicle of any kind belonging to his/her company cannot carry passengers without express permission from senior management. Insurance requirements make this rule absolutely mandatory.

An officer operating a vehicle must have a valid driver's license and should have no serious prior traffic violations.

When an officer is required to use his or her own car on official business, the officer should be reimbursed. The supervisor should tell the officer the rate of reimbursement *prior* to use of a personal vehicle.

EMERGENCIES

Every security officer should know:

1. How to call police and fire departments serving the area in which he or she is stationed.

2. How to give basic first aid.

3. Locations of the closest fire alarm boxes, all fire extinguishers and hoses and how to use them.

4. How to get around to *all* areas of the premises to which you are assigned and be able to direct others to all areas.

5. Locations of the closest telephone, two-way radio and switchboard.

6. Locations of all doors or exits.

7. How to close sprinkler system valves and their locations.

8. If any special hazards exist in the job area and what precautions are necessary.

9. Locations of all electrical power panels and how to shut off power in case of emergency.

10. How to report any unusual incidents to one's supervisor.

DISPLAYING AMERICAN FLAG

At facilities where the American flag is hoisted, it should be flown each working day. Normally, the flag is not displayed on Saturdays and Sundays unless the firm is working. Holidays such as Lincoln's and Washington's birthdays, Armed Forces Day, Memorial Day, Independence Day (July 4), Veterans Day and Flag Day will be observed by flying the flag regardless of the day of the week on which they fall.

The flag should be flown between sunrise and sunset. Company management will specify the exact time for raising and lowering the flag.

Questions regarding the flag should be referred to your supervisor.

All officers *must* familiarize themselves with the proper way to display the flag, handle it and fold it. Non-security executives appreciate receiving this information.

During the ceremony of raising or lowering the flag, uniformed officers who are observing *must* stand at attention and render a hand salute, or place their caps under their left arms and put their right hands over their hearts until the ceremony is completed. The hand salute with cap is preferable.

TRAINING

In today's high-tech world, a fascinating selection of literature, methodology and audio-visual training aids is available to teach

FLAG DISPLAY—At facilities where national emblem is flown, security officers must know correct way to raise and lower flag.

people all kinds of things.

Which techniques are best for training security officers?

Training a handful of employees in one place is challenging enough. But what approach makes sense for a big company or security contractor that has officers working three shifts around the clock throughout the United States and abroad? Compounding the problem is the fact that different officers have specialized duties based on specific facilities. A department store is different than a hospital. A brickyard is unlike a Hollywood studio. Protecting athletes and spectators at the Olympic Games contrasts with the security of a condominium.

California's Plant Protection. Inc./CPP Security Service faced such a training dilemma.

The firm found that traditional educational techniques, such as classroom instruction, job training teams and stacks of literature, were too costly. Whether these methods would penetrate the force at large was dubious.

Through trial and error, it was learned that a few simple one-on-one (management-to-employee) training approaches were very successful.

Security Lessons by Phone

In 1967, CPP solved part of its training problem by reaching for the phone. This technique is still used.

Three-minute security lessons and other topics affecting all employees are recorded weekly and put on automatic playback equipment leased nominally from the phone company. These messages are then available to anyone who calls that number.

Practical, usable information is slanted to facility protection officers and their level of responsibility. Recordings cover such subjects as "Reliability," "Reports," "Bomb Threats," "Discretion," "Elevator Emergencies," "Firearms Safety," "Fire Prevention," "Burglary," "Employee Theft" and "Airport Security." More than 100 topics related to the private security sector have been recorded. They're constantly kept up to date.

All posts served by the company receive a complete set of printed transcripts of the messages. Each is typed on a single page.

According to the telephone company (then Pacific Telephone), this program was the first use of automatic playback as a training tool.

The messages draw tremendous response. Firms that are not even clients request permission for their security officers to call and get the free lessons entitled "Security Subjects." Permission is always granted.

Here's a sample transcript of one of the weekly "Security Subjects" recorded for automatic playback on the telephone:

THIS IS CPP SECURITY SERVICE SUBJECT NUMBER 1 CONCERNING RELIABILITY

As officers of CPP Security Service, our greatest long-term asset to our company and our clients is RELIABILITY. Without RELIABILITY, all our other talents are of no value. Our neat appearance, alertness, ability to communicate, knowledge of instructions, etc., all go to waste if we fail to be on the job when scheduled or requested. Or, if we fail to perform our assigned duties—when we know we have the ability—we would violate every precept of RELIABILITY, LOYALTY and even HONESTY.

To ensure RELIABLE protective services to our clients, we do several things. Selection and checking our new officers is the first step. Others include an hourly call-in, periodic watchclock patrols, and frequent unannounced supervisory visits. Even so, the real responsibility for doing a RELIABLE job belongs to YOU.

Let me tell you why we chose to discuss RELIABILITY as a training subject. Not too long ago we heard about a manufacturer who had another security service. That other company lost their contract because one of their men was not RELIABLE. He chose to jeopardize his job and the jobs of his fellow officers by going to sleep at his post—with a blanket. "Only for a little while," he said later—after an executive of that company found him while visiting the plant during the off hours.

CPP Security Service officers must recognize the purpose for our hourly call-in and frequent watchclock patrols. They are to ensure your SAFETY first and, at the same time, our RELIABILITY. WE REFUSE TO BE "THAT OTHER COMPANY."

We continue to stress that we are a "TAKE PRIDE" company. We TAKE PRIDE in the fact that our men and women are the best, our service is the best, and our objectives are the best. We know that you cannot be a CPP security officer unless you take pride in your performance and RELIABILITY.

THIS HAS BEEN CPP SECURITY SERVICE SUBJECT NUMBER 1 CONCERNING RELIABILITY

Thomas W. Wathen
President

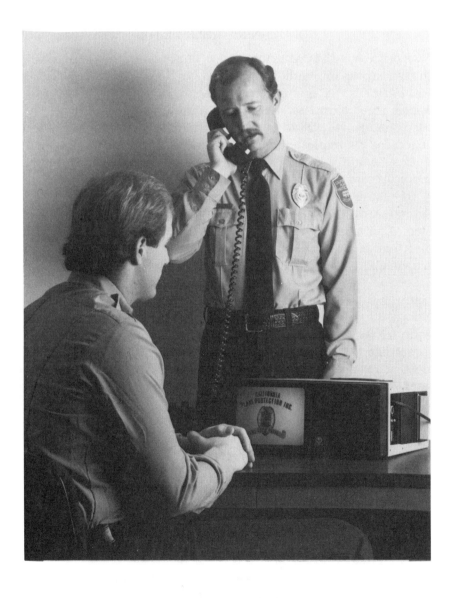

TRAINING FILM—Security officer (seated) views short training film at his duty post. Supervisor (with phone) relieves officer during showing.

Film Presentations

Another training aid that has proven highly effective for CPP Security Service & Pinkerton is a series of film presentations.

Informative contents, easy-to-use equipment, and distribution to every area office comprise the nub of this program. It's a convenient and inexpensive way to ensure that each security officer receives training that will help him/her do a better job.

Each 10- to 15-minute presentation is enclosed in a plastic cartridge combining a film strip and a magnetic sound tape. The projector resembles a small television set. It is a self-contained recycling projector with a built-in screen and sound speaker. Color photos and diagrams (slides) are synchronized with narration.

Typical subject titles include "Techniques of Patrols," "Fire-arms," "First Aid," "Fire Prevention and Control," "Hospital Security" and "Client Relations."

A supervisor takes the lightweight, portable projector to a security officer at his/her duty station and relieves the officer while the latter views the film.

To make sure each film is understood (and to have a record that the officer has seen and heard it), the supervisor gives a short quiz at the end of the presentation. These quick tests are written multiple-choice questions. Here's a sample test question on the film about hospital security:

"Radiology means (a) immediately, (b) x-ray department, (c) lunch time or (d) help!"

The right answer, of course, is (b).

These film strips also have been converted to video tape for viewing on video cassette recorders (VCRs) in Pinkerton's District offices at the time of hire.

POST ORDERS

Post orders cover specific requirements of a duty post. The director of an in-house security force usually oversees post orders for his personnel. A security contractor should prepare post orders for each assigned facility and submit them to the client for approval.

At the top of the orders should be telephone numbers for emergency services, the security officer's own supervision and cognizant organization management. Photographs of executives are very desirable and will enable officers to recognize senior management on sight.

The purpose of the post or patrol is usually stated.

Opening and closing procedures and hours of protection should be spelled out. Instructions should include patrol routes, clock key locations, and officers' duties by shift, day of the week and specific time.

Access control procedures for employees, visitors, vendors and vehicles during both working hours and after hours should be clearly written.

If the organization is a defense contractor or federal agency, post orders will alert security officers to provisions for protecting classified information (if required).

A requirement that an officer be armed, and the reason for it, should be stated in post orders.

Post orders also may include general instructions pertinent to the organization, local weather, socio-economic conditions in the neighborhood surrounding the facility, or other matters relative to the area.

Post Inspections

Periodic post inspections should be a regular procedure of firms with protective services. Purposes of such special inspections are to determine if existing policies and procedures are being met, to find out if all officers have adequate lines of identification and communication with their employer, and to assist security supervisors in establishing the best possible checklists for evaluating performance at each post.

The main aims of post inspections are to ensure that:

1. All officers are properly uniformed, badged, identified and equipped.

2. Telephone and radio communications are well-established and familiar to each security officer. Hourly call-ins for night and weekend assignments are almost always required.

3. All officers have received all of the training currently available.

4. Post orders and emergency numbers are up-to-date.

5. Each post is clean and neat, and reflects credit on the officer assigned to it.

CHAPTER 3

PUBLIC RELATIONS

CREATE A GOOD IMAGE

Building goodwill is one of your most important functions as a security officer.

More and more security officers are needed in busy places open to the public: airports, department stores, banks, hospitals and office buildings. Thus, your value as a goodwill ambassador, as well as protector, is magnified. Such simple courtesies as giving helpful directions become an important part of your work.

A sharp appearance, military bearing and courtesy will enhance your relations with people where you work. At the same time, your professionalism in dealing with the public helps to build a good image for the organization you protect. On duty, you represent them. You may be the first person a visitor meets. To that person, you *are* the company. Hence, you have an obligation to make a good impression.

Cultivate good relations with other employees at your workplace. After all, you're there to protect them. Look upon your association with them as a privilege. Learn who the top executives are and the functions they direct. Familiarize yourself with the organization and the facility layout.

Call people by name whenever possible. "Good morning, Mr. Brown." Small gestures like this will ingratiate you with people, regardless of rank. Be courteous to everyone, including your fellow officers.

MILITARY BEARING

Maintain a military bearing. Keep in mind that your main task is protecting. Your attitude should let everyone know that you intend to follow the rules, and that you expect everyone else to do

RECEPTIONIST—Being a corporate receptionist is a showcase role. Officer must be presentable, courteous, tactful and efficient.

the same. However, don't be so stern that you're abrasive. Exhibit take-charge, no-nonsense control, but also helpful politeness.

It's essential to be friendly, but never to the point where anyone might expect you to bend the rules. If you make the mistake of being too friendly, someone might try to put something over on you. Treat everyone alike.

BEING A RECEPTIONIST

Officers assigned to reception lobbies must display exceptional finesse in dealing with people. A neat appearance and good manners are "musts." The ability to handle a maze of situations promptly and smoothly also is invaluable. It's a showcase role.

If you look sharp and communicate efficiently, you'll make an immediate favorable impression.

One of the first things you should do as a receptionist is to put visitors at ease. You do this with a smile and a cheerful "Good morning (afternoon or evening)" which makes the visitor feel welcome. Then express a sincere desire to help in any way.

Most people who enter a business lobby come to buy or sell. It's important to direct a customer to the proper manager or department at once. Also help salesmen make the right contacts as soon as possible.

Much of your day as a receptionist is spent on the facility telephone. Here's a suggested way to announce a visitor: "Mr. Smith of the Smith Brothers Company is in the lobby to see Mr. Johnson."

That short message gives Johnson's secretary all the information she needs to alert her boss that someone is waiting to see him.

It is considered bad public relations to ask a visitor, "What do you want?" He feels uncomfortable explaining the purpose of his visit (which may be confidential) in the presence of strangers. A better technique, if the visitor is unexpected, is for someone to come to the lobby and address him privately. A secretary or assistant of the person the visitor wants to see should do this.

To save time and avoid embarrassment, the organization's policy on this matter should be explicit in your post orders.

Following are pointers to help you create a good impression and to perform well as a lobby receptionist:

- Be sure the lobby is neat at all times. Keep the reception desk uncluttered.

- Be sure you look presentable. Wear a smile as if it fits you.
- Give all visitors your complete attention. Make them feel welcome.
- Have current magazines or company literature on hand to make waiting less boring for visitors.
- Be sure all visitors sign the register, if a register is kept by the company you are protecting.
- Be sure proper visitors' badges are issued and returned, if required as a security measure.
- See that business cards and messages left for executives get to the right parties as soon as possible.
- Don't be overly familiar with employees or visitors. Be pleasant, but businesslike.
- Don't disclose privileged information of any kind.

POST ORDERS

Every special post has distinct requirements stipulated by security management. These vary from post to post and from company to company. Every propriety must be observed.

Make sure your duties—especially where you have extensive contact with the public—are clearly spelled out in your post orders.

Know what's expected of you, then make good practices habitual.

PLUS FACTORS

Good public relations is not complicated, nor should it be. It boils down to the application of common sense by each officer, in his or her way, to each day's routine.

An excellent starting point is a prideful attitude toward your job. That makes it easier for you to do a *good* job.

You'll find consistent development of these qualities extremely rewarding in your work:

Neat Appearance

Your appearance is a subtle, silent form of communication—visual communication. It conveys to other people a quick "reading" about you. How you look sparks an instant impression, positive or negative, in the mind of a beholder. Is your uniform clean and neat? Cap brim polished? Is your hair well groomed? All buttons buttoned? Are you wearing a proper uniform tie and stockings? Shoes shined? Take a hard look at yourself. If you were a stranger or one of your own supervisors, would you be pleased with your appearance?

The man or woman who looks sharp gets the most respect from the start.

Courtesy

Some people think military bearing and courtesy don't go together. While you are on duty, they *must* go hand in hand. Since you're employed to protect the lives and property of others, you must enforce certain controls. To do so, you must *look the part* in appearance and bearing. But you cannot forget the value of being courteous at all times.

How to be courteous is neither puzzling nor difficult. It means having a sincere desire to please. It means being cheerful with company personnel and the public. However, don't be overly talkative. Strive for disciplined politeness.

Learn to control your temper, no matter what the provocation. If someone gripes about something, listen to the complaint. Explain the company rules pleasantly but firmly. Show a willingness to help in any way you can.

Tidy Station

The appearance of your duty station is almost as important as your appearance. You and your work environment go together.

If you're stationed at a gate or an out-of-the-way place, you still come under scrutiny. In your work area, are the walls papered with risque photos and/or calendars? Are telephone numbers scrawled at random around the interior? Is the desk or counter cluttered with miscellaneous junk in which official business sometimes gets misplaced? Is your station well-equipped or cluttered with cooking and coffee-brewing utensils? Do you have a radio or television set that doesn't belong there? Are your post orders handy and neat or "dog-eared"? Does the roof leak? Are the windows clean? Does the woodwork need cleaning, polishing or painting?

Take a hard look at your station. Hopefully, you'll spruce it up so that it makes a good impression on those whose respect is valuable to you.

SOLID COMFORT—In real life, this cozy setup would defeat respect. How many wrong security practices can you spot in this cartoon?

Attentiveness

Attentiveness is the art of being a good listener. This is a capability you should master to handle people successfully.

When someone is explaining a problem to you, do you not interrupt before he has defined the problem?

If complex information is being given to you, do you ask the speaker politely to bear with you while you write down the main points?

Can you continue to listen to an unusual inquiry, even though you know you'll have to bow out of the situation?

Can you listen to a fast or strange talker and remember the gist of what he said?

If your answer is yes to all of these questions, then you're a good listener.

Patience

Patience is the quality of composure or forebearance.

Patience is keeping your "cool" when you're coping with an obnoxious person, a line of impatient people, a tangle of frustrating details, or any departure from easy routine.

Patience is calming down a distraught mother who has lost a child in an airport terminal. Composure is also called for to conduct a thorough search.

Patience is excusing yourself to answer the phone while you are signing-in and badging a VIP. His patience also may be sorely tested in this situation!

Tact

Tact is the ability to deal with others without offending. Tact entails sensitivity to other people's feelings. It rounds out patience.

Classical Example. The author learned of a textbook case of tact through a complimentary letter from the board chairman of a large client company.

The VIP had to meet the manager of one of the firm's suburban branches on a Sunday morning. They agreed by phone to get together at the manager's office. The plant was closed that day.

At the factory only one gate was open. The security officer on duty didn't know the visitor, but greeted him pleasantly. The stranger gave his name. He said he was an executive in the company (without revealing his position) and that he had an appointment with the plant manager.

The officer said no one was in the plant. Nevertheless, he phoned the manager's office. There was no answer.

The visitor asked if he could wait in the lobby. He said he was sure it would be alright.

"I'd hardly spoken the words before I realized there was no way for him to know I was telling the truth," the VIP wrote.

The security officer said that company rules required him to keep all visitors at the gate until he got permission for them to enter. He courteously asked the stranger to park near the gate and wait there.

"It occurred to me that the officer had done exactly the right thing," the VIP continued. "He'd been both polite and firm. By phoning the manager's office when he knew there would be no answer, he was trying to be helpful as well."

In a few minutes, the tardy manager arrived and explained that he'd had a flat tire and couldn't get to a phone.

The VIP closed his letter by praising the outstanding performance of the security officer.

That officer demonstrated a classical example of tact. He obeyed the rules, even though it meant keeping the chairman of the board outside one of his own facilities.

Discretion

One of the most important things a security officer must do is keep buttoned lips.

You must watch what you say, when and where you say it, and to whom you say it. That's discretion.

The dictionary defines discretion as prudence, especially cautious reserve in speech.

Unlike talkative persons who can't resist telling all they have seen, heard or done, security officers cannot reveal information loosely. Being gabby is contrary to the basic purpose of protecting.

High on the list of people to whom you shouldn't disclose information are poll takers, market survey researchers, union organizers and phone callers requesting unusual information.

Also don't talk freely with the press (see Press Relations later in this chapter).

Be courteous, be businesslike, but be wary of what you say to others. Avoid unauthorized disclosures.

Always be sure to report any attempt to get information from you.

Impartiality

Your control responsibilities require strict impartiality. Treat everyone alike. It's closely related to discretion.

A prime example of when to be impartial is during political campaigns. Avoid discussing politics with employees at the facility to which you are assigned. Your functions include controlling others. Your uniform is a symbol of authority. Your words and actions demand impartiality. Don't wear political buttons on your uniform. However, don't criticize employees with such baubles on their clothing.

On the positive side, it's commendable to take an interest in the issues and candidates. By all means, exercise your priceless heritage to vote. Just don't let your political bent interfere with your work. Your own sound judgment will tell you how far to go without impairing your effectiveness on the job.

Your impartiality while on duty makes you a more skillful controller of people—in short, a better officer.

Rapport with Fellow Officers

No other human relations are more vital to your function than harmony with your fellow officers.

Often recognition from them is the only "pat on the back" you get for a job well done. Hopefully, your colleagues will relay such compliments to your supervision.

You should cooperate with your fellow officers because, as a team, you provide superior security service. You depend on each other. Without *esprit de corps*—group enthusiasm—overall efficiency drops dramatically. The reason is very simple: loss of pride. Sagging self-esteem is mirrored in disregard for co-workers, and vice versa.

Because a rapidly growing number of females have become security officers, there has been a corresponding increase in incidents between the sexes. Male officers especially must be careful not to touch, make lewd remarks, use foul or blasphemous language or even make amorous advances to their fellow female officers. Such conduct could be considered as sexual harassment, violating state or federal laws. Supervisors are urged to watch for such infractions.

You'll find that rapport with your fellow officers, or lack of it, actually affects your disposition. Think about that. Do you want to be characterized as pleasant or sour? The choice is entirely up to you. Your disposition has a direct bearing on everything you do. If you practice cooperation, the biggest benefactor will be YOU!

Another thought worth remembering is that you and your fellow officers protect each other. Doing your job right and passing along sharp observations aids those who follow you on shift, your supervisors and your employer. A more efficient organization strengthens job security for all.

Reliability Restressed

The single most important quality demanded by your position is reliability.

You must be completely trustworthy. You're expected to be on duty when you're supposed to be. If not, you can't protect the firm's assets. In your specialty, reliability is your prime asset.

Desirable traits include attention to duty, alertness, promptness, strong loyalty, ample reporting, vigilant curiosity, inventiveness and temperance. Reliability ties them all together.

You are paid to be dependable.

PRESS RELATIONS

Many events at the company you serve may be newsworthy. Facility expansion. Impressive annual profits. Top management shuffle. A heroic employee. New product or service. A labor strike. A fire. A crime. News and feature topics abound.

One of the firm's major public relations goals is *favorable* mention in the mass media. The company generates its own news releases. Also the press is invited to the facility for special coverage.

On a fast-breaking story, reporters may show up uninvited. Often the first person they confront is you. They're smart and they're aggressive. They may pump you for information or take your picture without permission.

Your responsibility in this situation is clear. You're usually asked not to make statements to newspaper, magazine, radio or television reporters. Instead, direct them to the firm's public relations department or an executive named in your post orders.

Stay calm. Be courteous, but retain control. Explain the company rules. Tell reporters you'll call an authorized spokesman immediately to answer their questions. Don't be too cold or gruff. News media people resent the worn-out snub "no comment." Be friendly, but be discreet.

CHAPTER 4

COMMUNICATIONS AND REPORTS

YOUR GREATEST VALUE

Your greatest value as a security officer is your ability to communicate information accurately and promptly.

You communicate (report) by speaking and writing.

Besides being on the job, reporting is the most important responsibility you have. Good reports—oral and written—elevate you far above the ordinary security officer.

You are trained to protect people, facilities and sensitive information. You should be alert to anything and everything that spells trouble. You are the eyes, ears and even nose of the organization you protect. But your sharpest observations are worthless unless you report them to your supervisor, the security manager or, if urgency dictates, medical personnel, police, firemen or other emergency responders.

Communication Tools

Security officers communicate in many ways: face-to-face conversations, on the telephone and in writing. You also use special communication tools such as walkie-talkies, intercoms, two-way command post and car radios, and computer terminals. Communication equipment is covered fully in Chapter 14, Physical Security.

Learn to use the devices at your post well. Have telephone numbers you use often and emergency numbers handy for instant access. Learn the locations of interior and exterior telephones along your patrol route. Know how to reach key people in a hurry.

PERSPECTIVE

Humans start communicating at birth. Spanking a newborn baby's posterior elicits a loud wail. The infant communicates pain. That initial outcry activates breathing. One's first communication is highly satisfactory to all concerned parties within earshot.

To assume that everyone, after such an excellent start, will be an apt communicator is false logic. Ability to communicate grows as a person learns to meet the demands of life. Skillful communication is acquired. It doesn't happen spontaneously.

Communication is an exchange of messages between two people or among many. It involves sending and receiving.

A person talking to himself is not communicating. He's conducting a monologue.

Effective communications are easy to understand, accurate and prompt. Garbled messages are confusing. Incomplete messages leave the receiver groping for more details. Inaccurate messages can be dangerously misleading. No message at all is sheer vacuum.

INFORMATION LINKS

You are just one person with but one set of eyes and ears. No matter how efficient you are, you can't observe, know and control everything.

However, you're a member of a team—a network tied together and made strong by *effective* communications. That's why every scrap of information you report is potentially valuable. Your information, together with that gathered by your fellow officers, will give a more complete and meaningful picture of the situation at the facility you protect. Such team effort provides a better security overview.

You never know when something you report will prove to be invaluable—a vital link in a chain of information. For example, a security officer at a remote California post noticed an automobile in an unusual spot at an unusual hour near a neighboring plant. He jotted down the time, color and make of the car, and the fact that two men were with the car. Later, it was discovered that the nearby plant had been burglarized. The security officer's notes assisted the county sheriff in apprehending the burglars that same week.

Even though that incident occurred beyond the premises the

officer was protecting, his alertness reflected favorably on his entire organization. He was commended by his supervision, company management and law enforcement officials.

TELEPHONE TECHNIQUE

First impressions are important. A courteous approach enables you to accomplish your job easily and pleasantly.

Answering the telephone, like other personal contacts, affords you the opportunity to make a good first impression. Your civility and tact are valuable assets to you and the firm you protect.

Many of you use the telephone constantly during day shifts at lobbies and gates. Others are required to answer the telephone on evenings, weekends or holidays. Keep these factors in mind whenever you use the phone professionally:

1. As a security officer, you give and receive messages by phone. Talk to the person at the other end of the line as you would face-to-face.

2. Keep conversations brief. Avoid unnecessary chit-chat. That wastes valuable time, takes you away from your security function, and often keeps someone waiting while you're talking.

3. Be aware of people nearby who may be listening to your conversation. Make sure your overheard remarks don't create a bad impression.

4. Assume that every telephone call is important. You may have to answer the phone when you're busy. Never allow annoyance to show in your response. If you sound grumpy, the caller forms a negative opinion about you and the organization you represent.

Notice your method of answering the phone. Are you pleasant but brief? Is your voice distinct, or do you slur certain words, causing the caller to ask you to repeat what you said? Be pleasant, business-like, helpful and polite, but be distinct.

Identify yourself and the firm you serve immediately when you answer the phone. A plain "hello" won't do. A better answer is the name of the company followed by your own name, such as: "ABC Company, Officer Jones speaking." If you have a hard-to-pronounce name, say: "ABC Company, Security Office."

Ask your supervisor, if he has not done so, to include in your post orders the appropriate phrases you should use in telephone conversations.

It's a good idea to know the caller's identity and to understand the message so you can screen out "freaks" and channel bonafide inquiries to proper personnel.

For more pointers on telephone technique, see Being a Receptionist in Chapter 3, Public Relations.

Telephone Reports

Nights and weekends, it's good practice for contract security officers to phone reports to their area office every hour. These call-in reports protect the officer and keep his/her supervision well informed.

Telephone immediately to get help and to notify your command post in the event of an injury or illness, death, a fire, natural disaster (such as a flood), disturbance in a parking lot, improper activity anywhere within your vision, and any work stoppage, walkout or strike.

You should also phone your supervision immediately when you or a fellow officer has been abused for refusing entry to an intoxicated person. Security controllers also want to know (promptly by telephone) when any officer is unable to work because of illness, fatigue or intoxication.

Company management should not be bothered with matters like this. It's best to let your supervisor take care of these problems.

Post orders may require special reporting instructions at certain stations. Examples are executives who want immediate telephonic notification of such events as a death, fire, explosion, impending riot or news media inquiries.

WRITTEN REPORTS

Security officials to whom you report appreciate a variety of written information from you. Some of it may seem trivial or unimportant to you.

You should report everything out of the ordinary that comes to your attention. While facts are preferable to opinions, things you've observed or heard—even rumors—may cause you to have a strong hunch that something improper is going on or is about to happen. Maybe another officer has had the same hunch. That could add up to trouble ahead. So, by all means, tell your supervision.

Potential problems cannot be averted if they're not reported. Prompt reporting of anything faulty is the best insurance that it will be corrected quickly.

Security management wants to know about anything that varies from the normal—even if you've taken the required action and, seemingly, the incident is closed.

Later sections in this chapter spell out numerous things to report, as well as types of reports.

Writing Tips

If you think report writing is hard or dull, you're harboring unnecessary mental blocks. You needn't worry about your "literary" style or grammar. No one expects you to be an expert wordsmith. Your supervision is more interested in *what* you report than *how* you express it. You'll find that your observations will become sharper and you'll enjoy your work more if you practice—not fancy writing, but better reporting.

Here are some tips to help you write useful reports:

- Keep a notebook to record on-the-spot observances.
- Use legible handwriting. If you can't write plainly, print.
- Be accurate. Spell names correctly. State time precisely. Use civilian time (1 p.m.). Military time (1300) is not recognized in court.
- Write the way you talk.
- Tell it so it's easy to understand.
- Use words that are familiar to you.
- Use short words and sentences. Simple is better than complex. Big words and long sentences make communications foggy.
- Write reports that are clear, correct and complete.
- Be as brief as possible, but not at the sacrifice of thoroughness. To assure completeness, your information should answer these questions: Who? What? Where? When? Why? and How?
- Write to inform, not to impress.

WHAT TO REPORT

You've done your job well if you called the right people for help in an emergency.

When making your patrol rounds, let nothing escape your attention—faucets left on, gates that won't close, defective locks or doors, burned-out lights, trash accumulation, fire hazards, irregular employee activities and unusual visitors.

It's hard to imagine not finding *something* on each shift to report to security management.

Think of yourself as a human alarm system. Constantly snoop for safety hazards and any evidence of theft or potential theft. Then be sure to report *anything* that doesn't look right, even if it seems minor to you. Train yourself to eagle-eye details so you can spot abnormalities quickly.

Common Hazards

These are common hazards you should watch for *and* report:

- Slippery floors
- Tripping hazards such as hose lines or piping
- Inadequate warning signs or barriers at excavations or open manholes
- Missing or inoperative entrance and exit lights
- Poorly lighted stairs
- Loose handrails or guard rails
- Loose or broken wiring
- Defective ladders or scaffolding
- Leaks of water, steam, oil, gasoline or chemicals
- Unusual fumes
- Dangerously piled supplies or equipment
- Open or broken windows
- Unlocked doors and gates
- Unnecessary lights
- Electrical equipment left running
- Blocked aisles
- Blocked firefighting equipment
- Open fire doors
- Evidence of equipment overheating
- Company products, equipment or material apparently hidden or set aside under suspicious circumstances
- Evidence of illegal entry or trespass
- Uncovered containers of solvents

FIRE HAZARD—Smoking where flammables are stored is extremely dangerous. Luckily, security officer at right catches and reprimands this careless smoker.

- Oily rags
- Evidence of smoking in "no smoking" areas
- Roof leaks
- Unusual sounds
- Closed sprinkler valves
- Any unsafe condition.

What's an Incident?

What is a reportable incident? It is *anything* out of the ordinary! It's an accident, illness, auto wreck, a fist fight, drunken employee, fire, damaging wind or rain, an arrest by police, attempted theft, or vandalism anywhere on the job site. The list is endless.

You cannot write too many reports, only too few.

The officer who fails to report something extraordinary he/she has done, or seen, or heard on shift, is simply not doing a competent job.

Signs of Dishonesty

You should constantly be alert for telltale signs of dishonesty. They could indicate theft or vandalism. Reporting such suspicious activities to your supervisor will bring them to the attention of management. The security manager of the firm you are protecting counts on you to tell him what you've seen and heard while on duty. Your reports communicate this information.

Here are suspicious activities you should always report:

- Overly friendly employees who may be attempting to divert your attention
- Persons carrying packages or large purses in and out of a facility other than a retail store
- Frequent visits by employees to their cars during working hours
- Employees returning to the workplace during off-hours
- Loitering around parking areas or on the fringe of company premises.

Think Positively

Don't listen to the pessimist who tells you, "Why report? They (managers) never do anything about it anyway. Nobody cares."

Business owners care a great deal. Remember, one of the vital requisites for business success is controlling losses—protection of assets.

Your job is to report and report and report. Your communications are the core of protection services.

If you feel a problem you reported is being ignored or mishandled, mention it to your supervisor again. Ask if any further action is required on your part. Then let him or her take care of it.

Never bypass your boss and take up what you regard as an oversight directly with higher management. Such a blunder could provoke sticky repercussions.

NONDISCLOSURE

Treat Privileged Information Discreetly

The opposite of communicating is guarding your tongue. Watch what you say to others. Be discreet.

Tell your supervisor about everything you see and hear. Supervisors must know what's going on at your post. Your supervisor will keep the security manager informed.

But keep your reports "in the family." Don't share facts and rumors you collect with anyone not privileged to receive such information.

Don't say anything to newspaper, magazine, radio or TV reporters without proper authorization. The same goes for polltakers, union organizers, and people who simply phone and ask for unusual information. Any attempt to solicit information from you should be mentioned in your daily activity report.

TYPES OF REPORTS

Reporting procedures vary from company to company. A practical gauge for the number and quality of reports required is *adequate security*. No sensible director dilutes the enthusiasm and efficiency of his security force with too much paperwork. On the other hand, better protection is maintained with too much information than with too little.

Following are common types of reports, with notes on how to make them effective:

WRITTEN REPORTS—Better protection is maintained with adequate reporting. Here officer makes entries in Daily Activity Report covering his shift.

Daily Activity Report

Daily activity reports (see photo) cover each shift worked. The report should be completed on an on-going basis. It shouldn't be filled out in advance nor at the end of the shift when the officer's memory may be hazy.

Common sense is urged to make the report meaningful. Data recorded might include:

- Name and badge number of reporting officer
- Date and time of duty
- Name of officer relieved
- Time each Detex clock round begins
- Names of special visitors
- Safety or fire hazards noted
- Times of phone call-ins to command post
- Burned-out lights or defective locks, doors or gates
- Unusual incidents such as an accident or illness (these require a separate incident report for more details)
- Suggestions to improve security
- Contacts with any city, county, state or federal representatives—and the reason why
- Other items requested by management or stated in post orders.

Thorough reporting, regardless of the importance an officer attaches to an incident, is preferred over brevity.

A guiding rule of thumb is that a daily activity report is worth precisely the value of the information it contains. A security officer who turns in a poor report is presumed to have turned in a poor performance, too.

Incident Report

An incident report elaborates on a happening referred to in the daily activity report.

Details should include a description of the incident, action taken, and comments and recommendations.

To make sure all the facts are recorded, an officer should ascertain that these questions are answered: Who? What? Where? When? Why? and How?

The action taken should include who investigated, who was notified and whether or not the situation was corrected.

In his/her comments, an officer should indicate if further

OFFICER'S DAILY ACTIVITY REPORT

Corporate Offices: 6727 Odessa Avenue, Van Nuys, CA 91406

Date:_____ Shift: From _____ To _____

Client _____

	Yes	No	Were There Any	TIME
Items No. 1 through 13 must be checked (✓) Yes or No. Items checked Yes must be explained.				
1			New Instructions Received	
2			Fire Doors, Exits Blocked	
3			Other Fire Hazards	
4			Security, Exit Lights Out	
5			Other Safety Hazards	
6			Equipment Left On	
7			Window, Doors Unlocked	
8			Vaults, Safes Open	
9			Offices Unlocked	
10			Parking Violations	
11			Property Damaged	
12			Smoking Violations	
13			Defective Equipment	

SUBMITTED BY

_____

BADGE # _____

KEYS AND EQUIPMENT
RECEIVED IN GOOD
ORDER BY

_____

BADGE # _____

#012

WE TAKE PRIDE ®

PINKERTON INCIDENT REPORT FORM — illustrates simplicity but thoroughness recommended in reporting security infractions or unusual events.

action is needed. The officer might also recommend how future incidents of this kind can be prevented.

An incident report should be completed immediately after response has been taken to the incident.

A typical report form is that of Pinkerton's (see illustration). Some firms' incident reports are in checklist form.

Missing Property Report

A missing property report is filled out when an officer learns something of value is missing and presumed stolen.

Missing property can be company or personal property that is stolen, borrowed or just plain lost.

Highly valuable items and classified or proprietary information receive foremost consideration. But the disappearance of such things as desk pen sets, coffee pool change, even sandwiches, should be reported. Although these items may seem insignificant, their loss over a period of time could point to a pattern which might grow into more serious theft. Reporting such losses provides the basis for successful investigation and an early stop to pilferage. Losses due to pilferage amount to billions of dollars annually—hardly penny ante (see Chapter 9).

Sign-in Log or Visitors Register

Security officers use sign-in logs to record who is granted access to facilities. A visitors register is usually located in a company's lobby. At some industrial plants, sign-in logs also are kept at gates.

It is good security practice to require all visitors to sign in or be registered by the officer on duty. The same holds true for employees who show up before or after normal working hours.

Vehicular Traffic Log

A vehicular traffic log records movements of cars and trucks in and out of company premises. The log shows date, time in and out, description of vehicle or license number, and sometimes the name of an outside firm that owns or uses the vehicle.

Often an employer has a fleet of passenger cars operated by chauffeurs or other personnel, such as salesmen. These autos should be checked to ensure that only authorized persons are driving them. The vehicular log usually includes the identity of the driver, special passengers carried, and destination. Records also are kept on mileage.

Thoroughness of inspection depends upon the needs of management.

It's good security practice to inspect each vehicle for contraband. Each car and truck also should be inspected for external damage.

Employees have been known to use company vehicles as a means of stealing company property.

You may sometimes frown over the volume of details you have to log about vehicles. But keep in mind that the value of such completeness may show up later—in an accident investigation or tracing a crime.

In summary, your greatest value as a security officer is your ability to communicate information accurately and promptly.

ⓜ **MOTOROLA** *"10" SIGNALS*

10-4	OK-acknowledged.	**10-19**	Return to base.
10-6	Busy-Stand by.	**10-20**	What is your location?
10-7	Out of vehicle/service.	**10-22**	Disregard last message.
10-8	Back in vehicle/service.	**10-25**	Report in to/Call.
10-9	Repeat Message.	**10-26**	My ETA is.
10-10	Negative.	**10-31**	New assignment is/at.
10-11	Slower/Can't understand.	**10-96**	Need following parts/equipment.
10-14	My location is.	**10-**	_____
10-17	Enroute.	**10-**	_____

Remove backing and stick to sunvisor or dash

CHAPTER 5

PATROL TECHNIQUES

The rank or title of patrolman, which most security officers carry on their badges, is also a job description. The precise industrial security definition is "moving about or around a given area to maintain security."

Your clear understanding of *why* you are required to patrol will make your job easier and more meaningful and will make you a more effective officer.

The objective of a patrol is to protect buildings and their contents from fire and water damage, intruders, thieves or vandals.

RECORDING CLOCK SYSTEM

Most security officers are required by their post orders to patrol and to record their movements with a recording clock as they proceed to numbered key stations throughout the facilities entrusted to their protection. Each post should have a map or plot showing the locations of key stations and the frequency of required patrols.

There are very few assignments that do not require outside supervision and monitoring. Most posts, for instance, average less than 168 hours per week, or one officer around the clock.

During those hours when an officer is basically alone or working with only the maintenance people or a skeleton crew, the officer is usually required to patrol the area under his/her jurisdiction.

The recording clock system is designed to assist both the officer and his/her employer and is usually required by the fire insurance carrier.

The system usually consists of keys, each embossed with a

DETEX CLOCK—Key chained to a numbered station is inserted in Detex clock carried by security officer. Action records when he inspected a given area while on patrol.

different number or symbol, and a clock into which the keys are inserted and turned. The key imprints or punches its number on a paper disc or paper tape locked inside the clock. The keys are securely mounted, usually in small metal containers placed at strategic locations throughout the area to be patrolled.

Making one's rounds, an officer carries the clock and records his/her presence at all of the assigned key stations.

Computerization has been applied to the recording clock system to provide a fast electronic record of patrols. In one version, key stations are wired to a remote computer. The officer carries a key which he inserts at each station. This records the fact that he was at given checkpoints at certain times.

A newer method uses a coded strip as a control station. Each strip is about 3½ inches long, ¾-inch wide and ⅛-inch thick. It has a groove running down one side. Strips are installed on walls along the patrol route. Instead of a control clock, the officer carries a data acquisition unit. This hand-held device (about 8 by 3 by 1½ inches in size) has a snout-like fixture at one end that fits the groove in the wall strip. The data acquisition unit is inserted into and swiped along the groove. The portable unit reads and records data stored on each strip (such as date and time) by means of an electromagnetic system. It is battery-powered. The security officer turns in the unit at the end of his shift.

Many computer hookups and accessories are available. Information is easily transferred from a data acquisition unit to a computer, disc or cassette. A computer makes possible an instant readout on a video screen or a printout on paper.

CALL-IN PROCEDURE

An hourly call-in requirement is sound procedure for officers who work at night, on weekends or on holidays.

You would normally call your check-in point or the dispatcher at least once each hour. Checkers and dispatchers who receive your calls have a grave responsibility to you and your fellow officers. If you fail to call on schedule, they must react by calling you or calling your supervisor. If they fail to do these things, it may be at *your* expense.

If you become ill, have an accident or are involved in some trouble which prevents you from calling, the checker or dispatcher is not doing you a favor by not notifying supervision; they are not dependable for you. If you are in trouble, you need them to call someone to help you as soon as possible.

The officer who simply dozes will be awakened by the dispatcher's call, but if the dispatcher or checker fails to call, you will keep sleeping, miss a clock round, miss a prowler in the parking lot, or be caught asleep by management or your own supervisor—then you are in real trouble. If you are asleep, wouldn't you rather be awakened by the checkpoint or your own supervisor?

The call-in policy is designed for *your* protection, *your* safety and the collective reputations of you and your fellow officers. Since it is basically *yours*, be sure it is used to your advantage.

TENDING BUSINESS

While on patrol, you serve as the eyes, ears and in some cases the nose of the company's top management when they are not there. They count on you to tell them, through their security manager, what you observed while on patrol.

For example, did anyone unusual visit the facility? Did any employee come back to work late? Janitors leave early? Lights burned out anywhere? Any equipment overheated, broken down, or left running unattended? Any fire extinguishers blocked? Any doors found unlocked?

The facility needs patrols to ensure that you have penetrated, observed and inspected all areas which need protection.

Key stations should be located where they will provide maximal surveillance. This takes careful security planning. Such plans should meet all regulations governing safety or required by the organization's insurance carrier.

CORRECT PATROL PROCEDURES

Know Your Functions

Once you understand why patrols are necessary, you can proceed to the proper techniques—the *how to* part of your training.

It's essential that you know your functions and how to perform them. By knowing what is expected of you, you will know when to call your supervisor for assistance.

Before performing a patrol, you should be familiar with the general orders and post orders covering your place of assignment. Your supervisor or a qualified fellow officer should show you the basic layout of the facility and where to locate the various key stations. Follow his or her instructions carefully and keep your eyes open. Some patrol routes are complicated, and you don't want to be confused. Ask plenty of questions because each post is distinctly different.

The objective of a patrol is *not* merely to visit each key station like a robot. Don't blindfold yourself. *You must be alert, cautious and curious.* Be careful not to move too fast and risk overlooking something you should have seen, heard or smelled.

Above all, be sure to report or record anything improper or unusual that you discover.

Patrol Preparations

Before you begin a patrol, you must:

1. Know your general orders.
2. Know your post orders.
3. Know your patrol route.
4. Know the locations and purposes of all key stations.
5. Know the locations of emergency equipment and communications devices along the patrol route.
6. Have the right patrol aids. Items include:
   - Full uniform, with badge in plain view
   - Notebook and pen or pencil
   - Flashlight
   - Recording clock
   - Security keys
   - Pre-tested walkie-talkie or pager, if either is used
   - Special gear such as hard hat, safety glasses and whistle, if required
   - Properly serviced vehicle, if you're on auto patrol
   - Checklist of patrol items and areas to be inspected
7. Formally relieve your predecessor.

First Patrol Most Important

Your first patrol on each shift is the most important. Take your time. Be especially alert and curious during this patrol. Know what to look for. Dangerous situations or hazardous conditions should be discovered early so they can be corrected promptly. Be especially careful if production employees are leaving as you arrive. In their haste, departing employees often create potential security risks. You must observe careless oversights and nullify those that threaten security.

To ensure thoroughness, carry a checklist of the main things you're supposed to inspect or do. Take notes.

Some security firms print a safety checklist on the margin of an officer's daily activity report. The officer simply checks "yes" or "no" to a list of deficiencies. If an item is checked "yes," it must be explained. Typical entries include:

- Fire doors, exits blocked
- Other fire hazards
- Security, exit lights out
- Dangerous chemicals improperly stored
- Any safety hazards
- Equipment left on
- Windows, doors unlocked
- Vaults, safes open
- Offices unlocked
- Parking violations
- Property damaged
- Smoking violations
- Defective equipment.

The list might also indicate if new instructions were received. Another item is whether keys and patrol equipment received from the officer on the previous shift are in good working order.

Random Patrols

Your post orders indicate your patrol route. Sometimes it must be followed rigidly. However, many times the path can be varied. Always make your patrols when scheduled, but change the route whenever possible. Try not to be in the same place at regular intervals. Let's say your orders call for you to patrol Buildings A, B and C. Instead of routinely patrolling ABC in that order, alter your patrol pattern to ACB, BAC, CAB and CBA.

Random patrolling thwarts those who might depend on your

regularity to set a timetable for intrusion, theft, arson or vandalism. You can't possibly be everywhere at once. But a good way to upgrade patrol efficiency is to make your movements unpredictable. Especially if you're the only officer on your post.

Another way to achieve random patrol is to vary your lunch routine. If you spend half an hour eating at your station—always at the same time of day—a professional intruder won't expect you to intercept him elsewhere during that half hour. If permitted, it's a good idea to eat your lunch at a different facility location each day.

Take care to be truly random. Don't choose a few favorite locations or route patterns and fall into a "random routine." Sometimes double back—retrace your route in reverse. This helps to avoid a security breach shortly after you've left a given area. Intruders know that once you've used a certain recorder or clock key, you probably won't return to that area for about an hour. That gives them time to operate. Foil them by doubling back.

Patrol Precautions

To make your appointed rounds as safely and effectively as possible, you should observe these precautions:

1. Don't attempt to make rounds after dark without a good flashlight.

2. Be painstaking. Don't take shortcuts. You are more effective as a security officer if you proceed slowly and miss nothing.

3. Look for obstructions and low-lying ground hazards such as wires, piping and supports.

4. Go around obstructions, not over or under them.

5. Be careful of loose boards and unstable platforms.

6. Avoid slippery surfaces. Look where you walk.

7. Don't run down stairs, and always use the handrail.

8. Be careful climbing ladders. Check ladders before using them.

9. Avoid shadow areas of buildings. Walk a few feet away from the sides of buildings. When turning a blind corner, move out from it and peer down the side of the building before you turn. Glance back where you've been. Look into buildings as you patrol the grounds. Develop the habit of looking upward at building tops. When inside buildings, observe and listen before entering a room.

10. When opening a door, push it wide open ahead of you. Look inside and listen before entering. Watch for signs of intrusion. If you sense the presence of another person, call out, "Is someone here?" Do that *before* you fully enter a room. In this situation, don't turn on your flashlight too hastily. It could make you a target.

11. Find vantage points where you can stop and observe a large area without being seen.

12. Use your senses as you patrol—your eyes, ears and nose. Become familiar with normal sights, sounds and odors along your patrol route. Thus, you can readily sense when something is abnormal.

13. Give your inspection tour your full concentration.

14. If you're driving a vehicle during part of your patrol, don't let surveillance interfere with safe driving. It's better to stop your vehicle and investigate anything suspicious on foot.

What to Look For

Depending on the type of facility to which you are assigned, you will be expected to look out for certain things. Your post orders should identify special areas, equipment and processes that are unique to that post. A checklist is handy to help you remember.

Following are some general items to look for while on patrol to help you easily recognize adverse conditions. Your officer's manual should spell out a safety list.

1. **Fire and Fire Hazards.** These head the list of dangers you must watch for most carefully. Fires not only destroy property, they can destroy lives, jobs and even entire businesses.

Ask yourself these questions: Is there enough fire-fighting equipment spread around the facility? Is that equipment in the correct strategic locations? Has the equipment been checked and tagged in the past year? Is anything blocking the way to an extinguisher? Are any fire doors blocked open? If there is a sprinkler system, have you personally checked the riser each day to ensure that the valve has not been accidentally closed?

Sprinkler valves should be sealed open. If they are closed, no water can go through the sprinklers.

Checking for fire hazards is a big job, too. Flammables stored in the open, rags or other combustibles stored in such a way as to cause spontaneous combustion, soldering irons, coffee pots, even

SPRINKLER RISER—Regular inspection of sprinkler risers ensures that they'll work in event of fire.

fluorescent light ballasts can be hazardous.

Use your curiosity and imagination and you will find other things which might be fire hazards, such as overheated motors or ovens and bad electrical wiring.

2. **Safety Hazards.** People are a company's most valuable asset. Keeping the workplace safe for employees, vendors and visitors is one of your major protection duties. While on patrol, observe and note anything that is unsafe.

3. **Property Abuse.** Abuse of business property ranges from mild defacement of buildings to violent sabotage. Sabotage is the deliberate act of damaging or destroying a facility so as to hinder or halt production. Report all instances of property damage, no matter how slight. Examples include broken windows, fence holes, vehicular damage to buildings and barriers, oil leaks from machinery or storage drums, water damage and graffiti.

4. **Restricted Access.** Did you see anyone where he didn't belong, including an employee from a different shift? Did you notice anyone keeping an eye on the facility from the outside? Anyone loitering in the vicinity? Did an intoxicated person, or someone pretending to be drunk, try to get past you? These things deserve your attention. They should also be noted in your daily activity report.

Some areas may be closed or restricted because they contain proprietary or classified documents, processes or hardware. Be sure sensitive information is locked up and that all files and safes are secure in these areas. Also prohibit access to unauthorized persons.

5. **Perimeter Security.** This check is also imperative. Did you find and report any doors or windows that were left unlocked? Is the fence in good repair? Are gates and padlocks secure? Are the outside lights all working, and are they adequate to deter intrusion?

6. **Maintenance Discrepancies.** These are of primary concern to the facility engineer or maintenance superintendent. Common things in this category are leaky faucets or pipes, running or clogged toilets, burned-out lights, cracked or broken windows, doors that stick or locks that don't function.

You should know the locations of power transformers, circuit breakers (fuse boxes), light switches, elevator control switches and air conditioning switches. Inspect them often and report anything out of kilter promptly.

DANGER AREA—During patrol, security officer checks high voltage enclosure. He makes sure electric insulation and fence are intact and gate is locked.

7. **Vulnerable Areas.** These are areas that pose a potential extreme danger. A good example is a storage area for gas, oil, explosives or other unstable chemicals. A high voltage area is another example.

A good security plan also includes places in the facility where a criminal most likely would try to force entry. You should be extra watchful of these areas on every patrol.

The list of things to be on the lookout for is never-ending. In fact, it's almost a sure bet that you can find *something* to report— something of value and interest to management—every time you're on duty.

If you've been at the same post for a long time, you may be in a rut. It's described as "You can't see the forest for the trees." The point is, once you've grown used to seeing the same wrong things day after day, you no longer recognize them as wrong or discrepant. You won't spot those things on patrol, nor will you note them in your daily activity report.

Your job is to report anything and everything amiss, no matter how minor. If a discrepancy you find on patrol isn't corrected after a reasonable time, tell your supervisor. He or she will take up the matter with proper management and get you an answer.

REVIEW OF PATROL TECHNIQUES

Here's a quick review to reemphasize the main things to remember about patrolling:

- Your patrols must be made as scheduled. If they cannot be completed, an explanation must be entered in your daily activity report.
- Your first patrol on each shift is the most important. Be especially alert and curious during this patrol, and know what to look for. Dangerous situations or hazardous conditions should be discovered early so they can be corrected promptly.
- Use your checklist while on patrol.
- Make certain your telephone or radio is in good working order.
- Turn off any lights, equipment or machinery you are instructed to turn off.

- Be sure the facility you are protecting is secure: windows, doors and gates properly locked; skylights closed and secured.

- Fire equipment and sprinkler systems should be carefully checked.

- Fire doors or emergency exits must not be blocked.

- Evidence of smoking in "no smoking" areas should be reported. If you observe someone actually smoking, or find cigarette or cigar butts in such areas, you are obligated to report this careless disregard for company rules and the safety of fellow employees.

- Investigate any unusual smoke or odors (especially gas) you notice. If you cannot determine the cause, notify your supervisor and contact the maintenance foreman as soon as possible.

- Make sure all electrical or gas appliances not in use (hot plates, coffee makers, soldering irons) are disconnected or turned off.

- Remove any combustible materials such as papers, boxes, excelsior, sacks or rags if you find them near a furnace, heater, steam pipe or boiler. Then be sure to report that you found and corrected such an unsafe condition.

- Follow the same procedure as above if you find flammables (gasoline, paint, chemicals) stored in the open.

- Report and correct, if possible, *any* safety hazards you find: slippery spots on the floor, uncovered holes, cords, chains or pipes hanging too low, electrical wires frayed or in hazardous locations.

- Be extra watchful in areas vulnerable to extreme danger, such as where volatile chemicals or explosives are stored. Also be aware and maintain close surveillance of places where a burglar or vandal might try to break in.

No checklist would be complete without mentioning your responsibility to safeguard classified material. Defense contractors are entrusted by the federal government with confidential, secret and top secret information. You should be given specific post instructions.

On your patrol rounds, be sure to check safes, vaults, file cabinets or even entire restricted areas. Be alert to the fact that some careless people leave classified information, as well as company business secrets, unsecured. The firm you protect and its employees rely on you to help them avoid security breaches.

CHAPTER 6

FIREARMS

There are very few jobs today that require security officers to carry weapons. In fact, the author has helped lead the crusade to disarm security officers throughout the country.

However, this chapter is written for those officers who still need to carry firearms.

CHANGING TIMES

National surveys conducted in the early 1950s showed that about 50 percent of uniformed security officers in the United States were armed.

In those days, the security industry as a whole had little or no firearms training. State controls over the carrying and use of firearms were nonexistent.

Small security companies had the highest percentage of armed guards—mostly unschooled in gun use. Larger security forces, both contract and proprietary, were the only ones with weapon training programs. However, most firms that did train security personnel to handle sidearms tended to overstress marksmanship on the firing range. The responsibility aspect of firearms was almost totally neglected.

Consequently, the misuse of firearms by unqualified security officers produced a passel of lawsuits. The most severe litigation stemmed from the accidental killing of innocent bystanders.

Starting in the late 1970s, the number of private and in-house security officers allowed to carry guns steadily decreased. The reason for this decline was that many states passed laws requiring that all armed security officers be trained and licensed. Qualifying standards were established to get a license or permit to wear a sidearm.

Some firms found the cost of training officers to meet state standards prohibitive. It was deemed too time-consuming. Others abandoned extensive arming of security officers because experience showed it was unnecessary. Today fewer uniformed security officers carry weapons, and this trend is growing. Even so, the pros and cons remain controversial.

The nation's largest private security companies—authorize less than five percent of their force to carry firearms.

The philosophy behind this decision is that most security posts don't require a gun. The primary purpose of business protection is asset loss prevention, not law enforcement. In the majority of situations, the deterrent value of a pistol is outweighed by its hazards. Gun-toting heightens the risks of accidental death, injury and civil liability. Mishaps impair public image.

CALIFORNIA LAW IS MODEL

California legislated firearms training standards for security officers in 1974. The author is proud to have submitted recommendations leading to the enactment of this law. Many other states have adopted these regulations.

California's Bureau of Collections and Investigative Services issues applicants a firearms qualification card upon satisfactory completion of a training course. The course is prescribed by the State Department of Consumer Affairs.

A minimum of 7-14 hours of firearms training is required. Elements of the course include:

1. Moral and legal aspects of firearms usage (4 hours)

2. Firearms care and handling (2 hours)

3. Range qualification (time necessary to qualify, up to 8 hours).

An examination is given on all aspects of the course.

Firms and institutions approved by the State Commission on Peace Officers Standards and Training can train their own employees in the foregoing criteria.

STRICT PENNSYLVANIA GUN LAW

Pennsylvania also was one of the first states to mandate that security officers be trained and licensed to carry firearms. Its Lethal Weapons Training Act, passed in 1974, is among the strictest state gun laws for security personnel.

Applicant prescreening includes psychological testing by a licensed psychologist, a physical exam by a medical doctor, and a state police background check.

After a letter of clearance is issued, the following 35-hour course must be completed:

- Orientation (1 hour)
- Constitutional Law (2 hours)
- Pennsylvania Crimes Code (4 hours)
- Authority of Arrest (4 hours)
- Justification of Force (2 hours)
- Laws of Evidence (4 hours)
- Statements and Confessions (1 hour)
- Court Testimony (1 hour)
- Armed and Unarmed Self-Defense (3 hours)
- Introduction to Firearms (4 hours)
- Final Exam (1 hour)
- Combat Shooting (8 hours)

Refresher training is required annually, and complete re-certification is mandated every five years.

REALISTIC FIREARMS POLICIES

Pinkerton's basic firearms training is believed to be the most comprehensive for security officers in the State of California and elsewhere except for very special situations. All officers see and are given a written examination on a firearms training film. Those permitted to carry sidearms must comply with state regulations, including range qualification. Extra instructions, per client requirements, are given to officers assigned to special posts where a gun is mandatory, such as at defense installations and nuclear power plants. In addition, each armed officer must have an authorization in writing to carry a company-issued revolver.

Adherence to strict gun policies laid down in 1964 has contributed to the company's success and growth. These practices foreshadowed the national pattern in gun control standards for the private security sector.

Details of this pioneering firearms education follow:

Guns Are Dangerous

If you are authorized (in writing) to carry a gun on your present assignment, the single most important thing you must know is that you could kill or seriously injure someone with that weapon. Purposely or accidentally makes little difference. You could *kill*. The type of gun you use is safe, but people are not always safe when handling guns.

Only for Self Defense

Your weapon is *only* for self defense. Your job involves prevention, *not* apprehension.

Generally, officers don't need to carry sidearms while on duty. Company officials should be discouraged from requesting that you wear a weapon unless you actually need it for self defense on your post. The reason is simple: the weapon creates a potential danger to you and to the very people you are responsible for protecting.

All protection officers must have complete firearms training so that they fully understand when and how to use a gun. All the safety rules must be observed. Know the extra responsibilities you assume when you carry a gun.

What circumstances justify carrying a sidearm?

The first consideration is if your post is sufficiently hazardous to you personally. If you work *alone* at night in a facility that doesn't have a sensible protective perimeter, you may need a weapon for your own safety. Only security management can determine this for you and authorize you to carry a sidearm.

Secondly, if an employer insists on your wearing a weapon, his requirements should be so stipulated in your post orders.

In either case, you should be personally authorized, in writing, to carry the weapon you wear. You also must be trained in its use, trained in your limitations, trained and retrained, and constantly reminded that *your weapon is for self defense.*

At no time should a weapon be used to enforce a company's facility regulations. You may draw and use your gun only in self defense or to protect the life of someone else in your presence. You may not fire it for any other reason, even if a criminal temporarily escapes.

Preferred Pistol

The weapon recommended for security officers is a .38 special revolver with a 4-inch, 5-inch or 6-inch barrel. The security department or contractor should furnish sidearms needed. Automatics (semi-automatic) or revolvers of different calibers are not recommended. Neither should officers be allowed to carry other weapons such as a sap, blackjack, knife, brass knuckles or mace. Occasionally, nightsticks are issued as *defensive* weapons in lieu of revolvers. These sticks are very effective in the hands of a person who knows how to use them.

About the revolver itself, it weighs about 2 pounds and can be fired either by simply squeezing the trigger (double action) or cocking the hammer back each time, then pulling the trigger (single action).

Fictional Shootouts

You have probably seen movie gunslingers draw from the hip and shoot someone 50 or 100 yards away. Don't believe it. If it ever happens, it's pure luck. Handguns don't work that way. Records have been kept on the actual number of wounds, fatal and nonfatal, inflicted on people throughout the United States over a long period. The average distance at which these wounds were inflicted with handguns was 7 yards, or 21 feet!

Sidearm Care

The revolver requires relatively little attention. At most sporting goods stores you can find small kits that include patches for cleaning the bore, a brass brush to remove fouling from the barrel, and a bottle of oil specially designed for a handgun.

Keep your weapon in good shape. A gun that is rusty and fouled in the barrel may not do the job when you need it the most.

Gun Safety Rules

The main firearms safety precautions are:

1. Treat all guns as though they were loaded.

2. Never point a gun at anyone unless you intend to kill that person.

Preferred guns are designed so the trigger must be pulled before the hammer can strike the bullet primer. It's impossible to fire an uncocked pistol of this kind by dropping or bumping it. Hence, anyone who fires this weapon does so on purpose or is guilty of inexcusable carelessness. Don't cock the gun or hook your fingers

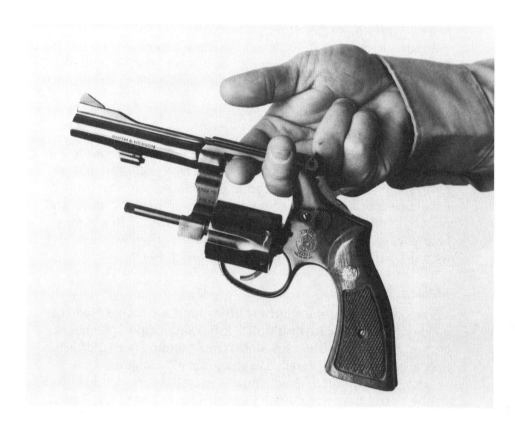

GUN SAFETY—When revolver is not in use, bullets should be removed and the cylinder hinged out. Accidents occur only with loaded guns.

around the trigger until you're ready to shoot. Never carry a gun in the holster with the hammer cocked.

When handling a revolver for any purpose other than firing it, make sure it's not loaded. Break open the cylinder and check to see if all the bullet chambers are empty. Don't glance casually and decide the gun isn't loaded—look again!

Continuous wearing of a gun may cause you to lose respect for it. Don't think that just because you're familiar with firearms the safety rules don't apply to you. All guns must be treated with the respect due a known loaded weapon. Most accidents occur with a gun thought to be unloaded.

When the weapon is out of the holster, the revolver's cylinder should always be hinged out (open) and unloaded, unless you are firing. Keep your fingers out of the trigger guard until you actually start shooting.

Periodically check the weapon to assure that the barrel and cylinder are clear of obstructions. Guns left in holsters for long periods accumulate dust and dirt which, when combined with either oil or moisture, harden and clog the action. Your gun could possibly explode if you fire it when such a condition exists.

At home, your gun should be kept unloaded in a safe and locked place where children and others cannot readily get to it. Members of the family should clearly understand who may handle the gun and then how to use it only in an emergency.

Outside the home, the gun should always be kept holstered. The law forbids carrying it in the waistband, in a trouser pocket, or in any way which is concealed. When going to and from your post in uniform, wear the weapon in its holster in plain sight. The gun must not be concealed in any way. Otherwise you must lock it in the trunk of your car. Please be certain to know what your state and local laws require.

Don't Brandish Weapon

Assume a readiness posture if faced with danger to yourself or others. But never brandish your weapon as a threat.

Don't play "cowboy" or "cop" on or off duty. Such antics erase your image as a professional protector.

Your gun is your responsibility at all times. When required, it's an important tool in your work. Never abuse your right to carry a firearm. Remember, too, that it can be dangerous.

Firing with a rest.

Firing offhand.

Firing from a crouch.

Shooting Proficiency

Now it's time to learn how to shoot effectively and accurately so you can use your gun correctly and safely when necessary.

You're not expected to be an expert, but you should learn enough to be effective. On the firing range you should be taught by a qualified instructor.

Instructions prior to firing should include:

- Firearms rules in your officer's manual
- Range and safety rules
- Complete explanation of the .38 caliber revolver and its ammunition
- Exact course of fire
- Procedure for benching weapons
- Targets and scoring methods.

Following are range qualification steps required for security officers by the State of California. Many other states have similar standards. If the state where you are employed has no firearms controls, these instructions will serve as a guide.

The range should have complete facilities. You should be able to fire all phases, using silhouette targets, from the 7-, 15- and 25-yard lines.

You will fire from 25 yards with a rest, from 15 yards offhand, and from 7 yards in a crouched position.

You step to the line and load your weapon carefully with the barrel always pointed down range. By the way, you will fire in 5-shot strings, and your instructor will give you only 5 rounds as a safety precaution. You will fire a total of 40 rounds, but the first 10 will be practice or sight-in shots.

The second 10 shots are to teach you to fire accurately without unduly exposing yourself to return fire from behind a barrier or wall. The first 5 rounds will be fired with the right wrist resting in the crook of the left thumb. Take all the time you need to be as accurate as possible, and you may cock the weapon for each shot, if you wish.

The second 5 rounds are from behind the left side of the barrier. Again, take your time and squeeze the trigger. You will be surprised how accurate you can be from these positions.

When you are used to the feel and sound of your weapon, you will move up to the 15-yard line. Here you will fire two 5-shot strings, but this time you'll only have 15 seconds for each string of

5 shots. This is plenty of time to cock, aim and fire the weapon carefully and accurately.

You will find that some practice dry firing with an unloaded weapon before you go to the range will be very helpful to you. Just be *safe* at all times and don't draw your weapon in the presence of other people, even if you know it's unloaded.

The third position is fast and from the hip. It is fired from only 7 yards, and you will point your gun instinctively just like you point your finger instead of aiming the gun. Each 5-shot string will be fired in only 10 seconds and in double action; that is, without cocking the weapon before each shot. This is plenty of time, however, to shoot carefully and accurately.

Scores are recorded between each string. Certificates are issued to all qualifying officers, but you're more interested in the general feel of the weapon than in your score.

RECAP

Now you've learned how to handle and fire your revolver safely. Review your officer's manual often if you have any questions, or ask your supervisor. If your post requires you to wear a sidearm indefinitely, you should return to the firing range at least once a year for a refresher course.

This is what you've learned:

1. Your gun could kill.

2. Draw your weapon only in self-defense or to protect the life of someone else.

3. Treat all guns as though they were loaded.

4. Never point a gun at anyone unless you intend to kill that person.

5. It's better for a criminal to escape than for you to kill or injure an innocent person.

6. Every officer who carries a handgun should be authorized to do so in writing.

You can take pride in the knowledge that you have professional qualifications in gun safety and use.

Note: The author nearly deleted this chapter entirely, since he is personally committed to a no firearms policy whenever possible. Regrettably, however, there are a few situations where prudence requires arming security officers. Even most banks have eliminated once traditional sidearms. The rule of thumb followed today lies in the question: "Whom do you want us to shoot?" Since the answer almost always is: "No one, of course!" —then weapons aren't needed at all.

CHAPTER 7

FIRST AID

SPECIAL TRAINING VALUABLE

Essential to Your Job

In an emergency situation, the first thing many people do is panic. Then they look for someone who knows what to do.

As a security officer, you must know what to do. You can't afford not to know. You must be ready for any and all situations and act swiftly and correctly.

This is particularly vital in cases involving on-the-job accidents, personal injuries, sudden illnesses or other mishaps requiring immediate, on-the-spot attention.

An essential part of your job is knowing the rudiments of first aid. First aid instruction should be part of your basic training as a security officer.

First aid is defined as immediate temporary care given by a trained person in case of sudden illness or accident before medical assistance is available. Such aid is given to prevent death or further injury, to relieve pain, and to counteract shock.

Red Cross, Firemen Helpful

To become competent in first aid requires many hours of training and practice. It's advisable to get this training from experts.

In most areas the American Red Cross, the local fire department and public health agencies provide training literature, films and personal instruction on first aid.

Whenever possible and pracitcal, all security officers should avail themselves of this valuable coaching as part of their training.

BASIC RESPONSIBILITIES

Get Qualified Help

Prompt communication is your key responsibility, since you're not expected to be an expert in caring for injured or ill persons.

Your first responsibility in most emergency situations is to call for qualified help.

The reason this policy is stressed is to limit your legal liability in case anything goes wrong. If an in-house security officer is sued, his employer also is liable. If you're a contract security officer, a suit may be filed against you, the contractor and the client company. It's very unfortunate that this situation exists, but it does.

If an accident or illness occurs within your area of responsibility, follow these primary instructions:

Refer all cases immediately to the company doctor or nurse if one is on the premises.

If medical personnel are not available at your facility, phone immediately for outside help. Your post orders should include emergency telephone numbers for local fire department paramedics, an ambulance service, a doctor and the nearest hospital. Be sure you know these emergency numbers or where to find them quickly when you start a new post. Some regions have a common number for all types of emergencies, such as 911.

If you're alone, need quick medical help and don't have emergency numbers, call the outside phone operator and ask for assistance. Just dial zero. State the nature of the emergency and the location. Relay all needed information correctly.

Report What Happened

Be sure to file prompt and complete reports on all accidents injuries and sudden illnesses that occur at your post.

Each emergency should be noted in your daily activity report and fully explained in an incident report.

Accuracy is a must. Security management will rely on your account of the details.

GENERAL POINTERS

Be Calm and Efficient

To give effective first aid, you must be in control of yourself and the situation. Show self-assurance.

Keep crowds away, but recruit bystanders for specific assistance; for example, calling for medical help if you cannot leave the victim.

Yield control to someone else if that person is more competent in first aid than you are. Then assist by controlling onlookers or granting any other request that person might make.

Be Careful, Kind, Gentle

Except in cases where it's necessary to work fast to save a life, be careful, kind and gentle. This approach will help to inspire confidence in the person you are treating. For him or her, this feeling of confidence is as important as the treatment itself.

Illegal Procedures

It is illegal for you to prescribe or hand out medicines. Even aspirin must be requested by the patient, assuming he is conscious. You must not recommend any medication.

Don't let the victim take any food or liquids until a doctor has seen the patient. Don't give the victim cigarettes, alcohol or any other substance. They might mask important symptoms.

Even though you're well-trained in first aid, remember you're a security officer, not a doctor, nurse or paramedic. That's why it's important for you to get qualified help.

MOST URGENT EMERGENCIES

If a life is threatened, haste is imperative. Follow these guidelines in dealing with critical cases:

1. Call for medical help. If a victim demands your immediate attention, ask someone on the scene to phone for you.

2. Treat the most serious threat to life first. For example, loss of breathing has priority over severe bleeding. (That's the prevailing medical opinion, although it's a split-hair decision on which there is not unanimous agreement.) In either case, seconds count.

3. If the victim is unconscious, check vital signs. Here are the ABCs of emergency life support:

    A. **Airway** must be opened if blocked.

    B. **Breathing** must be restored if it has stopped.

    C. **Circulation** must be restored if there is no pulse.

4. Stop extreme bleeding. Spurting blood indicates a severed artery. If such excessive bleeding isn't stopped, the victim will die in a few minutes.

5. Treat for shock. You do this by keeping the victim lying down, calm and comfortable.

(Note: Detailed first aid techniques for these and other emergencies are described in later paragraphs.)

6. Don't move an injured or unconscious person unless it's absolutely necessary to save his/her life. The victim may have broken bones or internal injuries that aren't obvious. Moving that person could cause further damage resulting in death.

If an out-of-control danger exists (such as a burning car or loose high-voltage wires), drag the victim to safety at once—if you can do so without being foolhardy.

7. Report the incident. As soon as the victim is in more competent hands, phone your supervisor. Jot down notes while the emergency is still fresh in your memory. Later, turn in required written reports.

RESTORE BREATHING

Breathing is essential to life. It carries oxygen into the lungs, then to the heart, and through blood circulation to the rest of the body. All body tissues require oxygen, but the brain needs more oxygen than any other tissue.

When the brain is deprived of oxygenated blood for 4-6 minutes, irreversible damage probably will occur. If no oxygen gets to the brain for more than 6 minutes, the victim usually dies.

Breathing may stop as a result of choking, heart attack, severe injury, electric shock, drug overdose, poisoning or drowning. All are potential killers.

Check Breathing and Pulse

If positioned otherwise, an unconscious person should immediately be rolled flat on his or her back. Keep the head aligned with the body to avoid a neck injury.

Try to awaken the victim. Shake his shoulder vigorously. Shout, "Can you hear me?"

If no response, check for signs of breathing. Look at the chest for breathing movements. If none is visible, place your ear near the victim's nose and mouth. Listen for breathing and feel exhaled air, if any, on your cheek.

Next, check the pulse. With one hand, hold back the victim's forehead. With the fingertips of your other hand, feel for a pulse on either side of the victim's neck just below the base of the jaw.

If you find a pulse, but the victim isn't breathing, immediately (1) open the airway and (2) start mouth-to-mouth rescue breathing.

If the victim isn't breathing and doesn't have a pulse, cardio-pulmonary resuscitation (CPR) is needed. If you don't know CPR, continue mouth-to-mouth revival on the chance that a pulse is present, but it is so weak you can't detect it.

Opening the Airway

Place one hand on the victim's forehead and push backward firmly. Place your other hand under the neck near the base of the skull and lift gently (see Figure 1). Tip the head until the chin points straight up. This should open the airway.

Fig. 1. Opening airway.

Coughing is a good sign. In the absence of coughing, listen again for any exhalation. If the airway is still blocked, try abdominal thrusts (Figure 2).

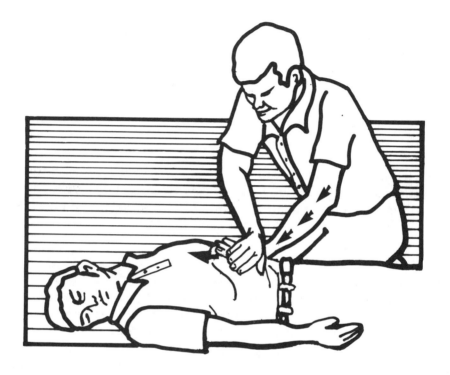

Fig. 2. Abdominal thrust

Place one of your hands on top of the other with the heel of your bottom hand between the navel and rib cage. Your fingers should point toward the victim's head. Press into the middle of the abdomen. Give 1-4 quick upward thrusts. Don't press either side or exert too much pressure, which might cause internal injuries.

(Note: The abdominal thrust is commonly called the Heimlich Maneuver, named after its developer, Dr. Henry Heimlich. How to perform abdominal thrusts on a conscious person is described under the heading, Remedy for Choking. In July 1985, the American Red Cross and American Heart Association agreed to no longer recommend back slaps for choking and CPR. The consensus is that back blows are unsafe. They could cause a piece of food or other foreign object stuck in the throat to lodge more firmly.)

If the victim has swallowed something that is blocking the air passage, perform a finger sweep. Hold the victim's mouth open with one hand, using your thumb to depress the tongue (Figure 3). With the index finger of your other hand, probe the victim's throat and remove any obstruction.

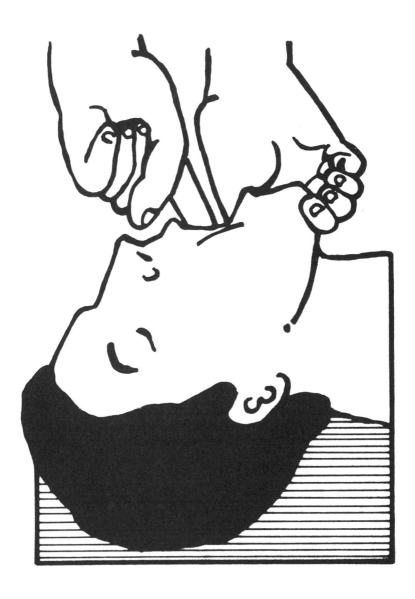

Fig. 3. Finger sweep.

Mouth-to-Mouth Rescue Breathing

Figure 4 illustrates mouth-to-mouth resuscitation.

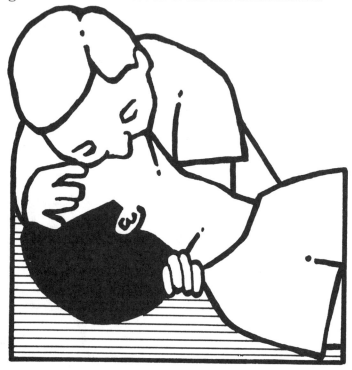

Fig. 4. Mouth-to-mouth resuscitation.

Hold the victim's forehead back while pinching the nose shut with the same hand. Keep the other hand under the victim's neck, lifting it gently to keep the airway open.

Take a deep breath, make a good seal on the victim's mouth, and give 4 quick initial breaths. Repeat a single breath every 5 seconds (12 breaths per minute). Blow air into the victim's lungs until you see the chest rise.

If you hear air escaping and see the chest fall, you'll know your rescue breathing is working. But continue until the victim fully revives or until help arrives.

In some cases, this rescue operation may take several hours. Remember, you're performing the breathing function for the victim. Without breathing for 4-6 minutes, he or she becomes a mental vegetable—any longer than that, a goner. Get professional medical help, even if the victim starts to breathe on his own.

Caution: A victim receiving mouth-to-mouth breathing or

abdominal thrusts may vomit. If he does, roll him onto his side to prevent choking. Clear his throat and mouth with your hooked index finger. Roll the victim back onto his back and continue mouth-to-mouth rescue breathing until you are relieved.

Remedy for Choking

A choking person is in distress—for good reason. Breathing is either difficult or impossible. When the air passage is totally blocked, the victim is only minutes away from unconsciousness and death. Choking is usually caused by food stuck in the throat.

Stand by, but don't interfere with, a choking victim who can speak, cough or breathe. If this condition persists, call for medical assistance.

If the choking victim can't talk, cough or breathe, he or she needs immediate help. The universal sign for this crisis is frantic hand-gestures toward the throat. Ask someone to phone for medical help while you try to relieve the victim.

The abdominal thrust (Heimlich Maneuver) is now the sole first-aid remedy for choking. Sharp back whacks are no longer recommended. They're considered dangerous.

Stand behind a conscious victim. Wrap your arms around his/her waist just below the rib cage (Figure 5). Clasp your hands

Fig. 5. Abdominal thrust (standing position).

together, with the bottom hand clenched into a fist. Press in and up in quick thrusts. Repeat until the victim is no longer choking or until medical help arrives.

If the victim faints, place him on his back and give abdominal thrusts with the heel of your hand as previously detailed in Opening the Airway. Continue until breathing is restored or until a medic takes charge.

HOW TO GIVE ONE-MAN CPR

You should be trained in cardiopulmonary resuscitation (CPR) by a qualified instructor.

CPR combines chest compressions with mouth-to-mouth rescue breathing. You're performing both artificial circulation and artificial respiration.

CPR is faster and easier when given to a victim by two rescuers. Since an emergency may require you to use it when you're working alone, the technique for giving one-man CPR to an adult victim is explained here.

Initial Seconds

Remember to call for help or have someone phone for you.

If the victim is down and unconscious, try to arouse him or her. If no response, look and listen for signs of breathing. If none is evident, open the airway and give 4 quick breaths. Listen again for breathing. Check the victim's pulse. If he isn't breathing and you can't find a heartbeat, start CPR.

Pay strict attention to small details. The right way is safe; the wrong way is dangerous.

Position of Victim

Leave the victim right where he is, unless an impending hazard makes it unsafe. He should be on a hard surface—the ground, the floor, or a spine board.

The victim must lie flat on his/her back. A vertical position hinders blood flow to the brain.

Position of Rescuer

Kneel at right angles close to the side of the victim's chest (Figure 6). Don't straddle the victim. Spread your knees about shoulder-width apart.

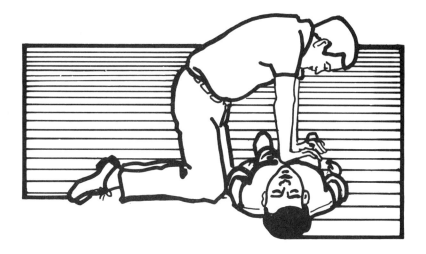

Fig. 6. Proper position of rescuer for CPR.

Practice how to position your hands (Figure 7) so you don't have to waste time in a real emergency. With the middle and index

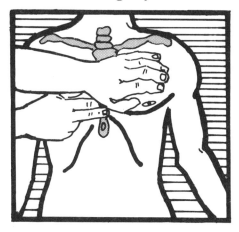

Fig. 7. Locating correct place on victim's chest to apply CPR compression.

finger of one of your hands, find the lower edge of the victim's rib cage on the side nearest you. Trace the edge of the ribs up to the notch where the ribs meet the breastbone. Place your middle finger on the notch, the index finger next to it.

Put the heel of your other hand next to the index finger. This is the bottom (compression) hand. Place it across the victim's chest, not parallel to his body. The heel of your compression hand is positioned over the lower half of the victim's sternum (breastbone)—the bone in the center of the chest to which the ribs are attached.

Now place your other hand on top of the compression hand. Interlocking your fingers may help to keep them off the rib wall. Pressure will be applied to the lower part of the sternum, but not the ribs themselves. *Warning:* Don't press below the rib notch, since that can damage abdominal organs.

Compression/Ventilation Technique

Deliver 15 rapid chest compressions, followed by 2 quick mouth-to-mouth lung inflations. For the ventilation portion, take a deep breath and deliver two lung inflations in rapid succession. Blow until the victim's chest starts to rise.

The ideal number of chest compressions is 60 per minute, according to the American Red Cross. Two full lung inflations take 4 to 5 seconds if the rescuer doesn't exhale between breaths. Allowing time for exhalation slows down the procedure. Usually, two rescuers work faster than one.

To establish a proper rhythm for one-man CPR, count "One and, two and, three and," etc., through 15. Each "numeral and" count equals about one second.

Press straight down about 1.5 to 2 inches. Your arms function like pistons. Your shoulders should be directly over the victim's breastbone. Bend from the hips, not the knees. Push smoothly.

Check the victim's pulse and breathing after the first minute and every few minutes thereafter.

Continue to alternate compressions and mouth-to-mouth respiration in a 15-to-2 ratio until the victim's circulation and breathing are restored or until help arrives.

Some victims cannot be revived, even if you start CPR immediately and apply it correctly. A massive heart attack, asphyxiation or a serious injury may be fatal, despite your best efforts. Recognize this fact and don't blame yourself for inept first aid if the victim expires.

Don't practice chest compressions on your relatives, friends or fellow officers. Without proper training, you could injure someone. Learn CPR correctly from an expert so you can use it effectively in an emergency.

Some posts have oxygen tanks and resuscitators. You should be taught how to use them efficiently.

HOW TO STOP BLEEDING

Stop severe bleeding with a clean bandage and direct pressure on the wound.

Make a pad of the cleanest material you can find. Sterile gauze is preferable, but a clean handkerchief, sanitary napkin or hastily-torn rag will do. If none of these is available, use your bare hand.

Hold the pad or your hand firmly on the wound until the bleeding stops (see Figure 8). It takes 5-15 minutes for the blood to clot.

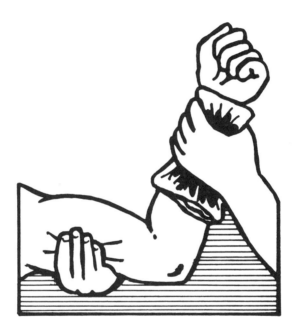

Fig. 8. Hold pad firmly on wound until bleeding stops.

If the first pad becomes blood-soaked, don't remove it. Put another one on top of it and keep pressing.

After the bleeding stops, bandage the pads right where they are, but don't wrap the bandage so tight it shuts off the circulation.

Assuming you've called for help, professional rescuers will clean the wound and rebandage it, if necessary. A doctor will do any stitching required.

If a hand, arm, foot or leg is bleeding, raise the limb so it's higher than the victim's heart. Gravity will slow the blood flow. Help the patient lie down.

Treat head injuries with more care. Don't press so hard that a possible bone chip might puncture the brain. Bleeding from an ear could indicate a skull fracture. A neck injury often accompanies a serious head injury. Don't twist the head or neck.

Severe nose bleeding can be stopped by pinching the nose with a thumb and index finger. Squeeze the nostrils firmly for at least 10 minutes.

Pressure on the wound controls bleeding in two ways:

1. It compresses the bleeding vessels, reducing the flow of blood into the damaged area.

2. It helps hold blood in the wound until clotting occurs.

Pressure Points

You can reduce bleeding by applying pressure to certain points on the body (Figure 9). These are points where arteries lie close to

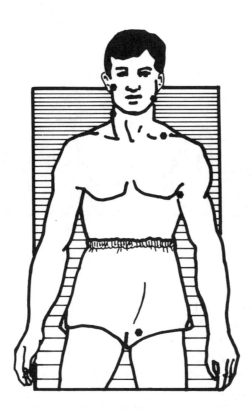

Fig. 9. Dots show pressure points to reduce bleeding.

bones. Sufficient finger pressure will slow down blood flow. Hemorrhage (profuse bleeding) can be controlled by pressure on these points until pressure dressings are applied to the wound.

Following are examples of how to stop bleeding in various parts of the body:

Scalp and Forehead. Press with forefinger or thumb just in front of the ear opening on the side near the bleeding.

Face Below Eyebrows. Press against the lower jaw just in front of the jawbone angle.

Neck or Throat. Press the bleeding side of the neck, even with the Adam's apple. Or, wrap your hand around the back of the neck and press both sides with your fingertips.

Shoulder. On the injured side, wrap your hand over the shoulder muscle near where it joins the neck. With your thumb and fingertips, squeeze this muscle.

Arm. Press fingers on the inner side of the arm just below the armpit.

Leg. Put the victim on his/her back. With the heel of one of your hands, press the victim's groin (inside of upper thigh).

Use a tourniquet *only as a last resort* after other methods of stopping the bleeding have failed. In the hands of an unskilled user, a tourniquet can be more harmful than helpful.

Tighten only until bleeding stops. Once the tourniquet is applied, don't remove it. For the information of medical attendants, attach a note or tag stating the exact time the tourniquet was applied.

SHOCK PREVENTION

Prevention of shock is important because shock can be more serious than the original injury.

Shock is a condition that may follow an accident or serious injury. Great weakness of the body is brought about by lack of blood circulation. Loss of blood may be due to external or internal bleeding. Severe burns cause large amounts of body fluids to be lost through seepage from the damaged area or from the blood into the tissue. This, too, will result in shock. Falling, collisions, electrocution, assault, bullet wounds, severed veins or arteries, muscle lacerations and broken bones often produce shock.

Shock Symptoms

Shock symptoms include:

- Pale face
- Cold sweat
- Nausea
- Mental confusion
- Weak and rapid pulse
- Irregular breathing
- Possible loss of consciousness

Shock is a Killer

Shock may follow any injury, or it may occur several hours after an injury. If not treated, shock can and often does result in death.

Shock can be aggravated by moving the victim. That could start or increase bleeding or cause pain. Leave handling to the medics.

Prolonged shock may be fatal, even though the injury causing the shock might not, in the absence of severe shock, have caused death.

First Aid for Shock

A shock victim should lie flat on his/her back. Elevate his legs about 12 inches, unless they're injured. Keep the person calm and comfortable, even if he seems recovered. Cover him with a blanket or coat to keep him warm. Clamminess accompanies shock, even on a hot day. If glare is a problem, provide shade. Keep curious onlookers away.

If a victim is short of breath and his neck isn't injured, put a pillow or folded blanket under his shoulders. Let his head and neck hang over the support. This keeps the airway open.

Never give food or drink, as they're unnecessary and could worsen the patient's condition.

Electric Shock

Electrocution can kill. The 110-volt electric current common in homes and offices is deadly.

When a person has been electrocuted, first call for medical aid.

Next, make sure the electricity is turned off. If an electrician is on the premises, have him do it. If none is available, shut off the power yourself at the circuit breaker or fuse box. You should know, in advance, where the master switches are located. A downed power line may prevent an immediate shutoff. In that case, call the electric company or ask someone to do it for you.

Don't touch the victim if the current is still on. If his life is imperiled, use a dry stick to move a "hot" line away from him. Drag him or her out of danger.

If the victim is conscious and breathing OK, treat him for shock as previously described.

If the victim is unconscious, check his breathing and pulse. If the breathing is weak or has stopped, give rescue breathing at once. If both breathing and circulation have stopped, give CPR until help arrives.

AIDING BURN VICTIMS

Burns can be one of the most severe injuries to which man is exposed. They're a common cause of death from accidents and fires in homes, schools and industry.

Most burns you encounter in your work probably will be minor. However, burns from scalding, explosions, fire or electricity can be fatal.

The most important thing to remember about burn victims is to *prevent shock and infection.* A seriously burned person should be kept as calm and comfortable as possible. Don't put anything on the burn. Keep it free from dirt.

Degrees of Burns

Burns are classified as first, second and third degree. The higher the degree, the worse the burn is. Here's a short description of each:

1. A first-degree burn produces redness.
2. A second-degree burn produces blistering.
3. A third-degree burn entirely destroys the skin and chars the tissue.

Emergency Procedures

Following are emergency steps and precautions to aid a person who has been burned:

- Call for medical help immediately.
- If the victim is severely burned, treat for shock. Keep him or

her lying down. Cover the patient with blankets, clean sheets or towels to conserve body heat.

- Don't try to remove clothing. It's too painful for the victim.
- Don't try to remove pieces of charred matter that stick to the burn.
- Don't try to clean the burn.
- Don't break any blisters.
- Don't put ointment or any other medication on the burn, including disinfectants.
- Let a doctor, nurse or paramedic dress the burn.

Special types of burns often require little more than good judgment. For example, molten metal is a daily hazard in foundries and metallurgical labs. A drop of molten metal anywhere on the body can cause a serious burn. In one's shoes, it creates havoc. Usually, the victim screams in agony and runs. He or she must be stopped. The worst thing to do for a burn of this kind is to apply water. The steam generated when the water contacts the hot metal (inside the shoe) burns the victim's foot more than the drop of metal would by itself. The correct thing to do is to remove the shoe quickly. The victim can rid himself of the hot object merely with a shake of his foot.

If you work where chemicals are used, learn the site's special emergency measures for treating chemical burns.

MOVING THE INJURED

Necessary for Safety

As previously stated, it's better not to move an injured person, especially when the gravity of the injury is unknown.

Some emergencies, however, make it imperative to move the victim at once. Examples are dragging injured people from burning vehicles or from the proximity of crumbling structures or potential explosions. Urgency will dictate the method of evacuation in such extreme cases.

Get adequate help to put a victim on a stretcher if he or she cannot walk. It's preferable to roll, rather than lift, an injured person onto a stretcher. Avoid bending any part of his/her body, since the slightest twist might increase the damage.

If a stretcher is not available, roll the victim onto a blanket, tarpaulin or large coat and drag the person to safety.

Emergency Transportation

It's a bad practice for a security officer to use his/her car or a company car to take a sick or injured person to a doctor or hospital. In so doing, you're really not helping the victim, either. This policy may seem nonsensical to you if you're faced with an emergency in which a human life hangs in the balance. But take a hard look at the alternatives, as well as things that could happen.

In the absence of a physician on the premises or available on rush notice, call an ambulance. An ambulance can get to you faster than you can drive to the hospital, without breaking traffic laws. Ambulance crews are trained for haste. They are medically competent and legally authorized to provide emergency assistance. You are not. You could have an accident on the way to the doctor or hospital. That could make you legally liable for further injury or death to the patient you are transporting.

Meanwhile, you have deserted your post.

Assuming you arrive safely, you and your employer are still liable if the victim suffers a lengthy disability or dies.

Because of the legal quagmire, most insurance policies void transporting stretcher cases in other than authorized emergency vehicles.

In a rare instance when you have no other alternative, call a taxi. At least a taxi is licensed to carry sick and injured passengers, as well as those that are healthy.

It's vital to get qualified help fast!

KEY FIRST AID DUTIES

To refresh your memory, here are the six most important things you must do in case of a serious injury or illness:

1. Call for qualified medical help.
2. Treat the most serious threat to life first.
3. Restore breathing and circulation if they have stopped.
4. Stop excessive bleeding.
5. Prevent or reduce shock.
6. Report what happened promptly and completely.

Your working knowledge of these basic first-aid measures could save the life of a sick or injured person.

CHAPTER 8

FIRE PREVENTION AND CONTROL

As a security officer, you're expected to protect property at your place of assignment against all possible damage or loss.

You're constantly alert to such human dangers as vandalism, theft and violence. You must also be alert for the silent signals which warn of the most disastrous of all attackers—FIRE!

Are you fire conscious? Do you always look for potential fire hazards? Are you certain you know how to call your local fire department without having to look around for the number? As a protection officer, you must be able to answer the foregoing questions with a firm yes.

PREVENTION'S FIRST DUTY

In the old days, the so-called "night watchman" had little or no training and not much to do except to detect fires. His only detection system was his nose.

Your job is to *prevent* fires, not just detect them. To do that, you must know the hazards.

All too often, the first noticeable signs of fire are the smell of smoke and the crackling of flames. The alert security officer, however, should note certain danger signs long before that late stage. To the alert officer, the smell of smoke should be one of the last signs of an impending fire. After all, almost anyone can detect a fire by smelling smoke.

It's your duty to know how to prevent, report and fight fires with the systems and equipment available at your post.

Your primary duty is to prevent fire by alertly spotting, correcting or reporting hazards. Your second duty, in case of fire, is to notify the fire department. Your last duty is to fight the fire, if that is possible.

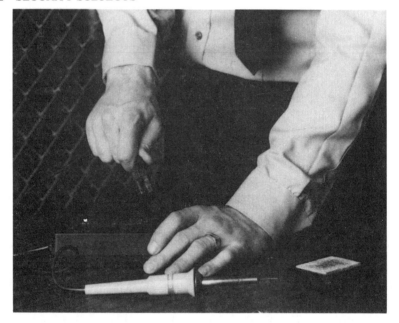

FIRE PREVENTION—Unplugging electric soldering iron left on is one of many ways to prevent fires.

Observe and Report Hazards

You should prepare a checklist of potential hazards at your present post and check these areas regularly.

Here are things to be on the lookout for:

- Paint lockers and spray booths
- Storage areas for flammables such as oil, gasoline, kerosene, alcohol, paint thinner, shellac and varnish
- Electrical appliances and tools left plugged in, such as coffee makers, hot plates and soldering irons
- Frayed, jumbled or haphazard electrical wiring
- Overheated machinery, motors or compressors
- Defective fluorescent light ballasts (they usually smoke and smell bad). Report such defects immediately and, if possible, turn off the light circuit until repairs are made.
- Improper storage or placement of combustibles such as oily rags, paper and packing materials. Grain, hay, sawdust, coal dust and large quantities of animal fodder are also highly combustible. All of the foregoing should be removed from high heat sources such as the sun, open heaters and steam pipes.

Know Firefighting Equipment

You should know, not only the locations of all available fire extinguishers, hoses and sprinkler system valves, but how to use them as well.

REPORT FIRES FAST

Remember, time is vital! The first five minutes are the most important, so report any fire immediately.

Only after you've notified the fire department should you attempt to fight the fire yourself. Without hesitation, report the fire first.

The only possible exception to this rule would be the immediate removal of persons in the fire area whose lives are endangered.

Telephone Report

Phone the local fire department, whose number you should know, or the operator, who is trained to handle emergency calls. Report the fire. Give your name, phone number and the address of the facility. Also give the exact location of the fire; for example, "Building 10 in the southwest corner of the plant." If possible, describe the nature of the fire; that is, combustible material, flammable liquid or electrical.

A handy acronym to remember in reporting a fire is TACT. It stands for Type, Address, Cross street and the Telephone number you are calling from.

Alarm Systems

If a telephone isn't available, use the nearest fire department pull box alarm, either on the property or on the street. You should know ahead of time where these fire alarm boxes are located.

One type of alarm box requires breaking a thin glass plate. Behind it is a switch which, when pulled, sets off a coded alarm in the local fire station. However, some alarms of this type ring only in the buildings they're placed in. Know the difference.

Don't forget, just breaking the glass doesn't set off the alarm. The switch has to be pulled. Be careful when you break the glass to avoid cutting yourself. Use a baton, the heel of your shoe, a rock or any other blunt object that's available. Don't try to break the glass with your elbow, fist or the heel of your hand.

Another type of alarm box simply requires an exposed lever to be pulled.

When you must use a street alarm box and it isn't prudent for you to leave your post, send a plant worker to turn in the alarm. Send a second person along afterwards to double-check.

It's imperative that you or someone you delegate be on hand to direct the firemen to the fire.

Many facilities have their own internal alarm or public address system. These are seldom connected with the fire department. Instead, they warn you and other personnel and send the plant's own fire brigade into action. You still must determine where the fire is and report it immediately to the local fire department.

Some buildings have automatic alarm systems that are set off by excessive heat, smoke or gasses. When a fire starts in an area with an overhead sprinkler system, the activation of the sprinkler system sets off an alarm, usually a bell on the outside of the building. Sometimes the alarm system is connected directly to the fire department or to an alarm company's central station, serving a dual purpose.

You must know the alarm systems in operation at your post, how they function, and what their limitations are.

Remember, time is vital. The first few minutes are the most important, so report any fire immediately.

Notify Your Supervisor

After phoning the fire department, call your supervisor. He or she will rush to your location and help notify executive personnel. After you've done this, proceed with specific emergency actions outlined in your post instructions.

FIGHTING FIRES

Minimize Dangers

Groups of curious workers can hamper firefighting efforts. For their own safety, ask them to leave the fire area at once. Usher them to safety in an orderly manner.

An internal alarm already may have alerted workers to an emergency. In some facilities, employees are drilled on how to evacuate in case of an emergency. At all times, on all shifts, you should know whether anyone is working in the plant and where.

A sudden fire or explosion could produce an additional danger: crumbling roof or walls. As the security officer on duty, one of your prime responsibilities is the safety of others. Exert every effort to assist those escaping from the danger area.

Here are some things you should also do after you've reported a fire:

If possible, prevent the fire from spreading. Close nearby windows and doors and remove combustible material. If the facility has fire doors, close them immediately.

Try to determine the cause of the fire quickly. If the origin is electrical, turn off the circuits, since an electrical fire can't be controlled until the current is stopped.

The same urgency applies to shutting off the power to machines and the gas to open-flame furnaces. Switches or shutoff valves, in most cases, are far enough away from equipment to provide safe access. You should know beforehand the exact locations of all main electrical switches and gas shutoff valves.

Direct Firemen

Even though you phone accurate information to the fire department, you or someone you delegate must be on hand to direct the firemen to the fire.

Some industrial facilities are large and complex and usually have more than one entrance. Also, locations of street and in-house fire hydrants vary in every case. By directing firemen when they arrive, a great deal of precious time can be saved.

Classes of Fires

Basic to your firefighting education is a knowledge of the kinds of fires and the type of extinguisher to use for each. Here are the four classes of fires and how to extinguish them:

1. **Class A fires** consume ordinary combustibles such as wood, paper or trash. They can be quenched with water-loaded extinguishers or hoses. An ABC multi-purpose powder extinguisher also will put out a Class A fire.

2. **Class B fires** are fed by flammable liquids such as gasoline, alcohol, solvents and oil. Douse these with carbon dioxide (CO_2) or a powder suppressor—but never with water.

Airport firemen use foam to smother an airplane fire, particularly when the jet fuel ignites. Foam also is used to snuff out vehicular fires and blazing spillage on highways. However, hand-held foam extinguishers are extinct in most places you'll be protecting.

3. **Class C fires** are electrical. Here again, water is forbidden. Multi-purpose dry chemicals, CO_2 or Halon vapor should be used.

4. **Class D fires** involve incendiary metallic elements such as sodium and magnesium. Facilities where these chemically active metals are kept usually have special extinguishing agents handy. If your post covers such a hazard, be sure you know where to find the neutralizers. Using the wrong thing could result in serious injury.

Types of Extinguishers

You must know how to use each type of fire extinguisher on your post. Read the instructions carefully. If you haven't actually used a particular type, ask your supervisor to demonstrate its use for you.

Whenever possible, it's a good idea to ask the fire extinguisher

EXTINGUISHER—Alert security officer douses fire in trash can. All extinguishers should be in good working order, and officers must know which types to use for various classes of fires.

serviceman to let you and your fellow officers use up old extinguishers just for the practice.

Here are the common types of extinguishers:

1. **The ABC multi-purpose extinguisher** may contain either dry chemical powder or liquified gas, depending on its size. As its name implies, it will suffocate Class A, B and C fires.

2. **The pump type extinguisher** is a round bucket with a handle on top and a hose. The bucket is full of water. Simply pump the handle while directing the hose nozzle at the base of the fire.

3. **Carbon dioxide extinguishers** can always be spotted by their horn-like nozzle attachment. Tanks contain liquid CO_2 under great pressure. They are most effective on Class B fires, as they cut off the supply of oxygen to the fire. Be careful never to hold the horn itself, because it gets extremely cold (-90 F). They can also be used on Class C electrical fires without danger of electrocution.

4. **Dry chemical extinguishers** are very effective on gasoline and oil fires (Class B). Since these powders are nonconductors, they can also be used on electrical fires. This type of extinguisher comes in various sizes from hand-held to large drums on wheels.

5. **A Halon extinguisher** is the best kind to put out fires in expensive electronic equipment, such as computers. The vapor will quench the fire without damaging the equipment.

Learn how to operate the extinguishers on your post. Here are some general operating tips:

- Pull the pin.
- Aim the nozzle, horn or hose at the base of the fire.
- Squeeze or press the handle.
- Sweep from side to side at the base of the fire.

Remember that water should never be applied to an electrical fire. Chances of a dangerous shock or electrocution are great. Besides, water helps spread the sparking.

REVIEW OF DUTIES

These are the main points to remember about fire prevention and control:

1. Your first duty is to prevent fire by finding, correcting or reporting fire hazards.

2. Your second duty, in case of fire, is to notify the fire department immediately.

3. Your last duty, when possible, is to fight the fire.

You'll find that the local fire department will be happy to assist you and your fellow officers in learning how to prevent and/or control fires. Most extinguisher companies offer demonstrations or training in the use of various extinguishers.

Your employer probably will arrange for this valuable technical instruction as part of your training.

If you have any questions about your responsibilities with respect to fire prevention or reporting fires, ask your supervisor for the answers.

Nothing is more important in your role as a protector than preventing a major or total loss of property by fire.

CHAPTER 9

THWARTING THEFT

TYPES OF THEFTS

Theft is the general term and **larceny** the legal term for the act of stealing. It means the unlawful taking away of another's property without the owner's consent and with the intention of depriving him of it.

Robbery, by legal definition, is the felonious taking of another's personal property from his person or immediate presence and against his will, accomplished by force or fear.

Burglary is breaking and entering a house or any other building with intent to commit a felony therein, whether the felony is actually committed or not. This crime is often committed at night.

Generally, employee theft falls into these categories:

1. **Pilferage**—stealing various small items that can be concealed on one's person or in lunch pails, briefcases and handbags.

2. **Collusion**—conspiracy among employees or with outsiders to defraud.

3. **Embezzlement**—theft of cash, negotiable securities or other valuables entrusted to one's care; taking by fraud for one's own use.

PILFERAGE

Pilferage has been called the "road to embezzlement" and for good reason. It actually is a form of embezzlement (a theft committed while in a position of trust). However, it's seldom done strictly for financial gain.

Oddly enough, pilferage is not thought of as a crime by most people. Usually, employees take items they're around daily. Workers disregard the actual value of these commonplace things

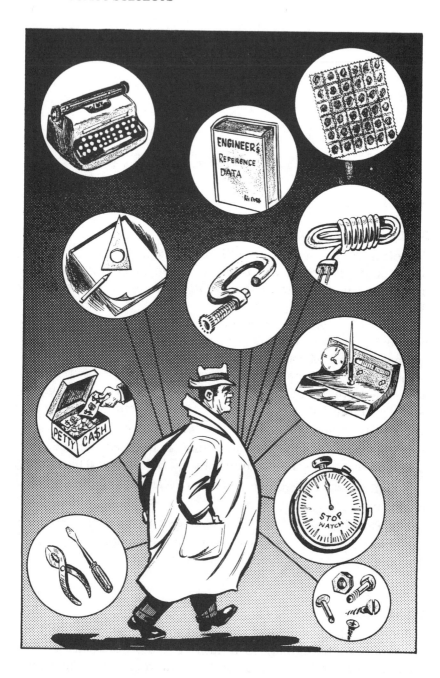

EMPLOYEE PILFERAGE—is the most costly security threat to business. Cartoon shows items commonly stolen. Also high on list are computers and software. Bulgy clothing is giveaway of concealed articles.

and come to think of them as their own. The moral aspect—that stealing is a crime—is totally ignored.

Business management is justifiably alarmed knowing that more losses are created by so-called "honest" people than by professional criminals. Obviously, many firms must tighten up their security to survive.

HIGH COST OF EMPLOYEE THEFT

Employee theft is the single most costly security threat to business today.

Most corporate theft is committed by ordinary employees. The expression "white-collar crime" is somewhat misleading. Stealing spans all occupations.

The annual cost of internal business theft is staggering. Hallcrest Systems, Inc., completed a 30-month study of private security for the U.S. Department of Justice in 1984. The study estimated that employees stole $67 billion from American firms in 1980 alone. That's more than six times the value of personal property stolen from homes (see graph).

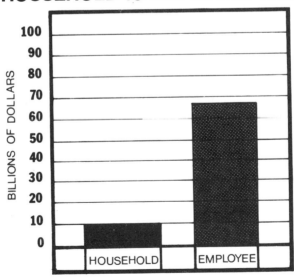

ANNUAL DRAIN—Estimated $67 billion stolen from firms by their employees dwarfs $10 billion value of things criminals steal from homes each year. Sources: FBI records (1983) and National Institute of Justice report (1984).

Minimal Risk

Economic crime is widespread for two main reasons:

1. It's easy. An armed robber may risk his life to get $50 out of a liquor store cash register. On the other hand, a computer operator can steal a $500 software disc from his/her employer with little or no risk. Many companies sweep their losses under the rug, rather than prosecute their employees.

2. Judges tend to give corporate thieves light punishment or none at all. The rap for bank embezzlement is often less than the sentence for bank robbery, although the embezzler may steal 10 times as much as the robber.

Theft Motives

Why do people steal from their employers?

One reason is that the average person has an exaggerated notion of how much profit corporations make. The national average business profit is about 4 percent before taxes. Net profit is even less. If employees are ignorant of a company's financial status, their guesses about profit margin will be unrealistically high.

In today's permissive society, the distinction between right and wrong is often blurred. Many employees regard petty theft as permissible, based on their liberal interpretation of "petty." Workers mistakenly believe that what they pilfer will not be missed and, since everyone else is doing it, they might as well get their share.

Temptation plays a part. Theft from a company seems easy and impersonal, with little chance of detection or actual apprehension. Dishonest people can't resist this temptation.

Another rationale is that theft of "insignificant" items partially compensates a person who thinks he deserves a higher wage or salary.

Typical Scams

Time-cheating is common among all employees, regardless of their specialties. Ben Franklin's advice that "time is money" is almost a forgotten axiom. Killing time is harder for wage earners who have to punch a time clock. That doesn't stop a dishonest employee from punching the timecard of a friend who is late for work or skips a shift entirely. If this deception succeeds, the company will pay the absentee for lost production time—a drain on profits.

Padding expense accounts is a ritual of people who travel for their employers. This misdeed usually is not intended to defraud the company, but to recover personal cash foolishly spent.

Kickbacks are as old as commerce. A kickback is a bribe for a business favor. It usually involves an unfair advantage. Example: a supplier pays a purchasing agent a secret fee for a big order. Quite likely, the supplier will then raise the price of his product to cover the kickback. This underhanded tactic ends up as a hidden cost to the agent's employer—a loss, really, that impairs the firm's competitive position.

Altering records offers many avenues of deceit. Bookkeepers who handle both billing and collections are often tempted to divert cash to themselves. Persons who control supplies also are in an ideal position to steal. The desired object can be anything the thief fancies. He or she steals it, falsifies the inventory record, then uses or sells the item.

An example of collusion is internal hijacking of air freight. Employees who handle bills of lading at an airport cargo terminal conspire with one or more truck drivers. Paper-shufflers find ways to cover up shipment losses. The trucker then diverts valuable merchandise which the schemers later split. Airplanes transport more freight of extraordinary value than any other means of carriage. Most air cargo theft is committed by air carrier employees.

Creation of a phantom payroll is a slick form of economic crime. It's hatched by someone in a supervisory position, such as a shop foreman. He adds phantom workers— nonexistent employees— to the payroll. Departmental paychecks come to him, and he hands them out to shop personnel. He pockets and later cashes the paychecks of fictitious workers he has contrived.

Another variation of ghost accounting is paying for maintenance parts and labor that were never ordered. The culprit works in disbursements. He or she writes, endorses and cashes company checks made out to fake persons and firms. Phony invoices are needed to pull off this scam.

Theft of proprietary or classified information and objects surpasses the petty class. A high-tech trade secret is often worth millions of dollars. If the information or device is a military secret, its loss could threaten national security. Hush-hush ideas, designs, models, hardware, software, inventions, literary works, musical compositions and financial secrets continue to be pirated — mostly by insiders.

Ways to defraud business are as unlimited as the imagination of the workforce. If employees spent as much ingenuity improving firms' profits as in stealing, the U.S. economy would boom. However, this high-stakes theft will flourish as long as the gains are relatively risk-free.

Domino Effect

Any employee is naive to assume that a theft can easily be absorbed. A wholesaler needs more than $10,000 in new sales to recoup a $250 loss in profits, according to Dr. Daniel R. Blake, Professor of Economics, California State University at Northridge.

Business owners and employees alike suffer losses. To stay in business, a company must raise prices or lay off workers, or both. Hence, employees must either work harder for the same money or take a pay cut. Promotions come to a halt.

Employee theft also has an adverse impact on the general public. Blake says economic crime hikes retail prices up to 15 percent and other goods and services as much as 30 percent. Thus, consumers end up paying more for everything.

Declining profits and jobs also weaken the local economy. Taxes that help to support schools and other community services are seriously undermined.

The ultimate bad news is when a company goes broke. About 80,000 American businesses file for bankruptcy each year. Of those, Blake estimates 16,000 (20 percent) fail because of crimes committed against them by employees.

HOW TO SPOT EMPLOYEE THEFT

As a security officer, you can take pride in knowing that you are helping to deter employee theft. To the employee, you represent the company's commitment to law and order. Even if some employees continue to steal, your image impresses the theft more strongly on their consciences. Your military bearing and conscientious attitude will help considerably to promote an atmosphere of responsibility among employees.

You should be constantly alert for these telltale signs of dishonesty:

- Overly friendly employees who may be trying to divert your attention from something they are stealing
- Persons carrying packages, purses or other large containers, conspicuous or not, in and out of the facility
- Visits by employees to their cars during working hours
- Employees returning to the facility during hours when they are not normally scheduled
- Employees who leave the premises by circuitous routes; that is, doors and gates which are out of the way from habitual exits
- Loitering around employee parking areas.

Be sure you make a written report of any such suspicious activities to your supervisor. He or she will bring it to the attention of proper management.

You must follow company instructions for inspecting packages and registering parcels. When this is required, the firm should issue a written directive.

PREVENTING EMPLOYEE THEFT

How can corporations prevent employees from stealing? The following measures will help:

1. **Pre-hire screening.** Careful screening of job applicants will weed out "bad apples" before they're hired. Personality tests and police background checks may cost a little more up front, but they greatly reduce losses in the long run.

2. **Know employees.** Be aware of their abilities and basic human needs.

3. **Adequate controls.** Establish tight controls on cash, merchandise and items with obvious value. Keep up-to-date computer accountability of all company property. Use spot checks and surprise audits to discourage dishonesty. Develop software to signal losses. Concentrate on items being taken.

Close monitoring of employees when they leave the workplace is required at many sites, notably defense and nuclear facilities. Wherever employee theft is rife, strict exit inspections should be enforced.

4. **Educational program.** Hold seminars to explain company economics to employees. Show them how their roles are linked to

the firm's success. Share key information with them. Teach them that honesty is just as important as getting to work on time. Trustworthiness is vital to company survival. Also spell out the penalties for dishonesty.

5. **Work incentives.** Find ways to reward honesty, reliability and good work. Create a sense of shared purpose among employees through bonuses, a stock purchase plan and profit sharing. Treat employees as goal partners instead of just labor units. The more pride they have in their jobs the less likely they are to steal.

6. **Police liaison.** If theft is suspected, get help from the local police or sheriff's department. Law enforcement agencies have detectives who specialize in investigating employee theft. In any case, report all thefts as a matter of policy. This action alone will serve as a deterrent.

7. **Prosecution.** Prosecute offenders whenever possible. Stealing is a crime, not a fringe benefit. Nothing drives that fact home to employees better than catching and prosecuting one of them for theft.

SECURITY OF OFFICE AREAS

Some general security precautions apply to nearly all office areas, whether they're guarded or not.

Pilferage and outright burglary are the two major security problems. Office pilferage can easily transcend the "petty" category. Thefts of electronic equipment are commonplace— ranging from a calculator to a computer, software, or computer components worth thousands of dollars. Unless controlled, such losses eclipse profits.

Security starts with close control of all keys. Where feasible, only one entrance should be used by persons authorized to enter during off hours. Keys to other entrances shouldn't be issued.

Inventories of all equipment and furnishings should be taken, identifying each piece by model, color and serial number. Sometimes security officers conduct these inventories while on patrol.

Bolting office machines to their stands or desks was once a standard practice. It should be again. Inexpensive bolts with locks are available.

Locking or attaching alarms to as many interior doors as possible is strongly recommended.

Only one person among janitorial or maintenance crews should be entrusted with keys. On night and early morning shifts, all of these people should enter at the same time. No one should be permitted to leave independently. The group should leave together.

It's also essential for these crews to have a special place to meet, leave personal belongings, eat and take breaks. Where appropriate, these people should be restricted to their own areas of responsibility. That is, personnel assigned to the second and third floors shouldn't be allowed on any other floor, except at the direction of their supervisor.

Janitors shouldn't take trash out of the building until their work is completely finished. Then a supervisor or security officer should accompany the refuse and personally assure that it's placed in trash bins.

THEFT BY OUTSIDERS

Your Presence Deters Theft

The mere presence of a uniformed security officer is a strong deterrent against theft by robbery or burglary at most facilities.

However, if you're present during a holdup, stay cool. If the robber is armed and you aren't, it's best to concede to the criminal's demands. Don't do anything rash that will further endanger yourself or others. Memorize enough details about the robber so you can give an accurate description to the police later.

If you are armed, don't draw your revolver unless it's necessary for self-defense or to protect the life of someone else. Remember, it's better to let a criminal escape temporarily than for you to injure or kill an innocent person.

For more pointers on what to do in the event of a robbery, see later section in this chapter under the heading, Security of Banks.

Burglary is another matter. That crime is committed when no resistance to theft is expected; in other words, after closing hours.

When Burglars Strike

By knowing the conditions a burglar considers ideal, you can take steps to counteract this crime. A burglar is most likely to strike under these circumstances:

- The criminal knows or believes there is something of value on the premises.

- The criminal is reasonably assured of privacy while in the act of stealing.

- Physical protection is sparse or nonexistent.

- Darkness and inadequate lighting will serve to conceal the crime.

- The criminal knows that the prospective victim is frequently careless about leaving valuable items lying around.

Burglary Prevention

Even with a uniformed officer on the premises, additional preventive measures should be taken. Here are routine security safeguards every organization should take to prevent burglary:

1. Check your building for entrances that aren't adequately protected by rugged locking devices or other physical barriers.

2. Always leave your facility well-illuminated at night, both inside and outside.

3. Be tidy and orderly. Keep nothing at your facility that's not needed in the normal conduct of business, especially valuable items. If these are necessary, secure them well.

4. Use a safe with a combination lock to store cash, checks and other negotiable valuables. Change combinations frequently.

5. Acquire a reputation for keeping little or no extra cash on hand.

6. Make frequent, irregular trips to the bank to deposit any money not necessary for the normal conduct of business.

7. Save carbon copies of charge receipts for 24 hours or more so you'll have a duplicate invoice if original vouchers are lost.

8. Log all checks accepted, as well as written, in case you want a fast tracer on a check you received or want to stop payment on one you wrote.

SECURITY OF BANKS

More and more, banks are using protective security officers during regular banking hours. These assignments require superior deportment and alertness because of the nature of the

BANK SECURITY—Security officer on banking floor is visible deterrent to robbery. Primary duty is to protect bank employees and customers.

banking business and because bank robberies are not as rare as most people think.

The following tips and procedures are offered to officers assigned to bank security posts:

1. Unless otherwise specified, the majority of banks today do not permit firearms. Therefore, you may not carry a revolver unless you're authorized, trained and qualified in its use. As you will see later in this list, the weapon is useless in most situations.

2. The appearance of the officer must be exceptional in all respects, since he/she will be in the public eye at all times. Officers should be carefully selected to represent the bank as well as possible. Weight in proportion to height, a clean-cut appearance and well-pressed, immaculate uniforms are but a few points to consider.

3. Courtesy, tact, curiosity and communication are requisites for bank duty. Being helpful and courteous, but vigilant at the same time, will bring you and the bank additional respect from customers.

4. Continual vigilance is the watchword here. Your prime function is to prevent a robbery. The officer must present a visible deterrent to potential robbers. Lunch breaks should be staggered from day to day. It is also imperative that the officer be accessible to the bank manager at all times. Your mere presence will dissuade most would-be robbers, especially if it's obvious that you're "on your toes." Very few robberies are committed, or even attempted, at banks where security officers are on duty.

5. More important than the protection of money is the protection of bank customers and employees. There are fewer robberies in banks where the security officer is exemplary in demeanor and continually visible on the banking floor. If you're confronted by an armed robber, first remember all the people around you. Everyone will be watching to see what you do. Protect by example. When appropriate, sound the alarm if one is available to you. Do *not* draw your weapon if you have one. Try your best to observe as much as possible about the robber(s). Note race, height, weight, age, eyes, hair, type and color of clothes and any obvious disguises. Also note any visible identifying marks such as scars or tattoos. Your primary job is not to apprehend, but to identify the robber at this point.

6. As the robber leaves, you must still protect people. Don't

shoot unless fired upon or unless your life or someone else's is threatened. If an escape vehicle is used and it's visible from the banking room floor, try to observe the license number. Barring that, get an accurate description of the getaway car. Your role now is to assist bank customers and employees in the aftermath of this crime. Normally, the bank will place calls to local and federal law enforcement agencies. However, the security officer should closely follow any instructions given by the bank manager and make a diligent effort to protect the crime scene.

7. As quickly as possible, document the observations you made of the robbery suspect(s) and anything unusual associated with this incident. If you're a contract security officer, notify your employer about this crime at your earliest convenience.

Leaving your post to pursue the robbers may increase the likelihood of a firefight in which innocent bystanders could be injured or killed. Such a tragedy would increase the liability to you and your security agency, as well as the bank.

PROTECTING RETAIL STORES*

Retail stores suffer the greatest losses due to business crime. Billions of dollars are lost each year by retailers nationwide due to employee theft and shoplifting.

Most retail security experts agree that shrinkage, the dollar amount of store merchandise that cannot be accounted for after an inventory, is caused by a combination of three factors:

1. **Employee dishonesty**—thefts of money and merchandise by store employees.

2. **Shoplifting**—thefts of merchandise by customers.

3. **Poor inventory control**—employees not following proper inventory control procedures designed to account for each piece of merchandise until it is sold.

In years past, the primary tools used by retailers to attack the shrinkage problem were plainclothes detectives whose main function was to detect incidents of shoplifting by customers.

---

*Ron L. Warren, CPP, Branch Manager of Security Consulting Services for Business Risks International, Inc. (BRI) of Nashville, Tenn., contributed this section. He has an 18-year background as a protection professional for retail stores. BRI provides a broad range of security investigative and consulting services to businesses and governments worldwide.

Losses continued to increase, and it became apparent that additional countermeasures were needed. Retail security managers and company financial personnel charged with inventory control began looking beyond theft by customers as the primary reason for losses.

Today's professional retail security manager must address employee theft and poor inventory control, as well as the detection and apprehension of shoplifters.

As a security officer working in a retail store, it is important for you to understand basic security risks associated with the retail industry and the appropriate loss prevention countermeasures retailers employ.

Employee Dishonesty

Many experts regard employee dishonesty as the leading cause of inventory shrinkage. Employees, who have access to and are entrusted with store merchandise and money, have more opportunity to steal than the customers. Employees steal by:

- Removing money from the cash register
- Removing merchandise from the store in bags, briefcases, boxes, or by simply wearing it
- Giving merchandise to friends and relatives
- Giving and receiving unauthorized discounts on merchandise
- Obtaining money from nonexistent returns (cash refunds)
- Voiding sales transactions.

Of course, these are only a few ways employees steal. More sophisticated methods are used by employees in management positions or in sensitive or critical areas such as accounts payable, computer center, shipping and receiving, credit department and mailroom.

Countermeasures to combat employee dishonesty include:

- Pre-employment screening
- Honesty testing
- Employee training and awareness programs
- Integrity shopping
- Effective cash control policies and procedures
- Employee package control procedures
- Closed-circuit television and recorder
- Paper controls such as sales tags, refunds and transfers

- Authorization procedures
- Creating a physical and mental presence of security at all times.

Most retail store managers believe the physical presence of uniformed security officers presents a powerful discouragement to thievery. Positioning a security officer at each entrance/exit of a store provides a strong psychological barrier against theft to employees and shoplifters alike. Placing a security officer at the employee entrance/exit before store opening and after store closing is extremely effective in reducing employee pilferage.

As a security officer, the important thing for you to remember is that to be effective, you must be alert at all times. Your presence and alertness will send a silent message to any thief that his stealing will not go undetected.

You must be polite but firm when enforcing store policies. Be friendly to employees; however, avoid becoming overly chummy. A favorite ploy of some dishonest employees is to establish a friendly, close relationship with a security officer, hoping the officer will become complacent, thereby rendering him or her ineffective.

Shoplifting

A shoplifter is any person who willfully takes possession of any goods, wares, or merchandise for sale by any store or other mercantile establishment with the intention of converting the same to his own use without paying the purchase price thereof. In short, shoplifting is *stealing.*

Millions of shoplifters are apprehended each year stealing from stores. More important, millions are not apprehended. Thefts of merchandise from retail stores go undetected because someone was lax in his/her responsibilities or was not adequately trained in loss prevention techniques. Many times, retail store management limits training of new employees to the sales and promotional aspects of the business, leaving the new employee unprepared to deal with shoplifting.

When asked why she didn't report the theft of a coat from the men's clothing department of a small retail store, one newly-hired employee said she just assumed that kind of thing happened all the time in retail stores and nothing could be done about it. It was later confirmed that no one had taken the time to explain to the new sales clerk her responsibilities in protecting company assets.

Recognizing a Shoplifter

There is no "average" shoplifter. Children as young as three, juveniles, senior citizens, rich people, poor people, housewives, students, business executives—people of all ages and economic backgrounds shoplift. Shoplifters do provide clues, however, in their behavior and the way they dress.

Suspicious behavior includes:

- Acting nervous
- Wandering eyes
- Asking for bags
- Walking behind counters
- Walking into the store in pairs and splitting up
- Constantly talking to sales clerk (could be a diversion).

Suspicious dress includes:

- Heavy coat on a warm day
- No outer garment on a cold day
- Coat draped over shoulder or arm
- Large-fitting clothes
- Raincoat on a clear day.

Shoplifters' Methods

Professional shoplifters develop techniques suitable to their unique skills in stealing a particular type of commodity. They plan their thefts well and sometimes use special devices to filch objects smoothly. By contrast, the amateur shoplifter uses much cruder methods, one of which is simply putting the stolen article in his pocket.

All retailing employees and security officers assigned to stores should be trained to detect a shoplifter, especially the professional. Here's a checklist of methods used by shoplifters:

1. Anything carried in the hands such as coats, gloves, newspapers and packages can be used as aids in palming merchandise.

2. To conceal merchandise, the shoplifter sometimes uses such containers as large purses, grocery bags, diaper bags, umbrellas, briefcases and similar devices.

3. The thief has a slit in the pocket of his coat. He puts his hand through this slit and carries stolen merchandise. It looks as though he has his hand in his pocket.

4. He tries on articles of clothing, dons an outer garment and wears it out of the store.

5. He or she goes into a jewelry store wearing no jewelry, walks out wearing stolen jewelry.

6. Two shoplifters may work together; while one is getting the clerk's attention, the other is shoplifting.

7. The shoplifter wears slacks, skirts or other garments with elastic waistbands, called "shoplifter's bloomers."

8. Thieves sometimes have hooks on the inside of coats, dresses, slips and other apparel.

9. A long coat may conceal merchandise hidden between the shoplifter's legs.

10. He walks into an unattended section of the store or an area close to an exit, picks up merchandise and hurries out the door.

Your Responsibility

Your job as a protection officer is to prevent losses, not to apprehend criminals.

Laws regarding the arrest and detention of suspected shoplifters vary from state to state. Shoplifting is generally classified as a larceny offense. The three elements of shoplifting are: (1) taking the merchandise; (2) carrying it out of the store; and (3) intent to deprive the store owner of such merchandise.

In some states the crime of shoplifting is considered a misdemeanor, in others a felony. Generally, misdemeanors are punishable by less than one year's imprisonment, while felonies are punishable by more than one year's imprisonment in the state penitentiary. But whenever you charge someone with shoplifting, you accuse that person of a crime for which he might go to jail.

Arresting someone for an offense he didn't commit can result in a false arrest lawsuit against the store, your employer (if you're a contract officer), and you. Consequently, *charging someone with shoplifting is a serious matter.*

It's usually the store manager's responsibility to execute the store's shoplifting procedure. Included in his instructions to employees should be specific guidelines on factors affecting the decision to make an arrest.

Since you, as a security officer in a retail store, may be called upon to help apprehend a suspected shoplifter, you should understand the elements that must be satisfied prior to stopping someone. Follow these precautions:

1. Actually see the person take the item. Don't guess. If you only think he took it, let him leave the store. Guessing could lead to a lawsuit.

2. See the person conceal the stolen property and know exactly where the item is concealed. This is very important in establishing proof of intent to steal.

3. Watch the person to be sure he hasn't changed his mind and gotten rid of the item. The fact that he picked up something and concealed it doesn't mean he'll have it at checkout. This person may be setting you up for a lawsuit. If he has ditched the item, don't stop him.

4. Be sure that the item has not been paid for before stopping the person. Make sure he has cleared the checkout area. His failure to pay for an item when he had the opportunity is further proof of intent to steal.

5. The item must be identified as property of the store.

6. The proprietor or his agent must be able to identify the merchandise.

Don't fall victim to the employee who rushes up to you and says, "Stop that person. I *think* he has a pair of pants under his coat." Generally, the person who witnesses the theft is the one who should stop the suspect—but only with adequate backup. Remember, all the elements of the crime must be satisfied before an arrest is made.

The best way to control shoplifting is to remove the opportunity to steal. It is common belief that cameras, mirrors, arrest warnings and alarm systems help to deter shoplifting. In some cases, they do. However, the most effective deterrents are customer service by conscientious, alert employees and the physical/mental presence of security in a store. Shoplifters don't want to be noticed. If store employees and you shower polite attention on all customers, potential shoplifters will often leave the store without stealing merchandise.

Note: As a private security officer, your power to arrest is very limited. Review section titled Citizen's Arrest in Chapter 2.

Poor Inventory Control

Inventory shortage is the difference between what records show and what is actually in the store by physical count. Shortages that occur because of poor paperwork control and bookkeeping errors are often referred to as book shortages. In the case of paperwork errors, there is usually no real physical loss of merchandise, just distorted inventory records. If not corrected, they can adversely affect profit.

Many retail stores create inventory shortage committees comprised of people from several departments (such as security, finance and merchandising) to study each department's loss record. Their goal is to reduce the amount of shortage due to paperwork distortion.

If you're a security officer stationed at a shipping or receiving dock or retail store exit, it's important to be aware that every piece of merchandise coming into and going out of the store should be accompanied by a piece of paper. At the shipping/receiving dock this may be an inter-store transfer, an invoice, a packing slip or a merchandise loan form. At the store exit, a typical paper is a sales tag. Your responsibilities at the dock may include breaking and verifying the seal on the delivery truck and matching the number of cartons received on a shipment against the waybill. At the store exit, you may simply be told to ensure that all merchandise carried through the doors by employees or customers is accompanied by a sales tag or other appropriate accounting document.

Remember that merchandise must be accounted for from the minute it arrives at the dock to the time it is sold to the customer. The final control is the sales tag. If that is not completed properly, it can also create a shortage. The absence of a sales receipt could signal a theft.

SHOPPING CENTER SECURITY

Richard Webster directs security at Plaza Camino Real, a 90-acre shopping center in Carlsbad, Calif. The mall comprises five major department stores and 135 specialty shops. Webster's normal crew is 12-15 proprietary security officers. He contracts extra help during holidays and special events. Here's what he had to say about his operations:

"The primary role of our uniformed security officers is public relations. We're an extension of mall management. The exemplary appearance and courteous services of our officers help to build public goodwill.

"Typical duties include directing customers to stores, maintaining a lost and found crib, helping people find their cars, reuniting lost children with their parents, and solving an endless list of human problems."

Combatting Theft

Burglary at the mall was reduced almost to zero, he said, when his force went to 24-hour security.

Merchandise losses follow a general national pattern—that is, far more goods are lost from internal theft than from shoplifting. Employee pilferage is combatted in several ways. Large stores have their own undercover security personnel. Electronic surveillance devices are widely used, as well as intrusion alarms. A daily computer inventory gives retailers a tighter rein on stock accountability. Uniformed security officers present a theft deterrent simply by being there.

Patrols

During business hours, Webster's team maintains a four-man patrol. Two of the officers are on foot and two cruise the grounds in a patrol car. This routine changes from time to time, depending on the level of congestion and any problems that crop up. Patrols also are conducted when stores are closed.

Liability Restrictions

Security officers at this shopping complex carry radios, but not firearms. Weapons are considered detrimental.

"To me, it doesn't make any sense to have an armed person in a crowded mall," Webster said. "The risk of shooting an innocent bystander is too high to take a chance."

Under lease terms, each store is responsible for its own inside protection. Assistance by mall security officers is limited due to liability problems. If a store plainclothes detective is in pursuit of a criminal, security officers summon police to the location and help track the culprit. Protection officers must avoid physical contact with an offender—except in extreme cases where the life or personal safety of the officer or a spectator is in jeopardy.

Webster added: "Many of the liability problems connected with shopping center security don't even involve theft from a store. An encounter that's nightmarish to us is the thief who grabs a customer's handbag in the parking lot. If you tackle that purse-snatcher and he goes down headfirst and is injured, the civil liability could be horrendous."

CONSTRUCTION SITE SECURITY

Losses of equipment and supplies at construction sites have declined in recent years. Contractors attribute this decrease in crime to the simple expedient of installing adequate security to prevent it. The key factor in this prevention campaign is assigning security officers to protect people, materials and property 24 hours a day.

Unique Problems

Construction sites provide unique security problems, but rules for protecting them generally apply to all such sites. Whether the development project is for housing, an office building, a hospital or a freeway, these basic steps should be taken:

1. A recording clock system must be installed, even for a single day.

2. A telephone must be available to report emergencies and to make your hourly check-in.

Main Purposes

Security officers are employed at construction sites for four principal reasons:

1. Prevention of fire

2. Prevention of vandalism

3. Prevention of theft (pilferage and burglary)

4. Safety. In late stages of construction, security officers control all access.

Accomplishing Objectives

To accomplish security objectives, the recording clock and telephone call-in systems must first be established.

Adequate shelter for the officer must be provided at the outset. It should be situated where you have a view of critical areas of the site. Ample heat and lights should be furnished.

To prevent fires, frequent patrolling of the most critical areas is required. Recording clock stations should be set up at all such points. An inspection checklist should be kept current with the construction superintendent.

Preventing vandalism requires you to be conspicuous to the general public. This means staying outside your shelter 90 percent of the time when weather permits. Warning signs also aid crime deterrence.

The same presence is needed to prevent pilferage and burglary. Construction workers often steal building supplies and power tools. Close accounting of these items, particularly at the end of each work shift, discourages this costly pilferage.

Knowing who to notify in case of trouble is vital. Usually, even a light rain should be reported to the site superintendent because of its effect on many aspects of construction. Be sure your emergency list is always current.

Adequate perimeter fencing and exterior lighting are prime protection aids.

Finally, you should also provide for yourself. Be prepared for bad weather with extra clothes—raincoat and boots when the season demands. Bring food, water and other things you need. Most sites are remote and poorly equipped, and you are usually alone.

Your responsibilities on a construction site are many, but following the rules will enable you to protect the property and gain the developer's respect.

THEFT BY COMPUTER

One negative spinoff from the mushrooming Information Age is theft committed with a computer.

The American Bar Association predicted that electronic theft would become one of the major crime problems of future decades. In a report·to Congress, the ABA stated, "It takes little imagination to realize the magnitude of the annual losses sustained on a nationwide basis."

Law enforcement agencies have turned up a spate of flagrant computer crimes. Examples:

- An expert programmer penetrated the computer code at a Los Angeles bank and transferred $10.2 million to his Swiss bank account by telephone.

- Four men in Virginia tapped the electronic mail accounts of several government, labor and corporate organizations.

- "Hackers" (youthful computer pirates) in Milwaukee gained electronic access to the files of a nuclear weapons research lab and 50 other facilities.

Linking computers with telephones is a marvelous convenience for rapid data exchange. But it also has made computer tampering easy.

Tighter computer security requires better system access control. That entails stricter accountability of equipment and users, as well as improved access codes.

As a defensive measure, some firms shut down their computers during after-work hours. However, many large operations have to stay on-line around the clock. They need 24-hour surveillance of each mainframe (central computer in a network) and all terminals in the system.

Better methods are being developed to track computer crime. Studies show that most violators are insiders. Preventive remedies include: (1) closer screening of personnel with access to computers, (2) motivation to discourage fraud, and (3) improved techniques to catch an electronic thief. Prosecution is a powerful deterrent.

Keeping pace with rapidly advancing technology, more security officers today are computer-trained. They operate computerized security monitoring systems. Others are specially trained to protect extensive computer installations.

This is the direction of the future.

AIRPORT BAGGAGE AND CARGO THEFT

Preventing theft of passenger baggage and air cargo are prime duties of security officers assigned to airports.

These specialties are covered fully in a separate chapter entitled Airport Security.

CHAPTER 10

PROTECTING INFORMATION

GUARD YOUR TONGUE

Keeping "buttoned lips" is one of the most basic things a security officer must practice.

It's contrary to the purpose of security to disclose any information to prying eyes and ears, friendly or not. A secret stays secret longer if fewer people know about it. Improper disclosure of any information, even unclassified, can result in the loss of or damage to the assets you're hired to protect. At the very least, it could be embarrassing.

Here's an example:

In an incident involving a potential theft, a security officer "just couldn't wait" to tell someone an investigation was in progress. He told the guys in the shop. They told their superintendent, who told the security manager. Since the investigation was not yet completed, the indiscretion unnecessarily embarrassed all department heads involved. Had the officer named a suspect who was innocent, the whole mess could have ended up in the courts.

You should refer requests for unusual information to the security manager or public relations manager of the facility you're protecting. Doing so adheres to the rules of most organizations. It's also advisable to refer police to the security manager. Cooperation with law enforcement authorities is strongly encouraged. Indeed, you can provide them with extra eyes and ears. But don't talk freely at the risk of blurting out indiscreet or incorrect information. Giving information to the police can be accomplished without betraying confidences. Be as helpful as possible, but let the security manager or other authorized executive decide what information is released.

MEETING THE PRESS

News reporters for print or broadcasting media might ask you all kinds of questions. Politely explain that company rules prohibit you from disclosing information to the press. Then call the public relations department. If the firm has no PR department, phone the security manager or other designated company spokesperson. Management personnel authorized to talk with news media representatives should be named in your post orders.

MILITARY CLASSIFIED MATTER

Security Clearances

Companies that have contracts with any branch of the Department of Defense (DOD) are often required to use and safeguard classified information—military secrets.

If you're assigned to protect such a facility, you'll need a security clearance. It's your access authorization. You cannot properly serve a defense contractor, according to federal regulations, without such a clearance. Appropriate clearance is mandatory for such duties as checking safes or file cabinets, inspecting restricted areas, burning classified waste or guarding the passage of classified data through gates.

You must have a clearance equivalent to the degree of information you're protecting. That is, if the highest level of information you're handling is secret, you must have a secret clearance.

Before or right after you're assigned to a defense facility, you'll be required to fill out a long federal security questionnaire to get your clearance. This questionnaire, which bares much of your life's history in detail, must be answered completely and truthfully. You will be thoroughly investigated by one or more federal agencies to confirm the accuracy of your answers. Omissions or lies will delay your clearance and may result in your dismissal.

Clearances are not automatically transferred from one company to another. If you are cleared and are employed by a different defense contractor, you'll have to apply for the transfer of your clearance to the new company. (Contract security officers may be assigned to a different client without having to transfer their clearances.) If your work at the second firm requires a higher level of authorization than you previously held, you'll have to reapply. Most security officers assigned to defense plants have a secret security clearance. If you leave defense employment for a period of one year, your clearance lapses and you have to apply all over again.

Need to Know

A security clearance is a respected trust. It doesn't, by itself, permit you to handle classified information. But if you have a need to know such information because of your duties, the clearance, in effect, verifies that Uncle Sam considers you reliable and trustworthy enough to protect that information.

Types of Classified Information

Pentagon regulations are changing constantly. Keeping the lid on sensitive information is always stringent. Your "bible" for protecting defense information is the U.S. Department of Defense Industrial Security Manual for Safeguarding Classified Information. That lengthy title is commonly shortened to the Industrial Security Manual (ISM).

The ISM goes into infinite detail on every aspect of protecting classified information.

Classified information is divided into three general degrees, as are security clearances. They are:

Top secret—the most sensitive defense information, the unauthorized disclosure of which would imperil the nation's security. Most security officers are not required to have this level.

Secret—information which could cause serious damage to the United States if disclosed to the wrong people. You will usually have this level of clearance if you work in a defense facility.

Confidential—the lowest classification of information which could be prejudicial to the United States if lost or disclosed to the wrong persons.

The government grants security clearances to companies and their facilities, as well as to individuals. It's wise for you to keep in mind that persistent carelessness in protecting classified information can result in a firm's losing its security clearance. The same applies to a person.

What to Safeguard

In the broadest sense, there are two things that constitute military secrets: data (information) and hardware, such as a

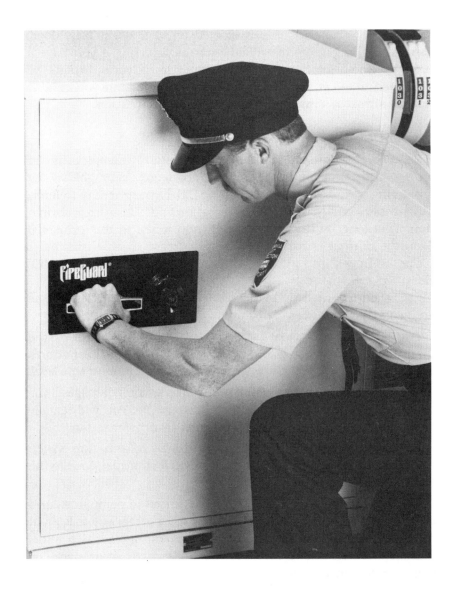

PROTECTING SECRETS—One of a security officer's most important duties is assuring that classified and proprietary data are locked up when not in use.

weapon or part of it.

Data can be in many forms: written words, formulas, codes, ciphers, maps, charts, diagrams, paintings, sketches, photographs, films and recordings. Computer programs (software) are another type of data.

Hardware is divisible into systems, subsystems and components.

As soon as you are assigned to a defense facility, familiarize yourself as soon as possible with the exact nature of the classified materials you're expected to protect and the specific procedures for safeguarding them at that plant. Each defense company usually has its own security manual, applying provisions of the DOD ISM to that firm's products and services.

Individual Responsibility

Protecting classified information is basically the responsibility of those to whom it is given in the course of their work.

You are often that responsible person. Your duty is very clear, or should be. Accountability for classified data entails round-the-clock control of it. Typical activities include storage in vaults, safes and locked files; receiving, forwarding, handling, reproduction and destruction.

If, for any reason, you cannot personally stand guard over classified information, lock it up. If you pass it along to another cleared person, be sure he/she has a need to know. Get a receipt from that person, the same as you would for money. Mailing requires a specific procedure, and again a receipt is mandatory.

You also are responsible for helping other people (employees) to keep secrets secure. Your duties may include checking vaults, safes, files and desks to ensure that classified matter is locked up. You'll want to make sure that windows and doors to restricted areas are not left open. You will be on the lookout for lock combinations employees carelessly scribble on their desk calendars. You almost certainly will be asked to inspect wastebaskets where secrets sometimes land as discarded sheets of paper, carbon paper, typewriter ribbons and tapes. You may be in charge of destroying classified waste deposited in special, locked containers. You also will examine things people carry.

Whatever your responsibilities, do them carefully and well. You're helping to protect Uncle Sam's defense secrets. Take pride in the fact that safeguarding secrets entrusted to you is an important contribution to our country's national security.

The organization you serve may have made a spectacular break-through in technology. That firm and its customer, our govern-ment, have a commitment to the people of the United States to shield advanced military systems from the spies of unfriendly nations. We all depend on a strong national defense as deterrence against powers that would destroy or enslave our society. Be proud of our nation's scientific resources. They bolster our freedom.

Legal Precedents

You have a legal obligation to safeguard classified information. The following types of federal laws regulate classified data, with stiff penalties spelled out for unauthorized disclosure:

- Espionage and sabotage acts
- Nuclear Energy (Title 10, Federal Code of Regulations)
- Mutual security pacts (with foreign nations)
- Internal Security Act
- Export acts
- Patent Secrecy Act
- Federal criminal statutes.

Don't Take Chances

Make certain you know your duties. Be sure they are properly described in your officer's manual and/or post orders. Don't run the risk of a possible security violation because of ignorance. If you have any doubts about a problem involving classified matter, call your supervisor or the security manager promptly. Your sense of responsibility must match the confidence shown in you by the federal government in granting your security clearance.

PROPRIETARY INFORMATION

Information a company considers to be private and confidential —that is, not to be revealed to competitors—is called proprietary information.

You're frequently responsible for the protection of such infor-mation. You must recognize that you're exposed to many business matters that are private in nature. You are obligated to be discreet. Things you see and hear on duty should be reported to your supervisor or the security manager. But never tell others about operations and happenings at the company to which you're assigned. It's nobody else's business, and that's the key. Guarding your tongue is acting in everyone's best interests. Doing so is expected and respected.

Typical Proprietary Matters

Here are some of the things corporations, particularly manufacturers, want to keep out of the hands of their competitors:

- New product designs
- Product performance
- Experimental models
- Advance product or service prices
- Unique research and development
- Pending bids on new contracts
- Sales and marketing strategies
- Concepts for new advertising campaigns
- Advance knowledge of imminent financial ventures
- Personnel records.

You must protect the confidentiality of everything in this list and more. Even the knowledge of unusual visitors, in some cases, must be kept hush-hush.

If you're aware of any leak in company trade secrets, report it to your supervisor, who will relay the indiscretion to proper management.

Remember, part of your job is protecting proprietary information because such knowledge is nobody else's business.

PRIVILEGED NUCLEAR INFORMATION

To be assigned to the protected area of a nuclear facility, you must be capable of obtaining a national security clearance. This entails rigid qualification requirements laid down by the U.S. Nuclear Regulatory Commission (NRC).

You'll have to learn techniques to prevent every possible breach of nuclear security. Each nuclear power plant has its own protection plan. All such plans are privileged information—not for public disclosure.

The NRC refers to proprietary matter as "safeguards information" (SGI). Within that designation are various grades of accessibility. For example, an NRC "Q" clearance is comparable to a DOD "top secret" clearance. A term-for-term comparison is impossible since the NRC has more labels for sensitive information than the DOD.

As a nuclear security officer, the level of safeguarded information entrusted to you will depend on your post and duties.

See Chapter 21, Nuclear Security.

CHAPTER 11

FACILITY SAFETY

As a security officer, you're expected to be alert at all times for any hazard or action that might lead to an industrial accident. Since your responsibility is prevention, you must report safety hazards, no matter how small, to protect employees and property.

Most facilities have safety programs, including written rules. You should familiarize yourself with these rules as soon as you are assigned to a company. Your safety role is a big one. Make certain you always report any unsafe thing or practice. You'll be glad you did.

Lists of common hazards to watch for were discussed in Chapter 4 (Communications and Reports) and Chapter 5 (Patrol Techniques). The biggest hazard to property is fire potential, covered in Chapter 8 (Fire Prevention and Control). If you must give emergency assistance to the victim of an industrial accident, follow instructions in Chapter 7 (First Aid).

Following are additional facts and pointers to help you spot and correct deficiencies which injure and kill plant employees.

THOUGHTLESS PEOPLE

Most industrial accidents don't just happen. They're caused by thoughtless or inconsiderate people who take unnecessary risks.

Common hazardous practices include:

- Horseplay among employees
- Running inside the facility
- Extra people riding or hanging onto plant vehicles
- Not wearing safety glasses or helmets when required
- Ignoring safety warning signs
- Removing or altering safety guards on machinery

- Overworking machinery or electrical equipment
- Disregard for personal safety of self or others in the proximity of danger.

Dangers of Horseplay

How the word "horseplay" relates to horses has been lost in our modern mechanized world. In an industrial complex, horseplay amounts to foolish, often dangerous, actions on the part of witless people.

The dangers of horseplay make it a security and safety risk that you must help to prevent.

Stories and articles abound of horseplay which ended in tragedy. Here are a few to remember:

- The old "hot foot" prank backfired. It ignited a worker in oil-soaked clothing into a human torch instantaneously. The victim's "best friend" had killed him.

- A playboy with an air hose permanently blinded a female co-worker. Just for laughs?

- Another joker slyly poured cleaning solvent into an associate's water cup. The thirsty man gulped down the contents and couldn't be saved. This same gag has been practiced with liquids ranging from urine to gasoline.

- The "boys" hid a steelworker's hard hat during lunchtime. Later a rivet accidentally dropped from several stories up, hit the hatless man on the head and killed him.

- Two clowns driving forklifts were drag racing in a warehouse. They spun around a blind corner, and one of them decapitated a deaf janitor who was sweeping the floor.

Unless stopped, horseplay inevitably leads to accidents. Running, chasing and playing catch often result in spills, bumps and bruises, if not broken bones.

Most companies won't tolerate horseplay. Those with published rules usually forbid such immature actions by employees under penalty of dismissal.

PHYSICAL SAFETY HAZARDS

Next to human carelessness, unsafe objects, substances, and mechanical/material defects rank high as causes of industrial accidents.

Watch out for obvious physical hazards. Note them during your patrols and report them in your daily activity reports. If immediate peril exists, promptly telephone the security manager, maintenance personnel or in-house firemen, depending on the nature of the hazard. If none of these is available, call your supervisor.

Here are examples of common physical hazards to report:

- Open holes in floors and open pits in the ground
- Protruding nails
- Blocked fire extinguishers, doors or other access
- Frayed electrical wires
- Low-hanging objects dangerous to pedestrians or vehicles
- Spillage which makes floors slippery
- Things one might trip over
- Unsecured oxygen or acetylene bottles
- Defective tools, equipment and materials
- Hazardous arrangement of tools, equipment and materials, or dangerous methods employed in their use
- Inadequate lighting or ventilation.

The list is endless—anything your good judgment tells you is unsafe or a potential safety hazard.

Hazardous Liquids and Gases

Many industrial liquids and gases can be very harmful, even fatal, if not properly controlled. Be on the lookout for misuse or accidental leakage of toxic liquids. Train your nose to detect lethal fumes. By so doing, you may save someone from serious illness or death.

Carbon tetrachloride formerly was used extensively as a cleaning agent. It was banned by the Federal Food and Drug Administration in 1970 as "injurious to all the cells of the body." There is no known antidote for carbon tetrachloride poisoning. If this risky chemical shows up where you work, report it at once.

The most common noxious vapor, according to the National Safety Council, is carbon monoxide. Toxic fumes are due to incomplete combustion in heating equipment and standing motor vehicles.

When burning, numerous plastics release deadly fumes.

Other potentially dangerous chemicals commonly used in factories include:

- Ammonia
- Turpentine
- Chlorine
- Formaldehyde
- Sulfuric acid
- Hydrofluoric acid
- Hydrochloric acid
- Trichloroethylene.

You can't be expected to memorize all the harmful substances. But learn the ones at your post, as well as how to control or counteract them.

ELEVATOR EMERGENCIES

You protect many facilities, besides office buildings, that have elevators. You should know what to do if something goes wrong.

Elevators are designed and built for inherent safety. They have automatic devices that will stop the elevator if an unsafe condition occurs. Occasionally, however, emergencies do occur. One example is when an elevator halts between floors due to a power outage.

Technical details of how to remove passengers safely in an emergency are usually described in literature issued by the elevator manufacturer. Read the manufacturer's instructions for the elevator(s) at your post.

Here are your duties as a security officer:

1. Be sure your post orders contain the telephone number of the building superintendent, facility engineer or maintenance manager. The title differs with each facility/organization. You must know how to reach the person in charge of the physical plant at all times.

2. Say an elevator stalls in its shaft. If pushing the "up" or "down" button doesn't correct the situation, call the building superintendent promptly. It may be necessary to notify the fire department.

3. Try to communicate with elevator passengers on the emergency elevator phone. Assure them that help is on the way and that they're safe if they don't panic or try to escape without help from the rescue squad.

4. Notify the elevator company by calling the emergency telephone number the firm has posted.

5. Stand by to assist the elevator mechanic or rescue squad.

6. Notify your supervisor and complete an incident report as soon as possible after the emergency. Try to include the names of stranded passengers, if possible.

NATIONAL ACCIDENT STATISTICS

The National Safety Council publishes an annual report called "Accident Facts" summarizing all types of accidents that happened the previous year. A mountain of statistics is collected from state and federal agencies. The sobering lesson in all this arithmetic is the pressing need for safety.

The council's findings on work accidents are particularly pertinent to this chapter. National accident patterns are given here, rather than statistics for a specific year.

Motor vehicle accidents—by far, the major cause of accidental death and injury—are a full-time occupational hazard for truckers, cabbies and others who earn their living driving. Some people drive company vehicles in the course of their work. While not work-related, off-the-job vehicular accidents to employees add up to whopping losses for them and their employers.

Accident Costs

All types of accidents cost the nation in excess of $95 billion annually. Cost factors include:

- Wage loss
- Medical expenses
- Insurance administration cost
- Property damage in motor vehicle accidents
- Fire loss
- Indirect loss from work accidents.

Insurance administration cost is the difference between premiums paid to insurance companies and claims paid out by them.

The indirect loss from work accidents is the money value of time lost by noninjured employees. It includes time spent filling out accident reports, giving first aid to injured workers, and time lost due to production slowdowns.

Causes of Accidental Deaths

The annual death toll from all accidents in the United States is more than 90,000.

Following are the causes of accidental deaths, with approximate percentages of the total in parentheses:

Accidental motor vehicle deaths. . . . . (50%)

Falls. . . . . (13%)

Drowning . . . . (7%)

Deaths associated with fires . . . . (5%)

Suffocation from swallowed objects . . . . (4%)

Poisons and drugs. . . . . (3%)

Accidental firearms deaths. . . . . (2%)

Gas and vapor asphyxiations . . . . (1%)

Other causes . . . . (15%)

Miscellaneous causes lumped under "other" include suffocation by means other than swallowed items, struck by falling objects, electrocution, air transport mishaps and medical complications.

Death From All Causes

The leading causes of death among all age groups are listed chronologically below. Note that accidents are the fourth leading cause. The top four killers account for 88 percent of annual deaths.

1. Heart disease
2. Cancer
3. Stroke
4. Accidents
5. Pneumonia
6. Diabetes
7. Cirrhosis of the liver
8. Arteriosclerosis
9. Suicide
10. Homicide

Deaths by Age and Sex

Accidents are the leading cause of death among all persons aged 1 to 44. Most fatalities in this age range are caused by motor vehicle accidents.

Among young people 15 to 24 years old, accidents claim more lives than all other causes combined. Four out of five accident victims in this age group are males.

Suicide and homicide death rates are higher for youths 15-24 than any other age group. In that age bracket, five of every six suicides are males. Young males who are murdered outnumber females about four to one.

Heart disease is the No. 1 killer of people 45 and older. Men who die from heart attacks outnumber women about three to one at ages 45-64 and two to one at ages 65-74. Among persons 75 and over, more women than men have fatal heart attacks.

Disabling Injuries

Disabling work injuries throughout the nation total about 1.9 million annually. Of these, over 11,000 are fatal and 70,000 result in some permanent impairment.

Nearly half of all injuries suffered by workers occur away from work. Causes of off-job injuries are about evenly divided among accidents in motor vehicles, in public places (no vehicle involved) and at home.

Here's an annual national summary of disabling injuries, lost production time and the estimated cost of these injuries:

Disabling injuries at work per year .... 1.9 million

Disabling injuries away from work............... 2.5 million

Production time lost (work injuries) .... 40 million days

Production time lost (off-job injuries) .... 50 million days

Future time lost* .... 110 million days

Direct costs .... $15.6 billion

Indirect costs** .... $15.6 billion

Cost per worker*** $320

*Future loss is the estimated time lost in future years from crippling injuries.

**Indirect costs represent the money value of time lost by workers other than those injured. Examples: employees who administer first aid, investigate accidents, write accident reports and process insurance paperwork.

***The $320 figure is the value of goods and services each worker must produce to offset the cost of work injuries. It is not the average cost of a work injury.

Body Parts Injured in Work Accidents

Injuries to the trunk occur most often, with finger and leg injuries next, according to state labor departments.

The range of body parts injured in work accidents follows. Percentages of total injuries are shown in parentheses.

1. Trunk .... (32%)
2. Fingers .... (14%)
3. Legs .... (13%)
4. Arms .... (9%)
5. Head, except eyes .... (6%)
6. Eyes .... (5%)
7. Hands .... (5%)
8. Feet .... (4%)
9. Toes .... (2%)
10. General .... (10%)

Disabling Injuries by Industry

People who work in service industries are the most susceptible to disabling injuries.

The following list shows the annual number of disabling injuries by industry group. Percentages of the total are in parentheses.

Service 410,000 (21%)

Trade 330,000 (17%)

Manufacturing 300,000 (16%)

Government 250,000 (13%)

Construction 220,000 (12%)

Agriculture 170,000 (9%)

Transportation and public utilities.............170,000 (9%)

Mining and quarrying 50,000 (3%)

TRAFFIC CONTROL SAFETY

Facility protection frequently requires you to perform traffic control duties. The basic purpose of such control is to speed traffic flow by eliminating vehicle congestion and/or assisting pedestrians in street crossings. Safety is a major factor.

Here are several points that will aid you to control traffic efficiently and safely:

Public streets are the province of the police or sheriff. Usually, security officers don't control traffic on such thoroughfares. At large facilities, however, it may be necessary for you to control traffic on public streets during short periods. It's the responsibility of facility management to get permission (or help a security contractor to get permission) for you to perform this duty. Law enforcement agencies recognize the need of large companies for extra traffic assistance during peak traffic hours.

Remember to do your work safely. This also entails being properly uniformed and equipped. The full uniform must be worn while controlling traffic. White gloves, caps and armbands of a high-visibility color are recommended. For better control at night or on dark days, fluorescent equipment is advisable: gloves, vest, cap covering and wand. Minimal use of a whistle is recommended.

Position yourself so traffic can flow past you, but stand where you're easily observable to drivers. It's generally better for you to stand on the side of traffic lanes, rather than between lanes.

Make your direction signals in a snappy, military way, not in a loose or sloppy fashion. *Don't over-control.* If traffic flows well by itself, stand erect on the sideline, watchful for problems, controlling only when necessary.

Be fair and impartial to all concerned. Favoritism will start horns blowing faster than any other problem.

Jot down license numbers and car descriptions of violators and troublemakers. Report those who regularly create problems in your daily activity report.

SECURITY OFFICERS VULNERABLE

You should know that you are expected to be safe by acting safely. Be cautious and report all safety hazards you find. Use the safety checklist at the beginning of each shift you work. If you don't find such a list, ask for one to be made or make one yourself. Be safe! You're setting a good example when you are.

CHAPTER 12

PERSONNEL CONTROL

IDENTIFICATION

Protecting life and property frequently requires that you identify employees and visitors entering and leaving the premises you guard.

Gate officers and receptionists have identification as their primary job (see section entitled Being a Receptionist in Chapter 3). Others such as night and weekend patrol officers must identify people who work after hours or persons who might seek admittance at odd hours.

Identification is important because, in most cases, your job is to restrict entry of unauthorized persons to the facility you protect. It's important to identify all people, since admitting the wrong person might cause a loss of a company's property or information.

Trespassing or suspicious loitering often portend theft or attempts to steal.

Most industrial firms use a badge or ID card system. Usually these badges or cards contain photos of the persons to whom they're issued. You mustn't take badges for granted. Neither should you stand so far away from persons entering your control area that you can't compare the badge and person. Close, rapid spot checks are desirable, as long as they're done courteously.

You've no doubt heard the story about the wag (employee) who pasted a picture of a monkey on his badge and slipped past the security checkpoint. Then he bragged about how easy it was to penetrate security. He broke security all right, because he welshed on his obligation to follow rules regarding access to the facility where he worked. He only proved his lack of concern for his employer.

You should, of course, be able to spot such obvious tricks.

Personal recognition is your most valuable aid in identification.

IDENTIFICATION—Security officer checks ID badge of employee at entrance to workplace.

You can do this easily in a small company. In a large firm where employees must wear badges and visitors must register, it's your job to see that these credential requirements are met, without excuses.

PERIMETER CONTROLS

The concept of a secure perimeter for protection is not new. In fact, it's one of the oldest tribal and military tactics in history.

Perimeter control has proven almost mandatory for any kind of nonretail business or an institution. Unfortunately, many business planners and architects overlook the value of a completely controlled perimeter to prevent losses. These controls are usually designed more for containing employees and assets than for keeping out trespassers.

You're often required to check a facility perimeter to make sure it's secure. You're responsible for assuring that all fences are in good repair and that all doors and windows on the edge of the property are locked or, if not guarded, controlled with an alarm. In other words, make sure no one can readily enter or leave the premises without your knowledge and consent.

If you're assigned to a post where you must ensure that people or materials don't get out illegally, use your imagination. If you wanted to get out without being detected, how would you do it? In all probability, an employee engaged in a forbidden act would take advantage of any loopholes you can envision. If you find an unauthorized exit—an unguarded, unlocked or nonalarmed door, gate or large low window—be sure to mention it in your daily activity report. Your supervisor and corporate management will be grateful for your keen observation.

The most common break in a secure perimeter is a door that can be opened easily from the inside and has no alarm on it to alert you to someone's departure. Another insecure access is a locked door to which nearly everyone has a key. Without correction, these deficiencies will make it almost impossible for you to maintain a secure perimeter.

If you have any doubts about the perimeter controls at your post, tell your supervisor. He or she should have the premises resurveyed and report any security flaws to management.

PERIMETER CHECK—Officer inspects barbed-wire loop on top of chain-link fence while on perimeter patrol.

PARKING AREA CONTROL

There should be a special place in heaven for the poor souls responsible for company parking areas.

No louder complaints are heard in security or personnel offices than the screams of employees outraged that their precious parking spots have been taken, or that things have been stolen from their cars.

As a security officer, you're sometimes in the middle of these tiffs—but you're supposed to be. You can make a security manager's life longer and happier if you know how to achieve good parking area control.

Your first responsibliity is to be patient. The second is to be courteous and tactful, yet firm, even in the face of outrageous and blasphemous behavior.

The company is responsible for establishing iron-clad rules concerning parking areas and ensuring that all employees are aware of these rules. Only then can you enforce them.

You're always responsible for protecting vehicles on the firm's property. You should be constantly alert for vandals, thieves, or just plain trespassers.

If your station doesn't permit visual observation of the parking area, then make frequent, unscheduled spot checks.

The presence of nonemployees who are "just taking a shortcut" across the lot should be reported in your daily activity report.

Everything stolen from cars and told to you by employees or visitors must be reported to the security manager promptly. Don't let these thefts go unreported, since the police or sheriff should be notified in every case.

If you observe vandalism or pilferage in the parking lot (or anywhere else), call for help and try to apprehend these offenders or order them away. If you're armed, under no circumstances threaten to use your weapon unless you are equally threatened and must defend yourself or others. Don't leave your post to chase criminals or suspects. These acts may be just a distraction to draw you away. Report the incident to the security manager and the police. Let them try to catch the guilty person(s). Your job is to get a good description of the suspect and his/her car. Also report the incident to your supervisor.

YULE SECURITY PROBLEMS

Merry Christmas and Happy New Year! Glad tidings of great joy. Yuletide is, indeed, a joyful holiday season for most people. Unfortunately, it brings a bundle of problems for security officers.

You're responsible for the safety and security of employees and authorized visitors all year round. This job gets tougher at Christmas time.

To make certain all the bases are covered, business firms should establish and publish policies applicable to the yule season. Are alcoholic beverages to be permitted inside the facility? Will celebrating be allowed in parking areas? If merry-making is okay, when can it get underway? How are you supposed to handle tipsy employees or visitors who want to reenter the premises after lunch, dinner or a party outside the facility?

Should wrapped gifts carried in and out of the facility be inspected? Are Christmas trees with electric lights permitted in interior work spaces? Must the trees and decorations be flame-proof?

Any extra or special schedules for you to meet? Whom do you call in case of an emergency when so many people leave the area during this festive season?

All these questions and more should be answered in advance by company management. Make sure you know how to cope with these situations before they arise. If the security manager doesn't tell you what to do, notify your supervisor so that he or she can ask for special instructions.

Your own personal behavior must be above reproach at all times, but especially during yule holidays. You'll get offers to have "just a little nip." Expect to receive an unusual amount of familiarity. Frankly, you're very vulnerable, but don't get coaxed into joining the revelry. You mustn't compromise your own integrity and the reputation of your fellow officers by taking part in celebrations.

At times, you have to be a master of diplomacy. This is particularly true in restraining undisciplined sexual advances. Sexual harassment committed by playful males against women should always be stopped. When celebrating, aggressive females occasionally throw propriety to the wind. They may try to shower you with affection (if you're a man). You must put them off good-naturedly, reminding them that you're on duty.

Remember, if you know the solutions to problems in advance, your Christmas will be much merrier.

TRESPASS PREVENTION

The penal code in the state where you're employed is specific about trespass.

As a security officer, you should be aware of at least the basic rules. You are frequently required to prevent or restrain trespass.

In most states, almost any type of property can be legally protected against trespass by posting proper warning signs. The exact wording and requirements for posting "no trespassing" signs are spelled out in the law.

The size of the sign and the way it's enclosed may vary from state to state. In California, for example, signs must not be less than 1 square foot in area, and the words "Trespassing, Loitering Forbidden by Law" must be stated in letters at least 2 inches high. Of course, the signs can be larger. They can also name the property owner and cite sections of the penal code covering trespass and loitering. Because of the inadequacy of small signs, larger ones are recommended.

Another specific in California law is that trespassers must be arrested by property owners or their agents, rather than the police.

If you have to arrest a trespasser, ask for immediate assistance from the local police or sheriff's office. Have law enforcement officers stand by in your presence to take over trespassers you're forced to arrest. In most cases, you should only assist members of management in such proceedings, inasmuch as the trespass is against company property.

Familiarize yourself with essentials of the trespass law in your state. Ask your supervisor for answers to specific situations you may anticipate at your post. You should also learn each company's procedure for counteracting trespass.

UNION ORGANIZING

The firm should give you clear instructions on what to do when labor unions attempt to organize company employees.

In general, you should serve as a neutral buffer during union organizing efforts.

Although you're not on anyone's side in the organizing drive, it's very clear who pays your salary. The owner's interests in protecting employees, property and other assets are your basic responsibilities.

Company rules for employee conduct have no bearing on union organizing per se. They're standard rules usually established long before the organizing began and must be followed by all who are authorized to enter the premises. Special rules for behavior or for movement of materials may be imposed by management during an organizing period.

You should be neither questioned nor liable for following your orders to maintain safety and order. Union organizers and industrial relations personnel are both very much aware of the federal statutes which govern an organizing effort.

Be polite and respectful to all concerned. Above all, maintain close liaison with the security manager.

Organizing efforts often start with the distribution of literature on or near the company's property, usually during shift changes. If you notice such activity, notify the security manager immediately. Make sure that literature is not being handed out on the premises. Union organizing is permitted on public sidewalks and streets, but usually not on company property.

If an organizing effort comes to your attention, report it to your supervisor promptly. You should be given special supervision and coaching at that time.

EMPLOYEE WALKOUTS OR STRIKES

General Procedures

When labor conflict arises between a company and its employees, your job becomes more difficult.

General policies recommended for security officers are:

1. You're employed to protect employees from injury and property from loss or damage. Those are your basic functions. Who you work for, and why, are never in question.

2. You're not against anyone. You have no personal stake in the dispute and harbor no ill will toward the pickets individually or collectively. You can't and won't interfere with the right to picket *off the company property.*

3. Don't become involved in the controversy. You are there simply to observe the activities of pickets at the company's perimeter and to report these activities to your supervisor.

Your uniform and your mere presence serve as reminders to all concerned that order must prevail and that no illegal acts will go unnoticed.

You shouldn't wear a firearm unless specifically ordered to do so by the firm that employs you. No one should ask you to bear a weapon without clearing such a request with security officials.

Your supervisor, in concurrence with corporate management, should spell out what you're supposed to do in the event of a strike at the facility you're protecting. Specific orders should be given to you in advance of a walkout, so you'll have a complete understanding of your role before a dispute develops.

Primary performance rules include:

- Be polite at all times.
- Don't lose your temper.
- Never discuss issues of the dispute with anyone.
- Avoid verbal exchange with strikers as much as possible.
- Report anything and everything that happens, for your own protection.
- Keep in constant touch with another officer by radio, telephone or visual observation.

Critical Period

Once labor stoppage occurs and pickets are posted, extra security coverage will be required to protect the facility and to help non-striking employees get into the plant. Maintaining operations will be difficult. This is the prime time for striking employees to create havoc.

Facility Protection

You'll be busier than a beaver. A well coordinated protection plan will have you roving the facility round the clock, checking entrances, windows and the entire perimeter. You should also check parking areas for nails and other hazards that might damage cars owned by non-striking employees.

Keep a checklist of things that should be monitored daily. It might include:

- Fire protection equipment
- Burglar alarm system
- Water lines
- Fuel supply
- Telephone system

- Heating, ventilating and air conditioning equipment.

One of the most vital areas to keep plant operations going is the shipping/receiving platform. You may be assigned to this post to maintain order.

Two-way radio communication is very useful to keep vehicular traffic moving in and out whenever there is a lag in picketing. This serves to avoid confrontation when a large group is present.

An hourly picket count by security officers will help security management chart picket activity and locations of strength around the clock. Other hourly checks should include perimeter lighting and defenses.

Review facility provisions for fire control prior to the strike. Fire-fighting equipment should be readily available at your post and throughout the facility in the event of arson attempts or malicious mischief such as stink bombs or firecrackers.

Be constantly alert for any actions by strikers resulting in property loss or damage or injuries to non-striking employees. Document details such as names, dates, time of day and place. Photographic documentation also is desirable, but that's not usually your responsibility. Specific things to watch for include:

- Throwing rocks at, scratching, denting or breaking windows of vehicles
- Weapons
- Property damage caused by unlawful entry attempts
- Vicious damage such as broken windows or vandalism on equipment
- Theft of company property
- Starting fires.

Monitoring Pickets

You may be asked to gather evidence on unruly or violent picketing. The facts you collect may be used in a legal enjoinment, so make sure your reports are detailed and accurate.

In general, get the names of pickets whenever possible. If a disturbance occurs, note the date, hour and place.

You can't know when disorder will erupt, but you should always closely monitor picket lines. Observe the number of pickets, where they form a line or congregate, and significant fluctuations in number. Describe the manner in which they're picketing (single file, arms locked, standing or moving). Record messages on picket signs.

If angry words are shouted to persons seeking entrance, try to identify the offending picket. Note any intimidations against non-striking employees. Also report when vehicles are stopped or blocked.

Observe and report unruliness such as drinking, noisiness and profanity.

Be on the lookout for violence or threatened violence. Get the facts straight, including statements from witnesses. Details are important. Document the following:

- Any actual assault
- Weapons involved, if any
- Besides name of person assaulted, identify, e.g., non-striking employee, company official, supplier or customer
- Circumstances leading up to the assault
- Description of the assault
- Nature and extent of injuries.

Document any arrests. Note how many police officers showed up and who was in charge. Describe how they handled the situation.

GAMBLING

One of your basic purposes is to protect business against loss. Loss prevention boosts profits.

Losses come in many forms. One of them is gambling. Gambling by employees, on or off company premises, represents a potential loss to any firm.

Most forms of gambling are illegal in all states other than Nevada and New Jersey. Exceptions are betting on horse races and lotteries in states where they're legal. Some versions of poker are legal in California.

Being caught and prosecuted for illegal gambling can be very costly in terms of time, money and embarrassment. A compulsive gambler often loses all worldly belongings, the respect of family and friends, and ultimately self-respect.

An employee who gambles and incurs heavy debts poses a threat to his/her employer because the bettor may resort to pilferage or embezzlement to cover gambling losses.

The distraction from business affairs and resultant loss of time can be extremely expensive, and it's demoralizing to other employees.

With these points in mind, be sure to report any signs of gambling. Your supervisor should be told promptly and confidentially so that he or she can take appropriate action with corporate management.

Be alert for these signs of gambling:

- Odds lines on sports, bet markers, cards, dice and racing handicap sheets you observe when on patrol.

- Money or markers changing hands in gatherings at lunchtime or during coffee breaks.

- Nonemployees such as food caterers, deliverymen and similar vendors who mingle suspiciously with employees during breaks or right before or after work.

- Employees who are continually borrowing, or trying to borrow, money from you or their fellow employees.

Your intent should be to prevent loss to the firm, rather than to meddle in the private lives of others or to cast aspersions on their activities.

All businesses should have a policy against gambling on company premises—except, of course, where it's legal, such as a Las Vegas or Atlantic City casino.

DRUG ABUSE

Alarmingly common today in all type of business are employees who are "stoned" on the job from use of drugs.

Alcoholic overindulgence in the workplace is an old problem long familiar to you. But the drug problem can prove more complicated. Drug abuse is not limited to young people. The truth is, blue- and white-collared workers of all ages are increasingly "hooked" on addictive substances.

Marijuana or hashish smoke is easy to detect by its pungent odor, similar to the sharp aroma of burning rope. "Pot" smokers frequently burn incense to disguise the smell of marijuana. On your rounds, teach your nose to be curious, especially in or near restrooms.

The pill problem is tougher to detect. The smallness of pills affords easy concealment. Without formal training, you can't tell one drug from another. However, you can learn to spot signs of drug use by the erratic behavior of employees.

Two kinds of prescriptive pills widely used illegally are called "uppers" and "downers." Uppers are amphetamines (pep pills). Benzedrine® and Dexedrine® are common examples. A stronger variety, methamphetamine, popularly known as "speed," is potentially lethal. All of these stimulants to the central nervous system cause the user's normal reactions to speed up—faster and louder talk, faster movements and brighter eyes. Dilated (enlarged) pupils in the eyes are a dead giveaway of drug use.

Downers are barbiturates (sleeping pills). These sedatives make users sleepy, dull, slow-witted and blurry in speech, as if they're drunk.

Lysergic acid (LSD) is a psychedelic drug used in the study of mental disorders. It is also widely abused. LSD in powder or liquid form can be applied to any food or beverage. While in the throes of the drug, "acid" users are easy to spot because they hallucinate, or have delusions. They're out of touch with reality. Their minds wander. They see, hear, taste, smell and feel way beyond the normal senses. Their "trips" can be beautiful or horrible. When "turned on," users of hallucinogens can be extremely dangerous to themselves and others.

Such behavioral extremes should be reported to the police to prevent injury or serious after-effects. Don't do this yourself. instructions that follow).

Users of hard narcotics (heroin, morphine, codeine) are seldom employed, unless they can afford or have access to drugs. Actually, cocaine use is very popular among the affluent, including celebrities. The street addict turns to crime to support his/her habit. You won't encounter many heavy junkies. But if you run across a syringe ("shooter") in a strange place, be sure to report it.

If you observe employee behavior that strongly suggests drug use, notify appropriate management immediately. If you detain a "stoned" employee in a lobby or at a gate, call the security manager, personnel office or the employee's immediate supervisor. Don't apprehend for any reason strictly on your own.

Be sure to make a few notes in your daily activity report. An incident report might be required if management takes any action on your observations and suspicions.

DRUG IDENTIFICATION

Various organizations provide charts, booklets and other types of literature which depict most of the illegal substances you should watch for. We suggest you find and keep such information at your post.

CHAPTER 13

WEATHER WORRIES

Sudden changes in the weather almost always affect the security officer and his/her protective functions. Regardless of your geographic location, weather can affect you and your duties. You should know the potential problems and be prepared in advance to cope with them.

HOT WEATHER

Hot or muggy weather is a challenge to your decorum, especially if you work outdoors or in a building with no air conditioning.

Dress as lightly as possible while still maintaining a proper uniform. If the heat and humidity are too oppressive, it may be advisable to bring a fresh change of clothes.

Be especially alert for fire during hot weather.

The people you deal with—employees and visitors—are more likely to be quick-tempered when the weather is suffocating. Though they're irritable, you must stay cool. At times, this may test your tact and patience to the hilt.

Most people take their vacations during the summer months. This often calls for personnel and scheduling realignments at a facility. It's important for you to be aware of such changes.

For those of you assigned to transportation terminals, resorts and tourist attractions, summer could be your busiest time of the year. Naturally, the increased workload magnifies your problems.

COLD WEATHER

You Need More Clothing

Chilly or frigid weather necessitates that you wear more clothes.

You must choose outer garments carefully so as not to detract from your appearance. Many uniformed officers have found that several layers of light clothes under the regular uniform is sufficient insulation against moderate cold. Except in areas of continuous subzero weather, a combination of multi-layer clothing with an all-wool melton jacket (short) is preferable, since it maintains a uniform appearance. Remember, your appearance is one of your greatest assets. Don't let chilly weather rob you of your effectiveness.

Freeze Multiplies Problems

Freezing brings ice, snow and a host of security and safety problems which you must identify, correct and/or report. For example, slippery sidewalks and roads affect the safety of employees. Glazed or snow-laden roads could also hinder you from getting to your post on time. Frozen pipes shut off water supply and could even cause a shutdown of operations. Cold also adversely affects many types of mechanical equipment, which you should observe on your patrol rounds and report.

Prepare Checklist

It's impossible to guess all the cold weather problems you might encounter in Vincennes, Indiana; Rochester, New York; or even in parts of Southern California. It is suggested that you prepare a list of things that need to be checked and a schedule of how often to check them. Completion of scheduled checks should then be recorded in your daily activity report. Your personal checklist should include reminders to yourself when to bring extra clothing or to take an alternate route to work.

Snow

Very few regions in the United States escape snowfall during winter months. Security officers at posts in mountain ranges surrounding Los Angeles have to cope with difficulties produced by snow just as do officers in northern states, the Rockies, Midwest, East and parts of the South.

Regardless of where you work, if snow is an annual menace, the precautions are basic: be prepared, be careful, and be mindful of the people and things you protect.

Your responsibilities include:

- Being able to get to your post

- Keeping warm
- Keeping pedestrian walks safe by notifying appropriate people of existing conditions
- Alerting building maintenance management to unusually heavy snow loads on roofs, as well as other safety hazards.

RAIN

Compound Problems

Rain brings transportation problems, flooded roads and parking areas, leaky roofs and many related problems.

Your job is to report problems caused by rain so company personnel can react and correct them. Bad leaks or flooding can halt production. This can be extremely costly if not corrected immediately.

If possible, where leaks may cause costly repairs to property, control them until corrective action can be taken.

Be prompt and complete in your reports to your supervisor and to facility managers.

Getting to Work

While rain brings transportation problems to everyone, it amplifies the security officer's problems. You *must* get to your job. Most people could just take the day off and not have to be temporarily replaced.

If the weather is rainy and you're uncertain of road conditions, you may want to start early for your post. You certainly will want to try to find out, by phone or radio, the condition of roads before you leave home.

Always remember to telephone your supervisor or the officer you're supposed to relieve if you are delayed by rain (or anything else). That's an important responsibility.

FOG

Fog is another weather worry you face. In really bad fog (ceiling zero) security problems are multiplied since visibility is limited for you, police, firemen and company personnel. However, burglars and vandals seem to have radar.

Double your watchfulness on foggy days and nights. If you do, you'll be ready for anything.

LEND A HELPING HAND

LEND HELPING HAND

You'll find that personal courtesies are especially appreciated by employees and visitors during inclement weather. Lending a helping hand will pay big dividends in respect and future co-operation.

Security officers who go out of their way to be helpful to others win much admiration. A splendid example is the officer who hangs up a sign to remind people entering an industrial complex to turn off their auto lights on foggy, rainy or dark mornings. Three cheers for the gatehouse officer who has these things:

- Jumper cables for dead batteries
- Telephone numbers of the automobile club and other towing services
- Paper towels to clean windshields
- A sympathetic ear for the endless troubles of others.

The idea is to be sensitive to the problems of people around you. By helping them, you establish good relationships with those whose respect you need to do your job efficiently. That includes almost everyone at your workplace.

COVER FOR THEFT

Foul weather of any kind heightens the incidence of employee pilferage. Be particularly aware of, and alert to, ways theft can occur during inclement weather.

Clothes, Haste Aid Pilferers

During cold or rainy weather, people wear more clothing and hurry through gates and lobbies. Employees dash into a facility to get out of bad weather, then rush out to their transportation after work. That's human nature.

Would-be thieves find this situation opportunistic for two reasons: (1) extra clothing offers better concealment of stolen items, and (2) a hasty retreat reduces exposure time.

Filchers will take advantage of you if you're not on your toes.

Some sort of shelter should be provided at every facility entrance so identification can be made unhurriedly. Otherwise, you run the risk of admitting an unauthorized intruder.

You may be lucky enough to spot a pilferer on the way out, but probably not. Long overcoats and raincoats can conceal a lot, and you cannot search. Take heart in knowing that the thief may "goof."

A sterling example was a too-greedy wire thief at an electronics complex. He wrapped so much wire around his body that he could barely move with the dead weight under his coat. The alert gate officer asked the perspiring, snail-paced employee to wait a moment. The wire heister collapsed under his burden before the officer had time to call the security manager's office.

Another classic bungle happened at a California aerospace plant. An enterprising employee waited for a rainy day to steal a 6-foot length of tubing. He was as tall as the pipe was long. He wore rubber boots and a plastic hooded raincoat. Hidden inside the raincoat, the tubing was inserted in one boot and extended along the man's back to the top of the hood. This made walking awkward. A little ramp by the gatehouse proved the thief's downfall—literally. He slipped and fell on the ramp. Like an upside-down turtle, he couldn't stand up.

Had he stolen two 3-foot sections of tubing—one in each boot—would the security officer have caught him?

Precautions Against Pilferage

Knowing the extra hazard of easy concealment should lead you to take extra precautions.

A potentially good first step is moving your post from the gatehouse to inside a facility door or the employee locker area during bad weather. Here inspection takes place before extra clothing is donned. (You cannot move your post without management approval, of course, but you can suggest such things.)

Asking management to request the cooperation of all employees in opening coats and jackets during checkout sometimes helps—but usually personal searches are forbidden.

Sharp alertness on your part for unusually bulky clothes on people you know by sight is a big deterrent. Remember, the psychology of confrontation is decidedly in your favor. If you stare suspiciously at most people, you may get an occasional guilty reaction. You can then politely ask the employee to stop for a moment while you inspect his lunch pail or her purse (if such practice is established as legitimate). A polite request that a coat or jacket be opened may bring results, but can't be pushed. If a person refuses and walks out, you have no authority, in most cases, to do anything except report your suspicions. It is recommended that an officer obtain his/her supervisor's permission before using the foregoing technique.

Use your daily activity report to log suspicious activity, and notify your supervisor.

For further information on preventing pilferage, review Chapter 9, Thwarting Theft.

CHAPTER 14

PHYSICAL SECURITY

UPGRADED TECHNIQUES

The Space Age and Computer Age have produced a bonanza of technical breakthroughs that have been a boon to business protection. Actually, the new technology has revolutionized security methods.

In the not-too-distant past, a night watchman had little else to aid him except his own senses, a flashlight or lantern, and maybe a telephone.

Today's security officer has much more going for him or her. Better planning of physical security and new electronic sensors, detectors and monitoring systems enable an officer to cover a wider area more efficiently. Not only has he/she greater surveillance, but faster detection of anything amiss. Instant communications link security forces around the clock and afford quick notification of management and emergency agencies. The same command and control technology that serves security officers also hastens response from police, firemen and medical personnel.

This chapter discusses state-of-the-art physical security. Some of these things are conventional protection aids of long standing. Others are recent technical innovations that have won wide acceptance in the security community.

STRUCTURAL BARRIERS

More than just housing royalty, ancient castles were fortresses. The huge stone structures were built to ward off invaders. In addition to unassailable ramparts, castles often were protected by natural barriers such as water or a mountain.

Though not war battlements, modern business facilities are strongholds, too. They must protect people and other assets from a host of misfortunes. Construction today affords the best possible safety from fire, weather, and natural disasters. Most buildings are designed to keep intruders (people and animals) out. Banks are nearly impregnable.

It would be ideal if architects and structural engineers gave design consideration to maximal internal and external security for every business facility. They should anticipate pilferage and bombs, as well as making a building burglar-proof. Unfortunately, such enlightened planning is rare.

It's impossible to build a barrier criminals can't penetrate, given enough time. The optimal solution is to make entry by force or stealth extremely difficult. A series of deterrents is preferable to just one barrier.

Better Building Materials

Standards set by state building codes and such private research groups as Underwriters' Laboratories, Inc., have generated constant improvements in building materials. Stronger masonry, metal, glass, walls, ceilings, floors and roofs enhance safety and security.

Walls

Walls and fences around a facility shield it from casual intruders and the public at large, but only serve as delaying barriers to professional thieves.

Enclosure walls are usually built of brick or concrete block. Aside from their aesthetic appeal, they're harder to ram with a vehicle than a wire fence. Also, making an entry hole in a masonry wall is either time-consuming or noisy.

Most building foundations and bearing/shear walls are made of reinforced concrete. Solid steel and reinforced concrete walls are the most impenetrable to bomb blasts. Engineering studies show that a steel plate 1 inch thick and a reinforced concrete wall 8 inches thick have equal resistance to the impact of high explosives.

Chain Link Fences

Industrial complexes are commonly surrounded by chain link fences.

The stronger and higher they are, the better. Additional deterrence is offered by topping them with various configurations of barbed wire. One is a barbed wire guard, or outrigger, that slants inward or outward at a 45-degree angle. Another combines those into a V-shaped barbed wire overhang. A third variation is coiled barbed wire or Razor Ribbon®.

How safe are these fences against vandals and thieves?

The U.S. Armed Forces have conducted a number of tests in recent years to find out how fast a two-man team can climb over a chain link fence, aided only with a blanket. Tests were performed on fences 8 feet high, topped with various barbed wire arrangements adding 8 to 24 inches to the fence's height. Penetration times varied from 4 to 12 seconds!

Such breaching tools as wire or bolt cutters would make access easier but, except for snipping a gate lock or chain, would take longer.

Secure Windows

It used to be routine for a thief to break a show window in a store, grab expensive display goods and flee.

A would-be burglar is somewhat stymied by laminated glass. It increases his/her exposure time. Laminated glass won't shatter even if struck with a hammer. This material is made by bonding one or more layers of a resilient plastic, such as vinyl, between sheets of glass. Auto windows are laminated.

Laminated glass in thicknesses from ¾ inch to 3 inches is bulletproof. The Bank Protection Act of 1968 requires that all drive-up and walk-up teller windows in banks be protected with bullet-resistant barriers at least 1-3/16 inches thick.

Under that statute, here's a general comparison of the thicknesses of laminated glass needed to resist fired bullets:

- Glass 1-3/16 inches thick—super .38 caliber pistol
- Glass 1-1/2 inches thick—.357 magnum revolver
- Glass 1-3/4 inches thick—.44 magnum revolver
- Glass 2 inches thick—30-06 high-power rifle.

A special type of laminated glass serves as an alarm window. The inside layer of glass is coated with a transparent oxide that conducts electricity. The current inhibits the alarm until the glass is broken.

Tempered glass is stronger than plate glass, but not as shatterproof as laminated glass. Since tempered glass won't break when people fall against it accidentally, it is widely used for entrance doors and pedestrian corridors.

Glass with a wire mesh imbedded in it is more fire-retardant than plain glass. Though not bulletproof, wired glass resists the impact of some large objects, such as a toppling person. That's why it's popular for shower doors.

Two high-strength plastics are excellent for security windows and safety glazing.

An acrylic (plexiglass) sheet is half the weight of glass and 17 times more resistant to breakage. Acrylic material withstands all kinds of weather and is long-lasting.

A polycarbonate sheet weighs half as much as glass, but has 300 times the impact-resistance of ordinary glass. This resin's superior toughness commends it for burglar-proofing applications. Polycarbonate material is less weather-resistant than plexiglass.

Since both of these plastics expand and contract due to temperature changes, sufficient clearance should be left in their frames.

LIGHTING

To be well protected, every facility should be adequately lighted in critical interior and exterior areas.

Effective night lighting of vulnerable perimeters makes it possible to reduce the number of security officers required to patrol the entire boundary of a factory or any other complex.

Modern incandescent and mercury vapor lights are available in many intensities for every need, from illuminating entrances and exits to floodlighting yard and parking areas.

Lights serve two purposes: (1) enable authorized personnel to conduct their work, and (2) discourage entry of unauthorized persons.

Some interior day lights and exterior night lights are fixed and continuous. Others are switched on only as needed.

Many types of emergency lighting are used, including the kind that automatically turns on when an intruder enters an area protected by an electronic detection system. His mere presence may instantly activate a floodlight, an audio alarm and a camera. Another type of emergency lighting is backup equipment to supply illumination when regular service fails.

Local power companies are very cooperative in helping customers to plan and engineer adequate protective lighting.

FLOODLIGHTING—Bright lights on exterior of industrial facility discourage nighttime burglary and vandalism.

LOCKS

The most common type of lock is one that opens with a key. Key locks may be built-in, such as in a door, or detachable. The detachable key lock has a shank that springs open when the key is turned in the lock. Padlocks are attached to hasps, bolts or chains to prevent unauthorized access.

For maximal security, any key lock should have a dead bolt (no spring). Key locks with springs, whether built-in or detachable, are the easiest to pick. They present no problem whatever to a professional thief. Even an amateur can pick one in seconds if someone shows him how.

Better protection is afforded if most doors in an industrial facility have neither an outside doorknob nor an outside keyway. Doors with heavy daily traffic should have double keyways, requiring a key to get out as well as in.

Combination locks, both built-in and detachable, are made in a variety of ways. The most common type has a dial, alternately turned right and left in circular motion through the correct sequence of numbers to open the lock. Another type of combination lock, like those used to lock bicycles, has numbers on a row of rotary discs. The numbers have to be lined up in proper sequence to open the lock. A third variation comprises a series of buttons that have to be punched in proper sequence.

A combination lock with nylon gears is superior. Its inner workings can't be fluoroscoped or x-rayed. Also preferable are combination locks permitting easy changing of combinations. The combinations should be changed frequently.

Fireproof and fortified, the sophisticated time locks in bank vaults are the ultimate in combination locks, but even they are occasionally penetrated by crafty burglars.

Many firms have doors and gates with electromechanical or electromagnetic locks. This type of lock is tripped by remote control. The electromechanical system combines the use of an electric current and a mechanical lock.

When charged, an electromagnet exerts up to 1,500 psi pull on a metal plate. Cutting off the current nullifies the locking device. In case of power failure, battery backup is used. Normally, these locks are engaged or disengaged by a pushbutton or key-operated switch.

Certain facilities, notably parking areas, have card key locks. A laminated plastic card containing magnetic foil serves as the key. Inserting this card into a slot electronically opens a gate or door. Some hotels use other variations of the card key, such as a rigid plastic strip with perforations matching the matrix of a door lock. Inserting the strip clears the lock tumbler pins, so the door can be opened simply by turning the knob. The newest system merely requires the card to be close to the "reader." It need not be inserted or even taken out of a wallet or purse to be "read."

Access to top secret areas has always been tightly controlled. One method requires both a card and a metal key to open a door. An additional requirement may be a frequently-changed access code. More recent identification equipment scans a person's face, voice, palm prints, fingerprints and even the retina of the eye. A computer memory core instantly reveals if that person is authorized to enter the restricted area.

SAFES AND VAULTS

Safes and vaults protect important business documents (deeds, titles, franchises, contracts, records). Vaults also are used to store art treasures and historical memorabilia. Very few industrial firms today keep large amounts of cash on hand.

The security of a safe or vault is measured by (1) its degree of fireproofing, (2) the surety of its combination lock, and (3) its resistance to penetration. A fireproof safe is preferable to one that is not. A built-in combination lock in a safe or vault is better than a detachable combination lock. A safe or vault should have a minimum resistance to tampering of one hour. If a thief can open a safe in less than one hour, that safe is unsafe. The more tamper-proof it is, the better it is.

Two- or four-drawer file cabinets with built-in key locks are the *least* secure. A better arrangement is a filing cabinet with a steel bar that secures all the drawers and is locked with a detachable combination lock. A fireproof cabinet with built-in combination locks for every drawer is even better.

The Department of Defense permits the steel bar and detachable combination lock arrangement for storing confidential and secret classified materials, providing such cabinets and locks are checked regularly.

ALARMS

The introduction of electric alarms early in the 20th century started a new era in the protection of banks and retail stores. However, the old-time burglar alarms were more often set off by unwary persons, animals and defective wiring than by burglars.

Today many efficient electronic sensors and detectors are used for security protection, fire prevention, safety, process control and environmental control.

There are six general types of sensing devices: electromechanical, sound wave/microwave, capacitance, vibration, audio and light.

These sensors can be grouped into three categories based on location. An integrated system protects:

1. The perimeter or point of entry (fence, door)
2. An area (room)
3. An object (safe, vault).

The following paragraphs describe the various types of alarm sensors commonly used today.

INTRUSION ALARMS—Four types of sensors to detect intruders are illustrated. From top, alarm systems are infrared (light and heat sensor), seismic (sensitive to vibration), ultrasonic (silent sound waves), and radar (tracks moving objects).

Electromechanical Sensors

Simple electromechanical sensors are descendants of the first burglar alarms. They're usually installed to protect openings (gates, doors, windows, skylights).

Breaking an electric current initiates an alarm. Typical is an intrusion switch. This device comprises two electrical contacts—one on the fixed surface and the other on the object that opens. Opening a door or window breaks the closed circuit and triggers an alarm.

Metallic tape that carries an electric current is sometimes installed around windows. Foil may trip up an amateur, but it's easily spotted by a professional thief. Other disadvantages are that it's time-consuming to apply, and blemishes may cause false alarms.

Wire and screen detectors can be used to detect forced entry at a fence or through an air duct. The tension on a single strand of wire or a screen sets off an alarm.

Another type of electromechanical sensor is a flat pressure mat. It's usually placed in front of a door, under carpeting or on stairs. Stepping on the mat activates an alarm.

Sound Wave/Microwave Sensors

Evenly-spaced sound waves are continuously transmitted and received. These are in a frequency higher than the human ear can hear; hence, this type of protector is also called an ultrasonic sensor. Any movement in the area covered disturbs the pattern, which starts an alarm. A sound wave sensor is strictly an indoor application. One drawback is that movement of air circulated by an air conditioner may cause a false alarm. More than one sensor may be needed for a large space.

A microwave unit (radar) operates on the same principle as an ultrasonic sensor. The main difference is in the type of signal used. Radar sends and receives an electronic beam, while an ultrasonic sensor uses sound waves. Another significant difference is that radar is an effective security aid both indoors and outdoors. Weather has no effect on a microwave signal.

Capacitance Sensor

This type of sensor uses a large condenser that stores and radiates an unnoticeable amount of electrical energy. The difference in the energy level between an antenna and ground coupling is measured constantly. An intruder absorbs some of the energy. This tips the capacitance balance, causing an alarm to sound. A capacitance sensor is practical only for indoor use. An electrical storm can cause a false alarm in an outdoor application.

Vibration Sensor

A super-sensitive sensor is installed on interior surfaces such as floors, walls, ceilings, safes or filing cabinets. The slightest vibration caused by an intruder attempting forcible entry is detected. The equipment is adjusted so that ordinary sounds are screened out. Vibrations caused by such unlawful acts as drilling or chiseling are picked up by an amplifier that activates an alarm. This type of detector is also called a seismic sensor.

Audio Sensor

An audio sensor works much the same as a vibration sensor, except that it picks up sounds audible to the human ear. Here again, a discriminator must be installed to screen out noises which might cause a false alarm.

Light Sensors

A photoelectric cell will protect large interior and exterior areas. This mechanism employs an intense beam of light. If the beam is broken, interrupting the light transmission, the resultant broken circuit triggers an alarm.

The photoelectric beam is invisible to an intruder. A visible light beam can be made invisible by putting an infrared filter over the source.

Using mirrors makes it possible to zigzag a photoelectric beam around a room or around a corner—a handy tool for protecting long corridors and warehouse interiors.

Outside units are built to resist weather.

Laser technology has been adapted to light-interruption alarms. A laser beam can be projected much farther than an ordinary beam of light. In general, laser optics cost less than photoelectric "eyes."

The foregoing sensors are the principal ones used for intrusion detection. However, there are others, a few of which should be mentioned.

Other Sensors

One thermal sensor is installed in a room where the temperature is kept below the normal heat of a human body (98.6F). If an intruder enters the area, his body temperature will activate an alarm.

This type of sensor lends itself admirably to the detection of an acetylene torch or a blowtorch.

A fairly new instrument checks the chemical content of the air in a given area. If human breath and sweat are detected, a meter records the change in the atmosphere, initiating an alarm. This sensitive sniffer is quite expensive.

Several radiation sensors have been introduced from time to time. They use radiation to detect an intruder. Most potential customers reject this type of sensor for fear of radiation poisoning. Actually, the amount of radioactive material is so slight it's considered harmless.

Monitoring alarms are widely used for safety. A typical application is a buzzer or red light which goes on when electrical circuits are overloaded. Hydrostatic monitors protect against explosion (if steam is involved) or warn of unwanted water in electrical systems. Elevators are equipped with monitors which reveal the slightest fault in cable, power or hydraulic systems. Some elevator alarms are local and others are wired to a remote station.

Eliminating False Alarms

False alarms are more likely to happen if only a single intrusion sensor is used.

Multiple applications eliminate this problem. The best method is to place two or more detectors in an area, unified so they all have to react to set off an alarm.

FIRE DETECTION

Fire Stages

A fire has four stages:

1. **Incipient stage**—invisible combustion gasses can be smelled, but there are no visible signs of fire.

2. **Smoldering stage**—smoke can be seen, but no flame.

3. **Flame stage**—the fire has now ignited.

4. **Heat stage**—the flames produce intense heat and quickly expand the air.

Types of Fire Sensors

The most effective sensors detect the first two fire stages promptly. Latent combustion and smoldering can progress for hours, or even days, before bursting into raging flames. The sooner a fire is detected and put out, the less damage it causes.

Here are the leading types of fire sensors:

- **Fixed temperature sensor**—initiates an alarm when the detection element reaches a certain temperature.

- **Rate-of-rise heat sensor**—triggers an alarm when the device senses that the temperature is rising faster than a given number of degrees per minute.

- **Combined thermal sensor**—combines features of fixed temperature and rate-of-rise sensors to track fast and slow fires.

- **Smoke detector**—an alarm is activated when smoke partially obscures a photoelectric beam.

- **Ionization chamber**—amplifies a tiny electric current produced by charged atoms, which sounds an alarm. This sensor detects air changes during an incipient fire stage.

- **Quartzoid bulb**—heat breaks the bulb, closing an electric circuit, which starts an alarm.

- **Water flow sensor**—an excessive flow of water in a sprinkler pipe causes a vane to actuate an alarm switch. A time-delay feature prevents false alarms due to variance in water pressure. Forerunners of this type of valve date back to the 19th century.

MIRRORS

Mirrors which aid business protection are of two main types: two-way and concave. The two-way mirror is a see-through mirror. It's placed in areas where an observer wants to watch the activities of other people without their knowing they're being watched. A concave mirror permits observation of a larger area than can be seen normally. With a concave mirror, for example, a store owner can see behind shelves and along aisles beyond the range of his natural eyesight. Concave mirrors improve safety in garages and parking structures, permitting drivers to see around corners. A security officer in a building can observe pedestrians along two or more hallways simultaneously with the aid of concave mirrors.

TELEPHONES

Telephones have become a necessity in business, including protection of a business. Telephone technology and services have improved appreciably in recent times. Now that Ma Bell's corporate structure has been splintered and a host of new competitors have entered the market, further advances are expected to flourish.

Use of the telephone by security officers is covered in several previous sections. See Telephone Technique and Telephone Reports in Chapter 4; Being a Receptionist, Chapter 3; Call-in Procedure, Chapter 5; and numerous references to phoning in case of an emergency. First use of telephone transcripts for training security officers is discussed under Training in Chapter 2.

Old-time switchboards are relics of the past. Dial phones have been replaced by push-button instruments. Self-answering phones take messages when the user is away. Other features include automatic dialing of programmed numbers, a display of time and date, and a timer to measure the length of each call. Business models offer multi-connection conference calls ("networking").

The most significant of all recent innovations is the linking of computers to telephone circuits. Using a device called a modem and an access code instantly ties far-flung computer terminals together via the phone lines. Individuals and corporations conduct business worldwide through the use of phone-aided computer relays.

All of these telephone advances have been applied to security services, enhancing communications and information transmittal and storage.

Perhaps you welcome the day when you can phone in your reports and they will automatically be printed and filed by computer. The technology is at hand, but cost-effective methodology isn't yet universal.

RADIO COMMUNICATIONS

Acquaint yourself with radio operation procedures furnished to you by your employer.

While you needn't study radio engineering, you should familiarize yourself with the radio system you use, whether at a fixed post or in an automobile equipped with two-way radio.

Radio signals require three basic devices: (1) a transmitter, (2) a receiver, and (3) antennas for both.

The transmitter provides the energy to send the signal. The antenna "spreads" the energy into the atmosphere. The receiver "catches" the signals and converts them into voice, printed word, or code messages.

Several types of radio units are used in security work. The most common is the base station/transceiver system. The base station is the transmitter, usually located in a central control station. The transceiver is a mobile unit installed in a patrol vehicle. All transceivers both send and receive. Another type called a pager only receives. Pagers are carried by security officers who are "on call." Response is by telephone.

Security and police radios operate on frequencies assigned by the Federal Communications Commission (FCC). Often several users are assigned the same frequency. Most frequencies are either VHF (very high frequency) or UHF (ultra-high frequency). Both VHF and UHF are "line of sight" equipment. That is, they operate best on flat ground with no obstructions such as hills, mountains or large buldings in the transmission path. The range of these radios is about 50 to 100 miles.

To overcome line of sight and distance, UHF messages are relayed via a "repeater." A repeater is an antenna placed on top of a tall structure, mountain, or other high ground. The base station transmits up to the repeater. The repeater receives the transmission, amplifies it and rebroadcasts the message to users' receivers. The transceiver can send a message back to the base station the same way.

Rules for Radio Use

A few rules are advisable to maintain efficiency in the use of radio equipment. Instructions should include:

MOBILE RADIO—Patrolman reports incident on car radio.

1. Report all incidents.

2. Whenever a patrol officer calls the police, all other units should remain off the air until the unit concerned gives an all clear. The only exception to this rule is in the event of another emergency.

3. Avoid unnecessary talking over the radio.

4. Hang microphones in holders provided for them when not in use.

5. Remember, frequencies are monitored by the FCC for abuses of radio procedure.

Radio Codes

Radio codes are used to keep messages brief and to the point. Each firm will have its own code for such messages as:

- Message clear and understood
- Receiving poorly
- All OK
- Stand by
- Awaiting instructions
- Repeat transmission
- Return to base
- What is your location?
- Disregard last transmission
- Proceed to (some designated location).

Generally, security managers assign code numbers to individual patrol officers. Blocks of numbers are assigned to geographical areas. This system speeds up transmission and identification.

CLOSED-CIRCUIT TELEVISION

Modern facilities use closed-circuit television (CCTV) for a number of security functions, mainly surveillance and access control.

An officer aided by one or more television monitors can control access to one or several gates or doors from a remote station. He/she identifies personnel on CCTV, then opens a gate or door by means of a remote switch.

CCTV also affords continuous surveillance of any critical area. With a small electric motor, the camera can be made to pan, or sweep, for wider coverage. Retailers employ CCTV to monitor merchandise. Banks use the device for robbery detection. Television cameras can be hidden to reveal pilferage or vandalism (e.g., graffiti on restroom walls) by employees.

Today's television equipment is compact and efficient. No longer is floodlighting necessary for a clear picture. Recent advances in infrared optical equipment make televising possible in dimly-lit areas.

STILL AND MOVIE CAMERAS

Cameras that take still and motion pictures have long been popular security devices.

Decades ago, an intruder knew he had been photographed when his presence triggered a photo flashbulb. Today a crook may or may not know when he/she is "on camera." Superb lenses and supersensitive film make it possible to shoot sharp pictures.

CCTV—Officer observes several areas at once on closed-circuit television.

Photos can be taken in the dark with infrared film. A telephoto lens lengthens the distance at which a subject can be photographed clearly. A wide-angle lens expands the area that can be photographed.

Still photos and movies greatly facilitate apprehension and conviction of a criminal. A clear picture of a crime being committed makes convincing prosecution evidence.

ELECTRONIC SCANNERS

Many industrial firms use electronic scanners to scan identification cards. Often the ID card scanners are employed along with television surveillance from a remote station.

More recently, holography has been applied to card scanning. This photographic method uses laser light to produce three-dimensional images. Holographic scanners are the kind used by grocery checkers.

Electronic scanners are also widely used in industry for product inspection and mail sorting.

Law enforcement agencies, including the FBI, use high-speed fingerprint scanners. This equipment is a great time-saver in identifying known or suspected criminals.

COMPUTER MONITORING

Today's talented security officers monitor hundreds of protection functions from sophisticated computer consoles. Two or more officers operate a computer control center that provides an automated security system for an entire facility. They're alerted to any system violations in a fraction of a second, aided by audio-visual signals, displays and printouts.

Automated Tasks

Practically any electromechanical device can be interfaced with a computer. Applications are limited only by imagination. Here are typical security tasks that can be performed automatically by computer:

- Lock and unlock doors
- Control personnel access
- Record employee attendance

COMPUTER CONSOLE—Today's protection officer controls numerous security functions by computer.

- Monitor all fire sensors
- Monitor all intrusion sensors
- Check key station patrols and warn of irregularities
- Turn lights on or off
- Start and stop machinery
- Detect and correct temperature/pressure extremes
- Control water level
- Provide a direct link to other security officers and emergency agencies.

Sharp Programs Vital

Normally, a computer monitoring system is tailored to each organization's needs. Hence, software offered by computer manufacturers usually is inadequate. Since a computer can't think or exercise judgment, its efficiency depends on the quality of its instructions. Good programming is a must. A common expression for lousy programming is "garbage in, garbage out." If computer tasks are complex, the software often costs more than the hardware.

Most security officers aren't trained to be computer programmers. Companies may use staff programmers or hire outside specialists to develop software for a protection system.

In the planning stage, design consideration should be given to future expansion. This will accommodate not only the firm's growing needs, but also the rapidly escalating state-of-the-art.

WHAT NEXT?

When this book went to press, electronics wizards were applying microprocessors to everything from kindergarten education to architectural design. What this bodes in future work innovations is mind-boggling. One prominent business forecaster predicted a major shift from smokestack industries to computer-related enterprises.

Following is a look at this technical stampede and its impact on security in years to come.

Computer Generations

Computers have gone through four generations: (1) vacuum tubes, (2) transistors, (3) integrated circuits, and (4) microprocessing.

Each later generation has shrunk the size of equipment. U.S. and Japanese microchip manufacturers announced that they would soon mass-produce megabit (million-bit) chips. A silicon chip about one-eighth the size of a postage stamp will contain enough microcircuitry to process a million bits of information. The storage capacity and speed of megabit chips are roughly four times that of previous chips.

A bit is a single number (0 or 1). Words are formed by combinations of those two numbers. Zero and one also correspond to "off" and "on" for instant switching.

Guessing what breakthrough will usher in fifth-generation computers stirs the imagination. A practical goal is a computer that's so easy to operate everyone will want one. Computer buffs are eager for simpler programming languages and memory capacity beyond the megabit chip. Some researchers predict a computer that will run on a "biochip"—a half-living, half-electronic cell.

Artificial Intelligence

A frantic race is on among worldwide industrial nations to create "smart" computers—machines with artificial intelligence. The Pentagon is the biggest U.S. spender on this research. Japan and Russia also have committed huge sums.

Experts regard today's computers as stupid. Researchers hope to replace these mechanical morons with computers that can see, hear, talk, plan and reason.

Thinkers are trying to find the roots of instinct and common sense. For example, how does a person know that a bucket with a hole in it will leak? What thought processes automatically prompt a person to close a car door?

The goal of the scientific community is to simulate human intelligence—to build a computer that can draw conclusions, make decisions and learn from experience. As baffling as this challenge seems, inventors are confident of victory within the next decade.

Countless uses for artificial intelligence are envisioned, from preventing nuclear war to diagnosing disease. Insiders say that the first nation to develop a truly "intelligent" computer will have awesome defense and economic advantages over rivals.

Protecting computer secrets shapes up as a colossal security task now and in the future.

Security Robot

A Massachusetts firm has built and tested a 4-foot-high, 400-pound security robot. It's expected to be used initially in prisons.

The robot makes its patrol rounds at 3 mph on three wheels. Unlike humans, it doesn't get sleepy or careless. It tracks security threats with infrared and ultrasonic sensors. Some models carry television cameras. An ammonia sniffer detects humans by their perspiration odor, no matter how faint.

Upon discovering an intruder, the rugged little machine says in a stern voice, "You have been detected." It relays all its findings back to a computer control room.

A sonar range finder guides the robot through buildings, recognizing landmarks programmed into its computer memory. The versatile automaton also can diagnose its own ailments.

Do you wonder if you'll ever be replaced by an R2D2 look-alike? You needn't fret. When robots are placed in security service, they'll perform functions that are boring or dangerous for humans. After all, robots need people to look after them.

Computerized Fingerprint Files

When this book was written, the FBI was in the process of auto-mating its mammoth collection of fingerprints. The bureau then had 22.8 million fingerprint cards in its criminal files, plus 35 million cards in other files. Many states were likely to follow suit. A few large cities already had efficient computerized fingerprint files. San Francisco installed its system in 1984. Other urban areas were raising money for this purpose.

A Los Angeles detective estimated that a manual search of the 1.7 million fingerprint cards the city had on file in 1985 would take 67 years. Hence, Los Angeles officials were planning auto-mation to speed up fingerprint searches.

An electronic brain (computer) can compare a fingerprint, or fragment of a print, with millions of others and come up with a match in seconds. The computer memorizes visual images of fingerprints. Each print also can be divided into quadrants that can be enlarged. A digital scanner counts 80-120 tiny points (minutiae) on each fingertip. Intricate fingerprint ridges, valleys, whorls and crisscross patterns are traced mathematically, speed-ing up identification.

This time-saver makes it possible to catch and prosecute many criminals who formerly got away.

Spy-Proof Phones

The kind of spy-proof telephones used by federal intelligence agencies may soon be available to private industry.

That word is from the National Security Agency (NSA) which commissioned a feasibility study in 1984.

In the past, phones equipped with secure coding devices were too costly for the average company. Each installation cost about $31,000 (at presstime). Researchers hired by the NSA forecast a future price as low as $2,000. The agency estimated that Uncle Sam and defense contractors would want about 500,000 of the new phones before they're available to other firms.

An NSA spokesman said the study was undertaken because Soviet electronic eavesdropping was thought to be on the rise. He explained that spying is made easier by a large number of voice communications via airwaves instead of wires. In other words, a cable phone system is less vulnerable to interception than a microwave-to-satellite network.

One method proposed for the secure phone system is to use a

computer capable of encoding and deciphering phone conversations automatically.

The NSA is the largest U.S. intelligence service. It was formed in 1952 to conduct worldwide electronic intelligence and to protect America from similar snooping by foreign powers.

Cellular Phones

Cellular phones were introduced in Chicago in 1983. This compact, portable communication tool promises all sorts of future applications. If and when the service rate is more affordable, the device could come in handy in your work.

Mobile radio telephones, including citizens-band (CB) radios, have a limited range. Only a small number of phones can be used at once over a wide geographic area. The advantage of cellular radio phones is that coverage is divided into smaller districts, called cells, and many phone calls can be made on the same waveband. You can call within your local area or anyplace in the world reachable by telephone. Transmissions are beamed to a satellite by microwave boosters.

While mobile phones in cars are stationary, you can carry a cellular phone anywhere you want to go. One model weighs less than 2 pounds and is small enough to fit in a man's coat pocket or a woman's purse.

Here are a few scenarios in which a cellular phone could aid you in your security duties:

1. Let's say you get into an auto fender-bender on your way to work. With your portable phone, you can quickly summon help and notify your supervisor and family.

2. You're posted at a remote construction site. Before a site phone is installed, a workman is injured. You can call an ambulance immediately on your cellular phone.

3. While on patrol, you discover a fire. It is already in the flaming stage. You can call the fire department on the spot, without waiting to get to the nearest facility phone.

4. You're guarding a big warehouse at night. While checking the perimeter, you see a burglar breaking into the building. He's unaware that you've seen him. He could be armed. With your cellular phone, you can call the police at once.

5. If you encounter an on-the-job problem you can't cope with — anytime or anyplace — you can call your supervisor for a prompt solution.

Super ID Card

In May 1985, five young men in Baltimore introduced a wallet-size plastic ID card capable of storing 500,000 words. Using a personal computer and digital scanner, the words can be displayed on a screen.

Initial use of the card was to store medical records. Market analysts reasoned that the same laser-optics used to create this coded disc could eliminate fake Social Security cards, driver's licenses, credit cards and passports. Publishers saw the potential for card-size books that can be read on video screens.

Presumably, a person could carry his lifelong employment and medical records—as well as all the information for his security clearance—in his wallet.

Biometric Identification

Many high-tech researchers are experimenting with devices that scan the human body to provide foolproof identification.

Employees in high-security jobs increasingly will be subjected to biometric inspection to verify who they are.

A federal laboratory in New Mexico uses an instrument that focuses on eye blood vessels to grant access to top secret areas.

The Rensselaer Polytechnic Institute in New York has designed a voice-activated lock. A device "reads" a person's voice sound-wave pattern similar to the way a computer scans a fingerprint. The lock opens when the voice scanner recognizes the speaker.

Apparently, direct voice-recognition works well, but some scepticism has been raised about the reliability of verifying a voice over the phone. As of now, this temporary hurdle was still under study.

Another invention measures the shape and pressures of a hand to activate an automatic bank-teller machine. Researchers believe each individual, besides having one-of-a-kind fingerprints, has a unique touch.

The success of these devices depends on cost, reliability and the whims of users.

Latest Security Cameras

It has been said that today's cameras will do everything but buy the film. Recent advances in electronics, optics and film quality have revolutionized still and movie photography. Much of this technology is a boon to security.

In the near future, it isn't farfetched to assume that a security officer could carry a television camera or video screen on his patrols. Lightweight television cameras already are in use as security monitors. An ultra-miniature TV set was introduced in 1985. It has a 2-inch screen and weighs just 7 ounces. It is battery-powered.

Another interesting R&D project is an infrared security camera that can "see" in the dark. It will be linked remotely with a computer printer that spits out an instant still photo of any intruder. This technology is now on the market.

Stock Certificate Detector

A Los Angeles company has developed what is believed to be the first automated system to detect bogus stock certificates, bonds and other securities. The system was expected to be fully operational in 1989.

Securities formerly were checked manually. The new high-speed system does two things: (1) electronically inspects certificates to verify their authenticity, and (2) prints coded data on newly issued certificates.

Authenticity is proven by scanning paper fiber patterns. The number of shares issued and other proprietary information are encoded on new certificates. A computer terminal is used for processing.

This innovation is hailed as the answer to securities counter-feiting. Today's photocopiers turn out fake certificates that are hard to distinguish from real ones. The new system takes the guesswork out of verification and, for the moment, defies duplication.

The technology has been approved by the Financial Industry Security Council.

CHAPTER 15

CROWD AND MOB CONTROL

Large-scale rioting isn't as common as it was in the 1960s. It was devastating then. After six days in 1965, the toll of the Watts riot in Los Angeles was 35 dead, 864 injured, and property damage of more than $200 million, with 600 buildings destroyed by fire. Looting was rampant, and thousands were arrested.

However, crowd control and prevention of violent mob action are still matters of serious concern for private security forces, as well as the police. The most common potential for a riot that you're likely to encounter is a striking workforce. Peaceful demonstrations against business firms sometimes get out of hand. So security precautions are necessary to prevent riots or to help control them once they start (see Employee Walkouts or Strikes, Chapter 12). Other demonstrators who could be dangerous are anti-war protesters lined up around a defense plant or anti-nuclear pickets at a nuclear facility.

If you've ever seen a riot, you'll never forget it. The specter of a mob running wild, buildings ablaze, vehicles overturned, windows shattered and bloody personal violence such as fistfights, clubbing, stabbing, shooting and bombing are terrifying. Such melees must be nipped in the bud.

What's the difference between a crowd and a mob? A crowd is a large assembly of people lacking personal identity. A mob is a disorderly or lawless crowd.

Examples of crowds are large numbers of people gathered to watch a game, show, parade, fire or an accident. The usual crowd has no leader. Each person is on his own. As long as everyone is orderly, the crowd is peaceable.

Crowd control requires that security personnel and police know these four things:

1. Reason for the gathering

2. The area occupied

3. Traits of people comprising the crowd

4. Identity of potential troublemakers.

Usually, the first three items above are no problem. The fourth, however, can be difficult. At a football game, for example, the purpose of the gathering is obvious. Security officers know the stadium and grounds well. Individuals and families are typical sports fans. It's easy to identify spectators who are for, or against, each team. But spotting agitators takes observation and/or advance tipoffs.

Mobs are either organized or spontaneous. Typical old-time mobs were lynching parties and early strike breakers. Unfortunately, the Ku Klux Klan is still with us, as well as other cults that thrive on turmoil.

As a security officer, you'll probably have little to do with organized mobs. Law enforcement agencies or the National Guard usually control such groups. However, you may become involved with a crowd that becomes a mob. Such a transition can occur very quickly, unless proper security procedures are employed.

Your objective in crowd control is to prevent the crowd from becoming a mob. To realize that objective, great self-control is necessary. Here are some do's and don'ts in this situation:

DO'S

1. Observe the crowd, not the event for which the crowd is gathered.

2. Note changes in the mood or attitude of the crowd.

3. Look for troublemakers—mob leader types.

4. Be impartial. Show no preferences whatever.

5. Whenever possible, keep outside the crowd.

6. Show respect for religious symbols, the American flag and state flags.

7. Keep agitators and leaders under constant surveillance.

8. Allow yourself to be seen, but don't swagger or strut. Maintain a relaxed posture.

DON'TS

1. Don't swear, argue or be dictatorial.

2. Don't engage in unnecesary conversation, even with friends.

3. Don't have body contact with crowd members.

4. Don't take sides.

5. Don't respond to baiting or gibes, but keep those persons under observation.

6. Don't be a decoy. Don't run to a reported trouble spot unless ordered by your supervisor. Walk quickly but calmly.

7. Don't permit loitering. Loiterers often become trouble-makers. Don't be fearful of noise, shouting, profanity, horns and the like. Mere noise is not mob action. In fact, noisemaking helps rowdy people to expend energy.

8. Unless ordered to do so, don't carry any kind of weapon. Weapons cause resentment, a dangerous emotion in a crowd. Besides, a weapon is of no use to you, alone in a crowd.

The reason for your presence in a crowd is to maintain order. Your uniform is a sign of authority and makes you stand out. Take jeers in stride. People in a crowd are more likely to tease than when alone. Even if taunts are brutal, that doesn't mean that mob action is imminent, unless you cause it by losing your head.

Be on the lookout for changes in crowd behavior that spell danger.

Troublemakers should be removed. That's not an easy task. First, be sure of the person or persons who are causing trouble. Warn them gently but firmly. Sense the crowd mood in relation to the agitators. Only when you feel that the crowd is unsympathetic to the rabble-rouser can you remove him/her. Even then, be careful.

If the crowd is in cahoots with the troublemaker and you sense a shift in mood to anger, call the police at once. They will assess the situation and use whatever tactics are needed for mob control. Your role then is to assist the police.

First aid crews should be on hand to tend any injuries, but avoid physical conflict. Leave that to the police. If you are not otherwise occupied, assist first aid efforts.

TRAFFIC FLOW

Traffic control is another important, but less obvious, form of crowd control.

When you control a mass of people, you must ensure that their movement flows smoothly, whether they're walking or in auto-mobiles. Avoid pedestrian and vehicular traffic jams. When people are prevented from moving, tempers flare and trouble follows.

A security force may have to add extra personnel to keep foot or auto traffic moving in an orderly manner. Traffic jam clearance crews should be available in case of stalled vehicles.

See section entitled Traffic Control Safety in Chapter 11, Facility Safety.

DEMONSTRATIONS

Demonstrating is a popular form of group protest in the United States. The First Amendment to the U.S. Constitution gives people the right to assemble. So any public gathering is legal, as long as it is peaceful and doesn't violate private property rights.

Demonstrations are generally of two kinds, nonviolent or violent. In a nonviolent demonstration, a group uses passive action to obtain its objectives. Sit-ins and stand-ins are examples. A violent demonstration is one in which a group employs force to attain its demands. Rioting is an example.

Definitions

These broad definitions describe participants in most demonstrations:

1. **Passivist:** A person who attempts to attain goals through nonviolent demonstration.

2. **Pacifist:** One who opposes war and the military.

3. **Activist:** A person who takes direct action to achieve a social, economic, or political end. Such action often disrupts normal societal operations, including those of a business or industrial facility.

4. **Militant:** A person who supports a cause through aggressive or violent action. He/she exhibits a complete disregard for the rights of others.

Security Against Demonstrators

In the event of a demonstration, particularly if it's tense at a facility you're protecting, the following steps are recommended:

1. Notify the security manager immediately. Ask for instructions on notifying other key executives and emergency agencies (police, firemen, public safety department). If the company has no security manager, alert the head of the firm, then call emergency

agencies you deem appropriate. An advance anti-demonstration plan will facilitate necessary action. If you're a contract officer, notify your own supervision as soon as possible.

2. Contact the right law enforcement agency for local jurisdiction. Police or sheriff's departments will assure that the demonstration is legal and counteract any violence. At a defense plant it may be necessary to call federal authorities such as the U.S. Marshal. Jurisdiction should be known in advance.

3. Follow orders of the policeman in command to restrain violent demonstrators to the extent necessary to protect life, company property or government property. Arrests will be directed by that official.

4. All security personnel involved in putting down an unruly demonstration should exercise restraint. Force should not be applied unless absolutely necessary to cope with the situation.

5. Non-employees on company property should be warned to depart or face trespassing charges. If trespassers resist, ask authorities to make arrests.

6. Company rules regarding participation by employees in demonstrations should be well understood in advance by all concerned. Follow instructions of appropriate management in enforcing these rules.

7. Classified materials should be locked and safeguarded at all times during demonstrations.

Overall Control

Following are general duties you may be asked to perform in cooperation with other personnel for overall protection of a facility during a demonstration:

- Control traffic
- Control employees
- Control demonstrators
- Protect critically essential areas such as power, water supply, communications, computer equipment and flammable or explosive stocks.

CAUSES OF MOB ACTION

The underlying causes of mob action are deceptive. The

incident that sparks a riot is merely a symptom of some deep-seated unrest, not the cause of it. The real cause smolders like a latent volcano before violence erupts.

Hot weather is said to have ignited long-standing frustrations which cascaded into the Watts riot.

Historically, almost any widespread grievance among people can trigger an uprising. These grievances usually involve prolonged adverse pressure on human livelihood or ideology, fomenting mass emotional tension.

Common roots of civil disorders are racial unrest, unemployment, discrimination (for any reason) and aggressive opposition to anything that is established (the law, business, religion, the military, government, and even dress codes).

America has a new generation of anarchists who revolt violently and senselessly against persons, places and things—often merely for the sake of change or just for "kicks."

RIOT PREVENTION

The old maxim, "An ounce of prevention is worth a pound of cure," is very apt in taking steps to minimize losses in the event of a riot.

Every company should have a long-range protection program. Proprietary or contract security management usually come up with an advance plan. Security officers should be thoroughly briefed on the anti-riot plan and their roles in it.

Company Preparations

The firm should evaluate all facilities and security personnel to make sure adequate security exists.

A key executive should be designated to take charge of anti-riot operations. This duty usually falls to the security manager. He/she should spearhead formulation of a plan and coordinate task groups assigned to carry it out. The firm that doesn't have a security department should call in a reliable contract security service for advice, planning and staffing.

Security personnel should make regular patrols. A radio/telephone reporting procedure, as well as television or computer monitors, should be tied to a central station to ensure cooperative action and to protect security officers in case of a disturbance.

All security personnel should know the telephone numbers of

the closest police and fire departments. Communications personnel should also have these emergency numbers at their fingertips.

Home telephone numbers of key executives should be known to security and communications personnel.

If the company keeps firearms, ammunition or explosives, it's imperative that the advice of law enforcement authorities be followed in safeguarding such stock.

The plan should include employee exit routes from the premises, then orderly auto retreats from the neighborhood.

Current inventory should be kept of all equipment and furniture, with each piece marked for identification in case it is stolen.

Flammable liquids and combustible materials should be secured in an isolated area specially constructed according to fire codes. In areas where fire damage potential is greatest, doors should be locked when not in use.

If security officers are not on 24-hour duty, all possible entrances, including skylights, should be connected to an intrusion alarm system. A fire alarm system with central monitoring is also a must for potentially hazardous areas.

Doors leading to back lots and alleys should be covered with sheet metal and have adequate locking devices. A dead bolt lock with no outside keyway, plus a crossbar, is suggested for maximal protection.

Burglar bars should be installed on all windows on the first floor, with the exception of large display windows. Hopefully, they're made of laminated glass. Merchandise should be removed from display areas at night and expandable metal gates pulled into place and padlocked.

When locking up a business at the end of the day, exterior and some interior lighting should be left on.

Safes and vaults should meet protection needs and should not be removable. The possibility of cash loss can be reduced or eliminated by making regular bank deposits and not keeping large sums at the place of business.

Duplicate copies of all important documents should be kept in a bank safety deposit box or other safe place away from company premises. Loss of such documents as contracts and receivable ledgers could ruin a business.

Security Officer Precautions

In protecting life and property, your basic purpose is prevention of losses. Your responsibilities are the same when confronted with mob action, but harder to accomplish.

In advance, be absolutely certain that physical security measures are adequate (see Chapter 14, Physical Security).

Does the facility to which you're assigned have adequate fire protection? Plenty of sprinklers, hoses, hydrants and extinguishers? Any fire fighting equipment on the roof? Are all doors reasonably vandal-proof? Are out-of-the-way doors and windows secured and alarmed against intrusion? Is the perimeter really secure, or does the fence have holes or missing barbed wire topping? Are the gates well padlocked? Are communications efficient? Do you know how to call police and firemen? Do you know where the nearest fire station and hospital are located? All these questions and more must be answered before mob destruction is thwarted.

If you have any doubts about security measures at your post, call your supervisor and discuss them at once.

Report Danger Signs

You must spot and report potential danger immediately so company management, with the help of the security department, can prepare for possible civil disorder. Your first responsibility is to alert your supervisor or notify law enforcement authorities.

Through news media and the "grapevine," you can stay aware of the social climate in your work area. If danger signals become obvious, indicating the need for emergency countermeasures, don't hesitate to call police. It's their job. They can evaluate the situation promptly.

Word of unrest among employees or suspicious activities of outsiders must be reported to your supervisor.

Mob action sometimes develops from what started out as a peaceful demonstration. Though they may be gang-led, most riots are spontaneous. Often a firm's involvement in a riot depends largely on its accessibility to rioters.

IF MOB ACTION ERUPTS

If a threatening situation comes without warning, your first job is to notify the police or sheriff. If the facility you're guarding is a defense plant and unauthorized persons have invaded the property, it may be necessary for you to notify the nearest federal marshal or attorney. As soon as possible, call your own supervision.

However grave the disorder, try not to panic. Your mere presence as a uniformed officer will help to instill confidence among employees, as well as to deter militants.

The second thing for you to remember is that your weapon is only for self-defense or the defense of another's life. Don't draw or reach for your revolver unless life-or-death necessity forces you to use it. Brandishing a weapon in an emotion-charged situation can be very dangerous. It could touch off violence, if violence had been avoided up to that moment.

Cooperate fully with law enforcement officers, firemen or medical personnel called to the scene.

If ordered by competent authority, assist in the evacuation of employees via exit routes planned in advance. If possible, leave in groups. Doors should be locked and windows rolled up in private cars.

All facility exits, including windows, should be securely locked and barred.

Retailers should remove cash from all registers and cash drawers and leave them open to view. Valuables that can't be taken out should be locked up in safes or vaults.

If merchants have time and their employees are not jeopardized, they should remove all merchandise from display windows. This will make the store less inviting to looters and may reduce the chance of broken windows or needlessly damaged areas.

Don't return to the premises until informed by the police or other reliable authority that the danger is over.

See Chapter 20 (Special Events Security) for more details on how to control crowds gathered to see spectator events.

CHAPTER 16

BOMB THREATS

Bombing and threats of bombs are serious security problems to American business and industry today. A new breed of extremists has bombed many facilities since 1980. An even greater number of bomb threats—a form of harrassment—have been received, most of which never materialized.

This chapter discusses security steps to ease the panic and disorder that a bomb threat can cause.

BOMBING BACKGROUND

Explosives have been used in assassinations probably ever since the Chinese invented gunpowder in the 9th century. Gunpowder has been used extensively in military operations since the 16th century. International terrorists have employed explosive devices for centuries. Although foreign terrorism has been rare in the United States, it now looms as a potential threat to asset protection (see "Specter of Terrorism" later in this chapter).

American history is replete with bombings. They were a common form of protest during the unrest that preceded and followed the Civil War. Early radicals bombed ethnic and religious groups. Old West outlaws bombed trains. Gangsters of the Prohibition Era bombed rivals, as well as victims who wouldn't submit to extortion. Gang criminals still favor bombing as a retaliatory weapon.

The most common explosive materials are dynamite, trinitrotoluene (TNT), nitroglycerin, gun/blasting powder and plastique.

Since they're so compact, today's bombs can easily be hidden. A quart-size explosive can do considerable damage, to say nothing of the chain reaction it may trigger. Pipe bombs and plastic charges are even smaller. Placement for maximal damage depends on the skill and daring of the bomber. Stairways, restrooms, and storerooms are likely hiding places if they're accessible to the public.

Delivery of a bomb to the site is the chief concern of security personnel. Once placed, the bomb is a real menace. The more vulnerable a facility is, the more it should be shielded from incursion. For example, all persons and vehicles are searched before they're admitted to protected areas of a nuclear power station. To complicate matters, an explosive device can be delivered by mail, vendors or service people.

BOMB EMERGENCY PLAN

Whether it's a hoax or real, a bomb threat can create hysteria.

The best defense against bombing is a well-organized bomb prevention plan. Every business firm and institution should formulate one in advance. A first-rate bomb emergency plan spells out procedures for:

1. Internal control (duties of security force, management and other employees).

2. Coordination with outside agencies (such as police bomb disposal unit).

Action Team

Each company should tailor its bomb reaction team to the firm's size, organizational structure and needs.

The first consideration is command and control—the ability and authority to act quickly and efficiently. A typical command post is headed by the security director and one senior member of management. Each should have an alternate.

An emergency control center should be set up in the best available hub for communciations. As a bare minimum, operations should be controlled with telephones and portable hand-held radios.

The command and control group should be small to hasten decision-making and action. Until fact is sorted from fiction, the fewer people who know about a bomb threat, the better. Other control personnel might include:

- Contract security manager (if appropriate)
- Facility superintendent

- Safety manager
- Evacuation controller
- Company doctor or nurse
- Chief of in-house fire brigade
- Department head, if location of bomb is known
- Switchboard operator.

Titles and responsibilities vary in every company. Hence, the management team assembled to cope with a bomb threat will be determined by practicality. The aim of the action team is to prevent losses (life and property). Logic dictates that sometimes a bomb threat is real.

As soon as the plan is firm, all participants should be briefed on their duties. Security officers will have key roles. If you're new at a post, find out if the organization has a bomb prevention plan. Learn your functions on the action team.

The bomb plan shouldn't be disclosed to all employees. Only those who will take part in the plan need to know about it. If it's common knowledge that everyone will be evacuated with pay in the event of a bomb scare, an employee might call in a phony threat just to get some time off.

Emergency Support

Outside emergency organizations should be contacted for advice and cognizance when the bomb plan is written. These include the police or sheriff, fire department, nearest hospital, telephone company and the FBI (if federal jurisdiction is involved).

This courtesy will establish good rapport with support people and ensure prompt aid if real danger occurs.

All security officers and communications personnel must know how to reach emergency agencies immediately.

Locating the Bomb

A good bomb plan includes a search procedure.

With all possible haste, appropriate law enforcement officials should be called to the scene to direct the search for a bomb. Many such agencies have squads specially trained and experienced in bomb threat investigations.

If the location of a threatened bomb is unknown and urgency dictates a search of critical areas until proper authorities arrive, this quest should be done by predesignated search teams. A list of

BOMB "NO-NO'S"

these teams should be readily available to security officers. The search should be conducted in a painstaking manner.

When the threat indicates the bomb has been placed in a specific area, the search should start there.

If a suspected bomb is located anywhere, the security manager should be notified immediately. The threatened area should be cleared of all personnel. No one should touch the suspicious object until the bomb disposal squad arrives.

Evacuation

An orderly evacuation of people threatened by a bomb blast should also be planned in advance.

Only a senior management official may give the order to evacuate a business facility.

If real or potential danger exists in a certain area, a security officer should make the determination to evacuate that area.

Depending on urgency, an evacuation order may be (1) broadcast over a public address system, (2) telephoned to department heads, or (3) delivered personally by security officers.

Supervision should direct a disciplined, systematic exodus of personnel to the nearest parking lot or clearing. Persons should remain in this location until advised to return to work or to go home.

Security officers should take necessary action to ensure that all classified and/or proprietary data are safeguarded.

RECEIVING A BOMB THREAT

Most bomb threats are delivered by telephone. The would-be bomber usually calls when someone can react to the threat. The phone offers the culprit a cloak of secrecy.

Each threat must be handled as if it's genuine, although most often it's just a hoax.

If you receive a bomb threat, don't panic. Keep your voice calm. Shield your conversation from non-security eavesdroppers. A bomb scare could stampede employees, which can cause more damage than some explosions.

Response Steps

Here's how to handle a call that a bomb has been planted in the facility where you work:

1. Start a telephone tape recorder, if you have one. Note the time.

2. Try to induce conversation. Keep the caller on the line as long as possible. Don't interrupt, except to ask the caller to speak louder, slower or to repeat. If you can, signal the phone company to trace the call.

3. Ask lots of questions (see list that follows). Show level-headed concern. Mainly, you want to know when the bomb is set to explode and where it is placed. The caller may or may not tell you. If you get this vital information, try to alert security management via a remote alarm while the threat is still in progress. If a fellow officer is nearby, use a code word.

4. Listen closely to the caller's message, voice and background noises. Take notes. Try to record the caller's exact words. Keep the caller talking until he/she hangs up.

5. Start phoning. Follow your post orders. Usually, the first person you must notify is the security manager. He or another executive will call the police or sheriff's bomb squad. If you're a contract security officer, get your supervision into the act promptly.

6. Fill out your bomb threat checklist (see form) as soon as it's practical, while details are still fresh in your memory.

Don't go looking for the bomb until you've completed your phone reports. The call could be a ploy to get you away from your post.

Questions to Caller

To keep a potential bomber talking, ask such questions as these:

- Why are you doing this? Point out that the explosion will injure or kill innocent people.
- If the caller indicates a personal problem, ask how you can help.
- When will the bomb go off?
- Where is it located?
- What kind of bomb is it? (The caller may want to brag about it.)
- Is the bomb in a briefcase, box or paper sack?
- When was it placed?

- How did you get it on the property? Are you an employee?
- Will you identify yourself? (If so, get name, address and phone number, if possible.)

Listen carefully to each answer. Answers may suggest other questions. Stretch out the conversation as long as the caller is willing to talk. The longer he/she talks, the less likely it is that a bomb has been planted.

Checklist Aids Recall

If you can't tape the call, a bomb threat checklist will help you recall the incident. Try to remember accurately as much as you can. This information will be useful in an investigation and may lead to apprehension of the threatener.

Be specific about details. For instance, if the caller had an accent, was it American such as southern drawl or Brooklynese? If the accent was foreign, try to identify it. If there were voices in the background, were they those of adults or children? One, a few, or many?

NOTIFICATION CHAIN

1. If a bomb threat call is received by anyone during working hours, the company security manager should be notified immediately. He will notify other management principals predesignated in the action plan.

2. If a bomb threat call is received during nonworking hours, the security officer on duty will immediately notify the following:

- Security manager
- Other management officials listed in the bomb emergency plan
- Local police or sheriff, as appropriate
- Federal Bureau of Investigation (if federal jurisdiction is involved).

3. During nonworking hours, the first management team member to arrive on the scene should notify the following:

- Company president
- Vice president or director of operations
- General counsel
- Other executives who, though not designated in the action plan, are vitally concerned about any emergency.

BOMB THREAT CHECKLIST

PERSON WHO RECEIVED CALL _____

Date_____ Time_____

      ☐ Local   ☐ Long Distance   ☐ Unknown

BOMB FACTS

When will bomb go off? _____

Where is it planted?_____

Method: ☐ remote control ☐ timer ☐ pressure ☐ other

Type bomb: ☐ dynamite ☐ powder ☐ TNT ☐ plastic
    ☐ nitroglycerin

Container: ☐ paper bag ☐ package ☐ box ☐ can ☐ bottle
    ☐ carton ☐ briefcase ☐ other

Delivery: ☐ in person ☐ U.S. mail ☐ other

CALLER'S IDENTITY

☐ Male   ☐ Female   ☐ Adult   ☐ Child

Name_____

Organization _____

Address _____

Phone Number (   ) _____

VOICE CHARACTERISTICS

TONE	MANNER	SPEECH
☐ loud	☐ calm	☐ fast
☐ soft	☐ angry	☐ slow
☐ high pitch	☐ rational	☐ coherent
☐ low pitch	☐ irrational	☐ incoherent
☐ raspy	☐ deliberate	☐ distinct
☐ nasal	☐ laughing	☐ muffled

LANGUAGE	ACCENT
☐ excellent	☐ USA
☐ good	☐ foreign
☐ fair	origin, if possible _____
☐ poor	
☐ cursing	
☐ obscene	

BACKGROUND NOISES

☐ quiet	☐ automobiles	☐ office machines
☐ noisy	☐ airplanes	☐ factory machines
☐ voices	☐ trains	☐ animals
☐ music	☐ construction	☐ other _____

The procedure for coping with a bomb threat will be determined by each firm's organizational structure and needs.

MAILED THREATS OR BOMBS

If a bomb threat is received by mail (or even hand-carried or just left on the premises), the person who opens it and realizes it is a threat should stop handling it immediately. Possibly, the sender's fingerprints can be lifted from the paper on which the warning is written. A police lab can also conduct other tests on the letter and its envelope.

Mailroom employees or others who handle mail routinely should be trained to be on the lookout for parcels that might contain bombs. Here are some of the telltale signs of a bomb-bearing package:

- Ticking sound
- Oil stains
- Strange odors
- Protruding wire or string
- Package unusually heavy for its size
- Package not symmetrical, as though homemade
- Scrawled handwriting or poor typing
- Addressee's name misspelled
- Wrong title for an executive
- Incorrect or foreign postage.

SPECTER OF TERRORISM

International terrorists murdered 4,261 victims during the years 1973-83, inclusive, according to the U.S. State Department. Nearly 40 percent of terrorist attacks in the 1970s were directed against U.S. interests. From 1980 to mid-1985, at least 320 Americans were slain by terrorists in foreign capitals around the world.

Most foreign terrorists prefer bold, swift attacks that result in shocking casualties. A horrid example was the suicidal bombing of the U.S. Marine Headquarters in Beirut, Lebanon, in October 1983. That truck-carried explosion killed 241 servicemen.

In June 1985, the State Department announced that 126 U.S. embassies and consulates worldwide would be renovated or relocated. Of these facilities, 75 needed to be completely rebuilt. The estimated total cost was $3.5 billion. The department's annual security budget of $129 million was expected to be tripled.

There is growing concern among federal crime watchers, including congressmen, that global terrorism will spread to America. FBI Director William H. Webster stated publicly that it's "entirely realistic" that Islamic terrorists could launch an attack inside the United States.

Moslem terrorists have bragged that no seat of government is beyond their reach. Jihad Shiites claimed responsibility for the 1985 bombings of a U.S. airline office and a Jewish synagogue in Copenhagen, Denmark. The leader of this terrorist group said, "Let them know that sooner or later we shall reach the heart of the White House, the Kremlin, the Elysee and No. 10 Downing Street."

The arrival of international terrorism on U.S. soil is a chilling thought. If it happens, corporations are possible targets, as well as government facilities. Alien terrorist strikes here will be very hard to stop. Fixing blame is no assurance that plotters will be caught and punished. More than likely, such raids will be ordered by foreign powers hostile to the West. Retaliation could escalate into a full-scale war.

The 1984 Summer Olympic Games proved that overwhelming security measures provide the best shield against imported terrorism.

U.S. terrorist incidents have declined in recent years. In the 1970s, the average was about 100 per year. There were 51 in 1982, 31 in 1983, and 7 in 1985, according to FBI records. Worldwide acts of terrorism ran about 800 per year when this book was published.

Bombings of 30 U.S. abortion clinics between May 1982 and July 1985 didn't meet the FBI's definition of terrorism. That definition is "the unlawful use of force or violence against persons or property to intimidate or coerce a government, the civilian population or any segment thereof in furtherance of political or social objectives."

FBI officials contended there was no evidence of a national conspiracy against the clinics. Thus, primary investigation fell to the Bureau of Alcohol, Tobacco and Firearms, a branch of the U.S. Treasury Department. This agency has federal jurisdiction in bombing and arson cases that don't fit the FBI definition of terrorist acts.

CHAPTER 17

DISASTER CONTROL

FLEXIBLE PLANNING

It's impossible to predict when a disaster will happen or the extent to which it will damage life and property. Hence, planning should be flexible to permit company management and the security force to follow their own judgment in the wake of a catastrophe.

However, it's sensible to have a plan. The main protective aims in a disaster are to (1) save lives, (2) administer first aid, and (3) minimize loss of property.

When calamity strikes, security officers may have to substitute as alternates to any position of authority necessary to achieve the above objectives.

TYPICAL DISASTERS

Disasters are both man-made and caused by the forces of nature. Following are typical examples:

- Fires
- Aircraft accidents
- Explosions
- Earthquakes
- Floods
- Landslides
- Tornadoes
- Hurricanes
- Tsunamis (huge destructive tidal waves).

Note: Enemy or terrorist attack by bombing also should be included as a reason for preplanning.

Sections that follow suggest general disaster control preparations for an industrial facility. Each firm should adapt these guidelines to its own locale, organization and needs.

CHAIN OF COMMAND

The following succession of command is recommended for most organizations or facilities in the event of a disaster:

- President/general manager
- Director of operations/executive vice president/asst. general manager
- Director of industrial relations
- Security manager
- Manager of plant engineering
- Maintenance supervisors.

Titles are not as important as *functions.* The primary concern is that a competent team is *predesignated.*

DUTIES AND PROCEDURES

At many facilities, when disaster strikes, security headquarters will:

1. Notify the in-house command/response team.
2. Notify security officers.
3. Call the fire department and police.
4. Request medical assistance.

All protection officers will aid as instructed or, in the absence of orders, as circumstances dictate.

In the event of fire, collapse of a building, airplane crash or explosion, you (security officer) should follow these general procedures:

- Evacuate the immediate area.
- Activate the fire alarm or phone the fire department.
- Call the office to which you report. Describe the incident and give the exact location.
- Attempt to control damage by using fire extinguishers or other appropriate equipment.
- Don't endanger yourself or others.

Cooperative Effort

Every security officer and all supervisory/management personnel of your facility should know the location of the nearest exit, fire alarm box and fire extinguisher. They should ensure that all employees know where these things are. Each extinguisher should be labeled as to its proper use and the type of fire for which it is intended. Supervisors should instruct workers how to use extinguishers. (You will know all the provisions of this paragraph applicable to your post.)

Supervisors and security officers shall direct employees to the best building exit in a safe and orderly manner. People should be assembled at a safe distance from the disaster site and should be restrained from curiosity roaming.

The security director, manager of plant engineering or other designee will control and coordinate all disastrous incidents in the plant (entire premises of a multi-building complex). He will also take charge of salvage operations. Other personnel should respond immediately if he asks them for help.

Maintenance supervisors will ensure that sprinkler risers and post indicator valves (PIVs) are open and are not shut off until ordered by the plant engineering manager or fire chief. Maintenance men will assist in controlling damage of structures, equipment and materials as directed by the plant engineering manager.

Be Prepared, Don't Panic

Sometimes security has advance warning of pending disasters such as hurricanes or tornadoes. In such cases, there is time to set up an emergency operations mode. However, most disasters occur suddenly with very little or no warning.

As a security officer, you must be prepared to shift from a normal mode of operation to emergency operating conditions *at once*. There is little time for deliberation in a disaster situation. Time works against you as in no other phase of security work. You must be prepared to *act*, quickly and intelligently.

Your greatest asset in preparing yourself for a disaster is your *imagination*. Imagine emergency situations *in advance*. See yourself *doing the right things* in those emergencies.

Your greatest liability in disasters is *panic*. Panic is intense fear. When you're frightened out of your wits, you tend to "freeze." Your judgment is deadlocked, and you make wrong responses. The worst kind of panic is that which causes you to run from the scene.

The best way to conquer intense fear is to prepare yourself, in advance, for any emergency. Advance *knowledge* of what to *expect* in various emergencies will help you to avoid panic and to react correctly.

EMERGENCY RESPONSE PRINCIPLES

1. Call the appropriate emergency response agency (fire department, police, hospital, et al), unless instructed that someone else is responsible for this notification.

2. Local police should always be notified in any emergency.

3. Notify the proper plant authorities (security manager or whoever is designated in your post orders).

4. Notify your duty supervisor.

5. Get ready to open perimeter gates for emergency response vehicles.

6. The greater the emergency, the more people you need to get involved. Don't be afraid to call anyone. Better to call than to regret later that you didn't.

7. Keep yourself calm at all times, especially when you're phoning or sending radio messages. Speak slowly and give the basic facts clearly and accurately. This is extremely important. Remember, you don't want to panic the people you call. If you panic, you're apt to send out unclear or incomplete messages.

8. Remember why you are there—to protect people and property. Do whatever you can to help people get to safety. Keep your voice calm and reassuring. Don't panic the people you're trying to help. If you do, you may cause them to injure themselves unnecessarily.

9. Do what you can to protect property not yet affected by the emergency.

10. Don't try to be a hero. Act intelligently and wisely. Follow the directions of those who assume command.

EXPLOSIONS

Explosions are the most terrifying of all unnatural disasters.

Depending on the intensity of the blast, expect the worst:

- Expect fire after an explosion.
- Expect another explosion to follow.
- Expect people to panic and run.
- Expect to see people bleeding as they run.
- Expect to see people lying about injured or dead.
- Expect extensive property damage (crumbled structures, wrecked equipment, broken glass and shocking disorder).
- Expect power, water, gas and communications outages.

The sudden, destructive force of an explosion usually causes immediate personal injuries and sends people running in panic. These people often hurt each other in their haste to escape through narrow passageways and doors.

Things vital to plant operation often are demolished. On-site personnel are helpless to fight a fire if water mains are ruptured and firefighting equipment is damaged. Nothing electrical will run when the power source is knocked out.

Your duty is to keep calm and notify emergency agencies. There's nothing you can do for persons killed at the blast site except to protect their personal property from theft. Do what you can for those whose injuries weren't fatal. Treat for shock and render whatever comfort you can (see Chapter 7, First Aid).

Keep people away from the area of the explosion. Don't go there yourself. Remember, there may be a second explosion or other danger in that area.

HURRICANES AND TORNADOES

In regions where dangerous windstorms are common, you will always have specific emergency instructions.

Hurricanes are tracked and reported long before they hit a given area. A hurricane usually reaches a wind velocity of 75-120 miles per hour. Buildings topple, roofs are torn off and blow away, telephone poles fall, and power lines are ripped from their moorings.

The safest refuge from a hurricane is a sturdy underground haven similar to a bomb shelter. A subway would be an excellent refuge, as well as the basement of any well-constructed building.

Tornadoes are more sudden. They're whirlwinds that literally pick up structures and carry them away. Both hurricanes and tornadoes are cyclonic winds and can reach 300 miles per hour.

Again, if you're in a cyclone area, you will have specific procedures to follow. Taking refuge in a deep underground shelter is the best way to avoid personal harm. There is absolutely nothing you can do about property protection during a cyclone. Local or state authorities usually prescribe preparations on radio and TV in advance—when there's any warning at all.

EARTHQUAKES

Earthquakes come without warning. A severe quake in an urban area will produce fires, explosions, building destruction, personal death and injury, and hazardous movement conditions. The first big shake is usually followed by subsequent temblors, or aftershocks. These vary in strength, but are capable of causing substantial damage to weakened structures.

During an earthquake, people are safer inside a building than on the street or a nearby parking lot—in the path of toppling debris or severed high-voltage lines. Supervisors should direct personnel to take cover under desks and tables or in halls and corridors away from windows.

Your chief work will come after the earthquake. Your main responsibility will be to aid the injured. Of course, you'll also be called upon to help out in other emergency conditions resulting from the quake. Your duty is to remain at your post as long as necessary to assist in getting matters under control.

A catastrophic earthquake may strain the availability of police, fire department and utility company personnel to respond to your facility in the face of widespread disaster. You and your co-workers may have to take over a number of tasks normally handled by professional emergency responders.

The only defense against an earthquake is preparation. If your post has an earthquake preparedness plan, study it carefully. That plan can save your life and the lives of many people under your protection.

QUAKE INSTRUCTIONS FOR OFFICERS

Knowledge of how to prepare and what to do in the event of an earthquake is the key to surviving such a disaster and lessening the hardships that will follow. You'll find the following guidelines helpful in becoming "quake safe" at home and at your post. This information will be valuable to your families and friends as well.

Before the Earthquake

Here are tips on **home** preparedness to be shared with your family:

- Most injuries incurred during the shaking are due to falling objects or shattered windows. Secure heavy bookcases, tall cabinets, appliances and water heaters to the wall with brackets, hooks or bolts. Place heavy or large objects close to the ground.
- Practice family emergency drills.
- Store sufficient food to last at least three days. A two-week supply is even better, as it can alleviate uncertainty and give a feeling of security during the post-disaster period.
- Keep about one-half gallon of water per day per person.
- Have a basic first aid kit.
- Have a flashlight with spare batteries.
- Have a portable radio with spare batteries.
- Know where the main gas and water valves are and have pipe and crescent wrenches to shut them off.

Preparations at **work** include:

- Check for possible hazards in your workplace that are similar to those at home, such as tall file cabinets that could fall and heavy objects placed overhead. Note these potential dangers in your daily activity report.
- Be completely familiar with emergency procedures in your post orders.
- Have a mini-survival kit available at work. A car survival kit is ideal and should contain such things as nonperishable food and water, extra clothes, flashlight, radio and sleeping bag/blankets.
- Be familiar with any disaster plans at the facility where you work. Help other officers and employees to be aware of preparedness for earthquakes and other disasters.

During the Earthquake

- Stay calm, don't panic, and help to reassure others. People always look to those in uniform for help and for confidence.
- If indoors, stay there; don't attempt to go outside. Never try to use an elevator or even a stairwell during the shaking.
- Get under a sturdy desk or table, or brace yourself in a corner or doorway.
- Stay clear of windows, bookcases, hanging plants and interior glass.
- If outside, move to an area clear of power lines, poles, walls and other falling debris.

After the Earthquake

At **home:**

- Check family members for injury.
- Check for hazards such as fires, leaks and spills.
- Put on sturdy shoes before moving about.
- Don't attempt to use the telephone.
- Turn on a battery-powered radio for information.
- Don't attempt to drive your vehicle.
- Be prepared for aftershocks.
- Cooperate with public safety efforts. Public services may be unavailable for substantial periods, so each family needs to be self-sufficient for as long as possible.
- If you and your family are OK, check your neighbors—they may need your help.

At **work:**

- Stay on the job! You'll have difficulty trying to return home.
- Check for injuries.
- Ascertain damage to facility.
- Comply with company emergency procedures.
- Check for any life-threatening hazards such as gas leaks, fires, chemical spills and shorting electrical wires.
- Try to maintain contact with central security at the facility (and your area office if you're a contract officer).
- Do what is possible to protect yourself, employees and the facility.

As previously mentioned, public services in the impacted area will not be available for an indefinite period, depending on the severity of the damage. Security officers on duty at the time of the earthquake will have the responsibility of lessening the damage at the facility. A security officer may find himself/herself remaining at work for an extended interval to ensure facility safety. A catastrophic earthquake will affect every aspect of the business community in the impacted area. Steps will be taken by management to get relief personnel into the field as soon as possible; however, many off-duty officers will be unable to respond due to road and structural damage or injury sustained during the earthquake. Standard forms of communication will be unavailable several hours to several days after the disaster. By working together, helping each other to prepare, and being aware of the potential consequences of a major disaster, the number of lives lost and damage suffered can be greatly reduced.

DISASTER PREPAREDNESS CHECKLIST

The following checklist was designed for private industry as part of the California Earthquake Response Plan in 1983. The author of this book chaired the Law Enforcement Security Committee of Governor George Deukmejian's Earthquake Task Force, which drafted the checklist. It serves as an aid to corporate disaster planners. The all-inclusive planning guidelines are adaptable to catastrophic disasters other than earthquakes.

Preparation for Disaster
1. Succession of management
2. Scenario development and exercises
3. Alternate headquarters establishment
4. Disaster training for employees
   —On site
   —At home
5. Practice evacuation drills
6. Clarification of responsibilities
7. Access rosters for specific areas
8. Transportation/evacuation plan
9. Communications plan
10. Support services plan

11. Medical plan
12. Fire plan
13. Security plan
14. Survival plan
15. Equipment shutdown/restoration plan.

Emergency Notification

1. Updated telephone roster
2. Notification system by work sections
3. Alternate means of communication
   - Emergency radio broadcasting system (list of stations to which employees should be tuned and liaison with stations to broadcast information)
   - CB/ham station(s)
   - Messenger
   - Define levels of emergency.

Assembly of Personnel

1. List of critical personnel
   - Assess response time.
   - Estimate if personnel are likely to have access to a destination. Appraise communications, roads and bridges enroute.
   - Determine if 24-hour coverage by technicians at plant is required.
2. Assembly areas
   - Primary and alternate
   - Chain of command/authority
3. Determination of who is not required
4. Priorities of assigned tasks
5. Identify people unavailable due to other commitments.

Priority of Tasks

1. Shutoff or restoration of utilities
   - Natural gas lines
   - Electricity
   - Water lines and fire hydrants

- Sewage and petroleum pipelines
- Waste disposal
- Traffic signals
- Microwave dishes
- Antennas
- Remote broadcast facilities
- Heating and air conditioning.

2. Medical assistance
   - First aid stations and mass-care centers
   - Medically-trained personnel on hand
   - Provide first aid and diagnosis.
   - Maintain list of emergency services:
     Hospitals
     Paramedics
     Fire department
     Police department and sheriff's office
     Local National Guard/Reserve units
     Civil Air Patrol
     Medical equipment.

3. Search and rescue
   - Trained search and rescue parties
   - Prestocked search and rescue equipment
   - Heavy rescue equipment operators available.

4. Reestablish communications
   - To employees/technicians
   - To emergency services
   - To others, such as customers, employee families.

5. Determine clear transportation routes
   - Site helipad
   - Routes to hospitals
   - Airdrop locations
   - Fuel and vehicle servicing considerations.

6. Survival equipment
   - Detection of potential hazards:
     Natural gas leaks
     Radiation leaks
     Toxic material

- Food
- Fresh water
- Lanterns and flashlights
- CB/ham radios
- Hand-held radios
- Medical equipment
- Cots and blankets
- Signaling devices
- Firefighting equipment.

Security

1. Maintain control of access to plant
   - Perimeter security
   - Crowd control
   - Determine downed security systems:
     Closed-circuit TV
     Alarms
     Remotely-controlled gate arms
     Traffic control
2. Safety of classified material
3. Protection of valuables and equipment
4. Intruder apprehension teams
5. Damage assessment teams.

Additional Considerations

1. Recurring disaster warning systems
   - Intercom
   - Horns and buzzers
2. Dead body staging
   - Coroner liaison
   - Identification, tagging, listing of bodies
3. Definition of authority
   - Legal powers
   - Financial authority
   - Authority to make alterations on facility structures
4. Mutual aid
   - Adjacent fires

- Liaison with adjacent facilities
- Sharing fuel and equipment
- Providing and receiving assistance teams.

NUCLEAR ATTACK

Destruction from a nuclear attack would be substantial, but maybe not total.

In general, a nuclear explosion produces these stages: blast, shock, fire damage and concentration of radioactive fallout.

Every industrial plant should have some kind of procedure to protect its personnel, as much as possible, in the event of a nuclear attack. Free literature on how to organize such protection is available from the nearest Federal Emergency Management Agency office or state and local civil defense authorities.

If warning is received that a nuclear attack is imminent, all equipment, except fire pumps, should be shut down and employees should be instructed to take refuge in designated shelters. If none is available, the last alternative is to crouch under a sturdy desk or table to avoid getting hit on the head by falling debris. People who survive a nuclear blast should remain in shelter areas until a clear alert is announced by local authorities, assuming officials also survive the holocaust.

In most disasters, the security force plays a major role in recovery operations. Critical functions include aiding the injured, perimeter security, crowd control, safety of classified or proprietary information, and protecting valuables and equipment.

CHAPTER 18

HOSPITAL SECURITY

BACKGROUND

Hospital security in the United States has gone through a kaleidoscopic evolution since 1900.

Up to about 1950, hospital protection was a maintenance function. As facilities grew, fire watchmen were hired. They reported to plant engineering. It's hard to believe, but a few hospitals still cling to that outmoded practice.

During the 1950s, law enforcement was seen as the most important aspect of hospital security. Off-duty policemen often moonlighted as hospital security officers.

Since 1960, there has been a growing awareness among hospital administrators that security is a specialized management service valuable to overall operation.

In the 1970s, the asset protection/management services approach expanded. The hospital security director became a member of top management. Safety was increasingly stressed.

Rapid changes are shaping up in the 1980s. Most hospitals are the not-for-profit type founded through civic donations or by churches. Many of these community hospitals are being replaced by investor-owned proprietary health care facilities. These corporate ventures are profit-oriented. Trend-setters seek better methods to trim costs. Viewed as a business investment, tight security cuts costs by reducing losses. Administrators have broadened the role of hospital protection and given it a new label, risk management.

The patient volume rises steadily in the nation's more than 7,000 hospitals, 20,000 nursing homes, and countless medical clinics. Some of the main reasons are: (1) a high incidence of motor vehicle accidents, (2) relatively unchecked violent crime, and (3) more elderly people.

Asset protection becomes even more complex. Security officers must be better trained to respond to these changes.

UNIQUE CHALLENGE

Hospital security is unlike industrial security in many ways. First of all, a hospital is open 24 hours every day. The perimeter is rarely fenced. Something is always going on, and much of the daily operation is laden with stress.

The people you're dealing with are patients, medical staff, administrative staff, aides, visitors, vendors and suppliers. The sick are incapacitated, and everyone else is in a hurry. Most have a problem.

It has been said that a hospital patient is an involuntary consumer. He or she would rather not be sick. They're there because of an emergency or on doctor's orders. In most cases, the physician selects the hospital. Another peeve is that the patient has no control over costs, which for years have risen faster than the national inflation rate. Relatives and friends who come to visit patients frequently complain about hospital routine. Overworked medical personnel sometimes get uptight. So the potential for lost tempers is extremely high.

ESSENTIAL OFFICER QUALITIES

Protecting a hospital requires a very special kind of security officer. Incidentally, at this writing, about 10 percent of all hospital security personnel are women. Their employment in this field is on the upswing.

Studies show that officers with the most savvy in security matters aren't necessarily the best candidates for a hospital post.

Russell L. Colling, in his book, *Hospital Security,** said the single most important trait a security officer needs in a health care setting is "caring."

Since patients are a hospital's prime concern, you must have compassion for them. Your caring about their well-being makes you part of the total health care system. To really care about others, you must first care about yourself. And you should care

---

*Copyright 1982 by Butterworth Publishers, Woburn, Mass. Quoted by permission.

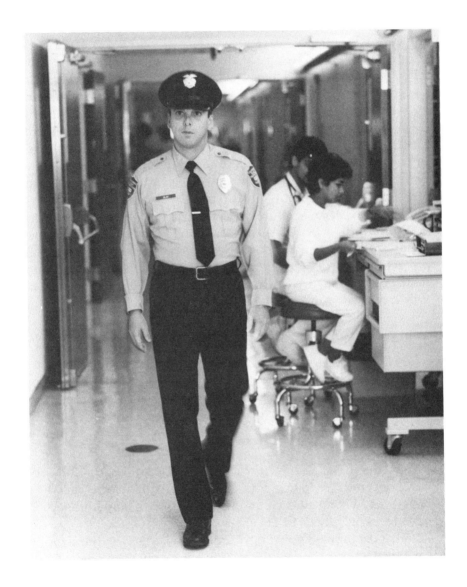

HOSPITAL DUTY—Security officer assigned to a hospital must have caring attitude toward patients, staff and public.

about your position. It's fitting to restress the basic philosophy stated in Chapter 1: TAKE PRIDE.

As a security officer, you are an important contributor to the hospital's employee and community relations. You are always in the eye of patients, the staff and visitors. Your exemplary appearance, attitude and conduct reflect favorably on the hospital's public image.

Be courteous and helpful at all times, especially when others are irritable. Tolerance is a major asset in hospital protection. A smile melts gloom. The amenities "please" and "thank you" never become trite. Your wording, and even the tone of your voice, can help maintain calm and efficiency in a hectic environment. Patient temperament ranges from meek to outrageous. Employees often work under pressure. Visitor anxiety sometimes boils to the point of hostility. Your politeness and dependability have a buffer effect on all with whom you interact.

Your uniform and military bearing will help deter misbehavior and unlawful acts. Usually, you won't be armed. Experience dictates that a gun is too dangerous to be useful in hospital protection. If the facility is in a high crime area, hospital management may insist that you carry a revolver. If so, you'll be fully qualified in its use (see Chapter 6).

NEW LEARNING CURVE

You'll have to learn lots of new things when you're assigned to a hospital. You can't learn everything overnight. But quickly find out as much as you can. The sooner you learn the ropes, the sooner you'll be effective in your job.

Facility Layout

You must first learn your way around. Learn the locations and functions of all departments. You will frequently be asked for directions. When you escort someone or deliver something, you'll have to know where to go.

Your post orders should have a floor plan showing the layout of the physical plant. It should pinpoint not only operational areas, but security checkpoints. These include entrances and exits, fire alarms, intrusion detectors, sprinkler risers, electrical control boxes, storage rooms and communication equipment.

Ask your supervisor or fellow employees to help familiarize you with your new surroundings.

Staff Personnel

It's also important to know who's who on the hospital staff. Learn the names of key medical and administrative personnel and their functions.

Your post orders should include an organization chart—preferably with photos of top management, so you can recognize them on sight.

As a starter, you should be personally acquainted with the security director and/or manager. You may not be introduced to other members of hospital management, but you should know who they are, especially if you work at a reception desk or in the visitor lobby. At the top of the list are the chief of the medical staff, the hospital administrator, assistant administrators, and the head of nursing service.

The larger a hospital is, the more specialized it becomes. In time, you'll learn who runs every function from admissions to housekeeping. Your knowledge of prime movers and hospital operation will increase your value as a security officer.

Medical Terms

You need to understand the most common medical terms used in a hospital. It will seem like learning a new language. You'll be expected to pick up this new lingo quickly so you can perform smoothly as an insider.

Your post orders should contain a minimal medical vocabulary or refer you to a source. Here are a few ordinary hospital expressions:

AMA—against medical advice (when patient leaves hospital against doctor's advice); also abbreviation for American Medical Association

Ambulatory—able to walk

Code blue—heart attack

Code red—fire

ECG or EKG—electrocardiogram, a heart monitor

EEG—electroencephalogram, a brain monitor

EMG—electromyogram, a muscle/nerve monitor

(Note: EEG/EKG/EMG often comprise a hospital department)

ER—emergency room

Geriatrics—treatment of the aged

Gurney—a four-wheel stretcher

IC or ICU—intensive care unit

IV—intravenous(ly), directly into a vein or veins

OB—obstetrics (maternity department)

OR—operating room

Pediatrics—children's unit

Radiology—x-ray department

Stat—immediately

Triage—a casualty sorting area

VS—vital signs (temperature, pulse, respiration).

SPECIFIC SITE TRAINING

Every hospital has specific policies designed to meet its service commitments efficiently. Therefore, it's a good idea for you to receive the same orientation given to all employees of any hospital to which you're assigned.

You should also know your legal responsibilities and the extent of your authority pertinent to hospital security. Laws vary from state to state and community to community.

Here are representative site training topics that deserve attention. They're not listed in order of importance.

1. Fire Codes and Standards
2. Basic Access Control
3. Visitor Control
4. Internal Theft
5. Use of Force
6. Disaster Control
7. Infection Control
8. Public Relations
9. Confidentiality
10. Verbal Intervention (how to "talk down" aggressive patients, others).

Following are comments on four of these topics. Others are covered in a later section, Typical Hospital Security Problems. Provisions of previous chapters that are applicable to hospital security are referenced for review.

Use of Force

Doctors and nurses sometimes ask security officers to help restrain patients. This may be necessary to administer medication or to stop patients from leaving the hospital when so doing is harmful to their health and safety. Restraint also may be necessary to control a violent patient.

You should be aware of hospital policies, as well as state and local laws concerning these situations.

The law is precise about your use of force in a custodial role. For example, here's a portion of the Pennsylvania Crimes Code, Section 509, titled "Use of Force by Person with Special Responsibility for Care, Discipline or Safety of Others":

"The use of force upon or toward the person of another is justified if...the force is used for the purpose of safeguarding or promoting the welfare of [an] incompetent person, including the prevention of his misconduct, or when such incompetent person is in a hospital or other institution for his care and custody, for the maintenance of reasonable discipline in such institution; and the force used is not designed to cause...death, serious bodily injury, disfigurement, extreme or unnecessary pain, mental distress or humiliation."

Other sections of the criminal code cover the use of force in self-protection, protecting a third party, protecting property, and making a citizen's arrest. Under Pennsylvania law, a private person such as a security officer "is justified in the use of *deadly force* [italics added] only when he believes that such force is necessary to prevent death or serious injury to himself or another."

Disaster Preparedness

Hospitals certified by the Joint Commission on Accreditation of Hospitals (JCAH) are required to stage at least two mock disasters each year. More may be mandated by hospital management.

These drills must be as realistic as possible. Internal and external catastrophes are simulated.

Practicing a make-believe disaster is not only difficult, but frustrating. A mock evacuation of a hospital takes lots of coordination, even if the "patients" are healthy stand-ins. Since the hospital must remain open for business, real emergencies constantly take precedence over sham exercises.

Typical security functions during or after a disaster are traffic control, Life Flight control, escort services and perimeter control. This is one time you'll fully understand the meaning of triage— the place where dead and injured victims are diagnosed and classified.

In an actual disaster, infection control is critical. Extreme care must be taken to (1) protect ill people, and (2) prevent the spread of disease.

If the hospital has a radiation decontamination policy, security probably holds down the perimeter. Each officer must know his or her specific role.

Review Chapter 17, Disaster Control.

Public Relations

Building public goodwill is a 24-hour responsibility at a hospital. It's no easy matter, due to the nature of the environment (sick people, countless stresses).

As a security officer, you're often the first person an outsider meets. Your neat appearance, courtesy and tact help to enhance the hospital's reputation. Good relations with patients is another plus factor.

You should know how to respond when media reporters phone or show up at the hospital. You're seldom, if ever, authorized to give statements to the press. Instead, refer reporters to a hospital official designated in your post orders. You should know how to contact this person at any hour, day or night. Be friendly and cooperative with reporters, but explain that you must follow hospital procedure. They appreciate prompt referral to an authorized spokesman. You may have to escort them to a certain individual or department.

See Chapter 3, Public Relations.

Confidentiality

Always respect the confidentiality of patient information. Treat it as proprietary information.

You should be instructed what to say when a family member inquires about a patient during an emergency that disrupts normal hospital routine.

Also keep mum about the status of employees, such as the reason an employee was disciplined or terminated.

Remember, guard your tongue. See Privileged Information (under Nondisclosure in Chapter 4, and Protecting Information (Chapter 10).

TYPICAL HOSPITAL SECURITY PROBLEMS

Every hospital is vulnerable to the same kinds of security violations. These infractions represent whopping losses in terms of life, property and prestige.

Prevention of such offenses is the justification for a security force.

Following are some of the most serious security problems facing the health care sector. Curbing these threats to operational success is largely a management responsibility. A case in point is the need for tighter control of hospital supplies, from drugs to bed sheets.

As a sharp security officer, you can be a big help in countering these detriments. Remember to be curious and alert at all times. Report everything that doesn't seem right to you, no matter how trivial. Your mere presence will deter wrongdoing in many situations. Maintaining order and safety are very important duties, too. You can't stamp our hospital crime entirely, but you certainly can make it harder to commit.

Assaults

Numerous types of assault, from scuffles to homicide, add up to a multi-headed monster in the hospital environment. Assaults account for most of the security-related lawsuits filed against health care facilities.

Sexual assaults on female nurses are frequently in the headlines. Rape and even murder occur both inside hospitals and on the grounds. Nurses aren't the only victims. Aides, other staff members, patients and visitors also are attacked. Patients are often helpless. They and others are particularly vulnerable at night.

Less publicized is serious conflict between various pairings of patients, staff, employees and visitors.

Painstaking internal and external patrols will help prevent or reduce assaults (see Patrol Techniques, Chapter 5). Frequency will be determined by need. Extra vigilance is called for at night. Pay particular attention to areas with high shrubs and low-hanging tree branches. This foliage offers perfect concealment for a would-be assailant.

Most fights can be averted by calming down antagonists—if you can talk to them before they start throwing punches. To settle a heated argument, (1) find out what the quarrel is about, (2) assess the crux of the problem, and (3) propose a solution that both parties can accept. The solution may be as simple as telling two angry people that loud argument is against hospital rules. It disturbs sick people. The worst thing to do is to take sides in the squabble. Act as a referee.

Knowing how to handle riled people is an art. It requires skillful tact and persuasiveness. You must recognize that most people aren't dunces, even if they're unreasonable at times. Don't scold or ridicule angry people. Instead, cater to their need for self-esteem. Calmly but firmly, divert their attention away from the source of their rage. Appeal to their emotional security. Make them feel that you're interested in them. You don't want them to hurt each other or get into trouble with the hospital and/or the law. Point out that good behavior on their part is the best way to win group approval —the respect of other people in the hospital.

Breaking up a fight that is already underway is another matter. If two patients are fighting, they must be separated. Scuffling may worsen their ailments. Medical personnel should be on hand. If the fight can be stopped without using physical force, that's ideal. However, if physical restraint is necessary, your help should be requested by someone on the medical staff. You should be aware of hospital policy and the legal limit of your support in this situation.

Knowing what to expect makes it easier for you to stay cool.

If a fight erupts between non-patients, whether inside the hospital or on the grounds, call the police immediately. Once blows are being exchanged, nothing you can say to the combatants is likely to subdue their tempers. If you intervene, the brawlers might pummel you. They're usually less inclined to assault armed police officers.

Theft

Employee pilferage is a major problem in most hospitals. Things commonly stolen are drugs, linen, food, tools (including surgical instruments), and maintenance supplies that can be used in the home.

The dollar extent of hospital pilferage is unknown, largely due to lack of accountability. Loss estimates range from 2 to 20 percent of a hospital's operating costs.

Armed robberies are increasing in and around hospitals. The two items most frequently sought are cash and drugs. Inside the hospital the cashier's office, cafeteria and pharmacy are the most likely targets.

Hospital burglaries are commonplace, too. The burglar's favorite target is operating room narcotics. The operating room is often isolated and closed down at night. Burglars bypass the cashier's office and pharmacy because alarms may protect those areas when they're closed. The gift shop, x-ray lab and storerooms also are vulnerable.

Theft of patients' belongings is another problem. Employees are sometimes at fault. More often, patients misplace things or send them home with visitors. Distress over a real or imagined theft can worsen a sick person's illness—a matter of more concern than the missing item. Generally, a hospital is not liable for articles a patient carries into the premises. But patient property presumed stolen tarnishes the hospital's reputation. Disgruntled patients have been known to create fictitious thefts in hopes of being reimbursed or to cast spite on the hospital.

Ways to combat all kinds of theft are spelled out in Chapter 9.

Kidnapping

Baby snatching is a dreaded menace for all facilities that provide obstetrical services. Although newborn infants are tagged, fingerprinted and footprinted to avoid mixups, precautions against abduction are lax in some maternity wards. Cases of white-clad kidnappers plucking babies from their hospital cribs are all too familiar.

There are two main reasons for baby stealing. One is the abnormal compulsion of a would-be mother who can't have children or has lost a child. The other is worse—selling babies for adoption.

Resourceful kidnappers have even found markets for cadavers and, in recent times, human organs.

Preventive measures against the heinous heist of babies from hospitals include:

- Round-the-clock surveillance by television monitoring (see Closed-Circuit Television, Chapter 14)

- A well-developed and monitored employee ID and visitor pass system (see Personnel Control, Chapter 12)

- An intrusion alarm triggered by unauthorized entry (see Alarms, Chapter 14)

- In the absence of electronic monitoring, frequent patrols (see Chapter 5).

As a protection officer, you must keep a sharp lookout for non-employees in areas where they don't belong. If you know all employees in the maternity ward during your shift, you can spot an imposter in hospital garb. Identify any suspicious stranger by asking for his/her employee ID card or visitor's pass.

Fires

During the past decade, the damage caused by fires in medical facilities has sparked a rash of new government regulations.

Much of the blame has been laid on faulty or obsolete construction. However, surveys show that most fires in hospitals and nursing homes start in patients' rooms. Careless tobacco smokers are the principal culprits. The second major cause is defective electrical wiring.

Arson figures prominently in health institution fires. Psychotic patients are sometimes at fault. Employees, former employees and union agitators also are on record as hospital arsonists. They're often motivated by revenge.

As a security officer, you're thoroughly trained in fire prevention and control (see Chapter 8). Be sure you know the location of all firefighting equipment at your post and how to use it. Fire vigilance is extra critical in a medical facility. Most patients are bedridden and unable to flee from a blaze. Thus, a fire poses a bigger risk to a hospital than to other business establishments.

Drug Abuse

Today drug abuse is widespread throughout society. It is alarming in the health field because it represents a threat to the quality of patient care. Another disturbing aspect is that the ready availability of drugs at some medical facilities encourages illicit traffic.

Some hospitals are a major source for street drugs, mainly amphetamines (pep pills) and barbiturates (sleeping pills). Employees obtain these pills by dipping into uncontrolled supplies, forging requisitions, or manipulating inventories.

Unfortunately, a few medical personnel, including doctors and nurses, are addicted to hard narcotics (heroin, codeine and morphine).

Easy access to these drugs compounds the problem. The more

people who have keys to drug cabinets, the less secure the supply becomes. The best-run organizations maintain strict account-ability of narcotics. Too often though, narcotics and dangerous drugs are so taken for granted that safeguarding them lapses.

While internal control of drug distribution is a hospital management function, you can help to clamp the lid on abuses. You do this through keen observation. Notice employees who are "stoned." Giveaway signs are slurred speech, dilated eye pupils, uneven gait, extremely happy/sad and no tolerance for frustra-tions. Be alert for illegal drug trafficking. Observe suspicious-looking outsiders who are overly chummy with employees. Then report accurately what you saw to your supervisor. Let him/her relay your findings to proper channels. You're not being a stool pigeon. You're doing your job right.

Another abusive problem you often have to cope with is the drunken visitor. He or she can be a pain in the neck anytime, but frequently shows up in the wee hours after the bars close. Try to escort the tipsy individual out of the hospital with as little disturbance as possible. If the person gets belligerent, call the police.

Review the Drug Abuse section in Chapter 12 for more tips on how to recognize and combat this problem.

Bomb Threats

Hospitals are the brunt of hundreds of bomb threats annually nationwide.

Common threat motives are revenge, extortion, and merely a desire to create excitement.

It's an exasperating problem. Each threat must be treated as though the perpetrator has, indeed, planted an explosive. Most threats never materialize, but a few medical facilities are actually bombed every year. And that's tragic.

The slightest hint of a bomb can cause serious medical reper-cussions among bedridden patients. If a search is made, a "cover story" must be developed in advance. Only search members and administrators should know the real reason for the investigation. The search should not be discussed in public areas for fear that word will reach patients, employees and visitors. Panic could ensue.

Surveys indicate that hospital bomb threats follow a familiar pattern. Large hospitals (400-600 beds) are the most frequent targets. Most threats are phoned, usually during or right after evening visiting hours. Most callers don't specify the bomb's location. If a site is mentioned, it's usually a patient area. Over half of the callers won't give a reason for wanting to bomb the facility. Among stated reasons, employee gripes top the list.

Chapter 16 covers fully security steps that should be taken before, during and after a bomb threat.

Safety

Safety is a demanding and never-ending responsibility in all health care facilities, especially hospitals. It has a big bearing on a medical facility's reputation. The patient who suffers an accidental injury at a hospital has cause to ponder the irony of that twist in fate. Hospitals are legally required to have safe premises. Every precaution must be taken to guard against accidents to patients, employees and visitors. Accidents cost money. They represent hefty losses in manhours, lawsuits, insurance increases and public goodwill. A hospital whose safety record is too flagrant could lose its accreditation.

Falling is the most common type of patient accident. Patients usually fall close to their beds. The older the patient is, the more susceptible he or she is to falls.

An estimated one-fourth of hospital employee accidents involve lifting materials or patients. Other types of hospital employee accidents parallel those in industry (see National Accident Statistics, Chapter 11).

Visitor accidents range from vehicular mishaps in the parking lot to tripping on slippery floors.

It's lamentable that most hospitals don't have full-time safety personnel.

Hence, accident prevention, investigation and reporting are largely medical staff and security duties.

On your internal and external patrol rounds, observe and report any hazard that conceivably could cause an accident. To refresh your memory on unsafe conditions, see Common Hazards, Chapter 4, and Physical Safety Hazards, Chapter 11.

Special hazards exist in a hospital that you won't find in most other facilities. Flammable anesthetic gas and oxygen are examples. Ask questions to learn about the storage and possible peril of chemicals used in lab work. ,

Nurses write reports on accidents involving patients, since that entails patient care. Summoning medical help may fall to you if the patient has an accident on the hospital grounds. Also get medical aid quickly for accident victims who are employees or visitors. Any employee or visitor accident resulting in an injury creates another patient, of course. At least treatment is at hand.

Be sure to write a factual incident report to your supervision on any accident you attend. Also note it in your daily activity report (see Chapter 4). Accuracy is critical in your written reports on hospital accidents. Your account may later be used in litigation, especially if you witnessed the unfortunate happening.

Fire prevention is another important safety consideration, covered in earlier paragraphs.

Emergency Room Security

A hospital's emergency room (ER) poses several special security problems.

One is theft of patients' personal belongings. Emergency victims are admitted and treated hurriedly. The pace is so fast that the medical staff can't be concerned with protecting such valuables as cash and jewelry. Thieves may be dishonest employees or relatives/friends who sometimes take patients to the emergency entrance.

Another invitation to ER theft is the availability of prescription pads.

Since most hospitals don't post a security officer fulltime in this area, a rigid system of visitor control and possibly television monitoring are needed.

Occasionally, emergency patients are under arrest. An example is a person charged with felony drunk driving in a motor vehicle accident. Since the offender is injured, police deliver him to the hospital for emergency treatment. What's the security procedure for his custody while he's in the hospital?

Some large-city jails have hospital units fully staffed and equipped for emergency surgery. In those places, patients who are under arrest are locked behind bars.

In other areas, the local police or sheriff's department contracts with a private security company to provide officers whose sole duty is guarding prisoners at community hospitals.

Most hospitals don't have jail cells. Detention wings are fairly common. These facilities have single rooms, each with only one door. Either there are no windows or the floor is so high an injured prisoner would be afraid to attempt an escape. A security officer is stationed outside the door at all times.

Police may order extra restraints for patients considered dangerous. It's not unusual to strap down a prisoner who is under the influence of hallucinogens like LSD. Handcuffing a patient to his bed is another safeguard. An additional device is a knee brace. It locks when the prisoner stands up, preventing him from running away.

DIVERSE DUTIES

Your duties will depend on the type and size of medical facility to which you're assigned. Expect to perform a few or all of the following services:

- Access control—monitoring entry and exit of patients, hospital personnel, visitors, vendors and delivery people
- Personnel escorts
- Internal and external patrols
- Parking and traffic control
- Police liaison
- Package control (observation only)
- Employee locker inspection (only by management mandate)
- Lock and key control
- After hours receiving/storage security
- Elevator control (during shutdown hours)
- Lost and found control
- Flag raising and lowering
- Body removal—safeguarding a deceased person's personal property after it has been inventoried, escorting transport of the body within the facility, and granting premise access to the undertaker.

CHAPTER 19

AIRPORT SECURITY

There are 4,798 public airports and 10,678 private airports in the United States.* These range from small general aviation facilities to large international terminals.

Protecting them is highly specialized, since all are closely regulated by federal laws. Airport operations and interstate flight are governed by the Federal Aviation Administration (FAA), an arm of the U.S. Department of Transportation.

A major airport poses security problems unlike those at any other kind of facility. One big difference is the preponderance of open space. Ticketing, baggage, concourse and hangar areas have vast expanses of open floor space. Runways occupy miles of open land.

Another unusual aspect is that you serve both local and federal government authorities, corporate clients and the public. You must have a finely-tuned sense of responsibility toward airport management, the airlines, FAA officials, on-site police and passengers. Most big airports are operated by cities.

OFFICER SELECTION

Security officers selected for airport duty must have these physical and behavioral qualities:

- Neat appearance
- Military bearing
- Courtesy
- Dignity

---

*Source: Statistical Abstract of the United States, Census Bureau, U.S. Department of Commerce (1983).

- Tolerance
- Tact
- Alertness.

SCOPE OF DUTIES

This chapter discusses key duties you will have at a large air terminal. Each facility must have an FAA-approved security program, regardless of size. The two main functions you'll perform are:

1. Preboard screening of passengers and their carry-on articles

2. Facility and perimeter protection.

Passenger screening is the responsibility of air carriers—the various airlines. Facility security is the responsibility of the airport operator.

The purpose of an airline security program is to prevent aircraft hijacking, sabotage and related criminal acts. The primary function of a security officer assigned to predeparture screening is to prevent dangerous and/or unauthorized articles from being brought aboard an aircraft. Examples of forbidden items are weapons, explosives and flammables.

Special Training

By FAA mandate, security officers must receive special training to be passenger/baggage screeners. Passengers are screened with metal detectors (magnetometers). Baggage goes through x-ray examination. To learn the equipment and procedures, a checker must have at least 8 hours of training in the presence of a qualified screener. A new screener needs about 40 hours of on-the-job experience before he/she can work unsupervised.

Recurrent training is given at least annually. Airlines must test all screeners every 6 months.

Higher on the skills ladder is a checkpoint security supervisor (CSS), an FAA designation. The FAA minimum requirement for CSS qualification is 24 hours of instruction. Most of these security officers are former screeners.

A checkpoint security supervisor is usually armed. He or she can supervise the screening process without a law enforcement officer (LEO) being present. A CSS detects and detains, whereas an officer assigned to perimeter control deters and reports. A CSS is commissioned to conduct body searches (physical patdowns or frisks), if necessary. An arrest for an offense is usually made by a LEO stationed at the preboard checkpoint or nearby.

Some checkpoint security officers are deputized with full police powers. Hawaii permits private security officers under contract to the State Department of Transportation to make arrests at all Hawaiian airports (at the time of this writing).

However, most airport security officers have no authority other than that of a private citizen. They support, rather than replace, on-site law enforcement officers. The LEO responds to the request of screening personnel for assistance.

CSS training includes an FAA slide presentation. In addition, here are the main topics covered in the FAA-approved instructional course for CSS certification:

- Glossary of terms
- FAA rules and regulations
- Legal authority
- Client policies
- Interview and investigation techniques
- Report writing
- Radio and telephone communications
- LEO credential verification and bypass procedures for airport/airline concessionaires
- Patdown searching techniques
- Disposition of weapons
- Handling physical evidence
- Human and public relations.

Sterile Concourse

The term "sterile" is applied to floor space beyond the screening checkpoint—a restricted zone between an airport's public areas and flight aprons. Public access to a sterile area is barred until people are cleared to enter.

Initially, airline officials considered three options for placement of screening personnel and equipment: the sterile concourse, boarding area, and gate.

The sterile concourse proved to be the best answer. Stationing law enforcement officers, screeners and detection gear at each boarding area or gate was simply too costly. A screening checkpoint at the entrance to a concourse accommodates more passengers with less manpower.

An added security advantage of the sterile concourse is that it delays storming a plane. The increased distance between the screening checkpoint and the boarding gate gives police and airline personnel more time to react to a hijacking attempt.

HISTORY OF SKYJACKING

The first known hijacking of an airplane took place in Peru in 1930.

During the late 1940s, numerous planes were stolen by people seeking to escape from behind the Iron Curtain.

From 1930 to 1967, there were only 12 attempts to hijack U.S. planes, seven of which were successful, according to FAA records. The FAA definition of a successful hijacking is when the hijacker controls the flight and reaches his destination or objective.

The first hijacking of an American commercial aircraft occurred in 1961. A wave of successful airliner hijackings hit U.S. and foreign carriers during the period 1968 to 1972. The peak year for seizure of the big U.S. passenger planes was 1969. That year there were 40 attempts, 32 of them successful.

Hijackers favored Cuba as a haven until word filtered back that terrorists who landed there were promptly jailed.

Motives for hijacking an aircraft include extortion of cash, political protest and fleeing a felony.

The master stroke—the final straw in the annals of U.S. air piracy—was the infamous "Dan Cooper" caper.

On the afternoon of November 24, 1971, a man boarded a Northwest Orient flight from Portland, Oregon, to Seattle, Washington. He bought his ticket under the alias Dan Cooper. When the plane was taxiing for takeoff, he demanded $200,000 and four parachutes. He showed two stewardesses what appeared to be a bomb in his briefcase. He said he would blow up the aircraft if his demands weren't met.

In Seattle he got the money while holding most of the crew as hostages. All 35 passengers and two crew members were allowed to deplane. Cooper ordered the pilot to fly to Reno, Nevada. The remaining crew had to stay in the front cabin with the curtain drawn. Somewhere over Northwest timberlands, Dan Cooper bailed out and has never been heard of since.

This case was unique because Cooper was the first air pirate to escape by parachute. Not only was he never apprehended, but not even identified.

Cooper's feat encouraged a surge of U.S. aircraft hijackings, resulting in extortion demands of more than $8 million. During that period, $5,355,000 was forked over—all of which was recovered, except Cooper's $200,000.

Sky Marshals

Uncle Sam instituted several emergency measures to combat the growing incidence of skyjackings.

In September 1970, President Nixon ordered armed federal personnel on U.S. commercial flights. The initial force was recruited from the FAA, Customs Service, FBI, Secret Service, CIA and the Defense Department. These men became known as sky marshals. Eventually, government marshals were replaced by a civilian corps called Customs Security Officers because they were trained by the U.S. Customs Service.

The Sky Marshal Program reached its authorized level in August 1971, with an airborne complement of 1,500. In addition, 230 U.S. marshals were stationed at airports.

While the program helped to reduce the success rate of sky-jackings, it obviously wasn't the optimal solution. There were more hijacking attempts on U.S. planes in 1972 than in 1971— 31 versus 27. However, the success rate fell from 44 percent in 1971 to 30 percent in 1972. Both years were improvements over 1970 when the success rate was 68 percent.

One embarrassing incident was the in-flight hijacking of a plane carrying both a sky marshal and an FBI agent.

Airline officials were constantly fearful that a high-altitude shootout would be disastrous. Another drawback of the Sky Marshal Program was that there weren't enough marshals to cover adequately the volume of air travel.

Many aviation security experts felt that the best defense against plane hijacking was on the ground, not in the air. Later experience proved this logic correct.

First Total Screening

On December 5, 1972, the FAA issued two emergency regulations. One ordered air carriers to start screening all passengers and their carry-on articles within 30 days. The other gave airport operators 60 days to assign at least one police officer to each passenger boarding checkpoint. This dual edict imposed overwhelming logistics and funding problems. Airline and airport executives, naturally, protested.

Despite hectic makeshifts, the first day of 100 percent screening of passengers and carry-on luggage occurred on January 5, 1973. Although there were delays, all scheduled airliners took off. The public displayed admirable patience. It was clear that most American travelers were fed up with air piracy and welcomed strict protection measures, even if inconvenient.

Shortly thereafter, the government approved carrier surcharges to pay for the increased security costs.

Preboard screening didn't put a permanent lid on airplane hijacking, but the decline was dramatic. It should be noted that private security officers were hired to implement this program successfully.

NEW FEDERAL LAW

After the rash of 1968-72 skyjackings, Congress passed a new law that significantly updated the Federal Aviation Act of 1958. Public Law 93-366 was signed into law on August 5, 1974. Title 1 of that law is called the Anti-hijacking Act of 1974. Title 2 is known as the Air Transportation Security Act of 1974.

This legislation is implemented by Federal Aviation Regulations (FARs) issued by the Federal Aviation Administration. Here are abstracts of FARs pertinent to preboard screening:

FAR 107 requires each U.S. airport operator to have a security program to protect persons and property traveling by air transportation against criminal violence and aircraft piracy.

FAR 121 orders U.S. air carriers (firms providing regular passenger service on large planes) to screen all passengers and their carry-on items to prevent weapons, explosives or incendiary devices from being brought aboard aircraft.

FAR 129 requires foreign airlines to conduct predeparture screening of passengers and their carry-on luggage on flights to and from the United States. Many foreign air carriers comply with this rule to show good faith in international mutual protection pacts. However, security screening at some foreign airports leaves much to be desired.

FAR 108 permits specially-trained security officers to handle routine screening duties formerly performed solely by law enforcement officers. This regulation doesn't cancel the need for police at preboard checkpoints, but sanctions flexible support.

Passenger planes are vulnerable to hijacking both on the ground and in flight. Public Law 93-366 changed the legal definition of "in flight." The previous wording was "from the time power is applied for takeoff until the landing run ends." The new version under PL 93-366 is "from the moment when all external doors are closed following embarkation until the moment when one such door is opened for debarkation." This provision makes it easier to prosecute a hijacker apprehended in the plane before takeoff.

AIR PIRACY IN 1980s

Cuban refugees stepped up air piracy of American passenger planes in 1980 and 1983 (see chart). Most of these hijackings took place in the United States, according to the FAA. Many lawless Cubans who were granted asylum in this country by President Jimmy Carter hijacked U.S. transports to return to Cuba.

HIJACKED U.S. AIRLINERS, 1980-85

Year	Attempts	Successful
1980	21	13
1981	7	1
1982	9	3
1983	18	13
1984	5	4
1985	4	1

Source: FAA

Massive Kidnapping

On June 14, 1985, two Lebanese radicals hijacked TWA Flight

847 bound from Athens to Rome, and diverted the plane to Beirut. On board were 153 passengers, 104 of them Americans. Thirty-nine American hostages were held in Lebanon for 17 days. Terrorists brutally beat and killed a U.S. Navy diver, Robert Stethem, and threw his body upon the tarmac at the Beirut Airport. The Amal Militia demanded the release of 1,195 Lebanese prisoners, mostly Shiites, jailed in Israel.

With the help of Syria (normally anti-American), the captives were transported from Beirut to Damascus to Frankfurt, West Germany, then flown home. Israel eventually released all of its Shiite prisoners, but not at the request of the United States.

This episode of wanton terrorism shocked and aroused the entire American nation.

U.S. Tightens Security

Responding to the hijacking of TWA Flight 847 and five other terrorist incidents within three weeks, the FAA directed U.S. airlines to take these steps to tighten security:

- Eliminate curbside baggage check-ins for international flights.
- Refuse any baggage on both domestic and international flights not checked in by ticketed passengers.
- Increase manual inspection of carry-on bags, in addition to x-ray examination.
- Match all passengers and their baggage.
- Either a 24-hour hold or manual and x-ray inspection of freight, cargo and mail carried on passenger flights (not applicable to perishable items from known shippers).
- Increase security training for airline personnel.

Transportation Secretary Elizabeth Hanford Dole banned the sale in the United States of any airline tickets to Lebanon and suspended the authority of Middle East Airlines (Lebanese carrier) in this country.

She also suggested additional sky marshals.

Congressmen were busy drafting legislation to toughen international airport security. One measure called for the State Department to study foreign airports and publish a travel advisory on those where security is loose. Another proposal was to bar U.S. jetliners from landing at airports that receive traffic from nations deemed to be bad security risks.

The Airline Pilots Association recommended that Congress allot $20 million more for FAA security research and programs.

PASSENGER SCREENING

An FAA sign is posted at the point where passengers are inspected. It reads:

- IT IS A CRIME to carry a concealed weapon aboard aircraft.
- Federal safety rules require inspection of persons and hand-carried articles passing an inspection point.
- Inspection may be refused.
- Persons refusing inspection will not be permitted to pass the inspection point.

Often friends and relatives accompany passengers to the boarding area, so they, too, must be screened.

The decision to accept or reject any passenger rests with the air carrier. This responsibility includes upholding federal safety regulations. Thus, passenger screening is conducted by an air carrier representative. This representative can be an airline employee or agent (security officer contracted to represent the company). Here is the screening procedure:

Step 1: The person is inspected by means of either a walk-through or hand-held metal detector. If the person being screened doesn't trigger the detector's sound alarm, he or she is cleared to proceed beyond the screening point. If the alarm is activated, the person must be reprocessed.

Step 2. The individual causing the alarm is asked to divest his/her person of metal, then is reprocessed through a walk-through metal detector. The screener has the option to use a hand wand. If the second inspection fails to initiate an alarm, the person is permitted to proceed. However, if metal is still detected, additional screening is necessary.

Step 3. The person again is requested to remove all metal. A hand-held metal detector is then passed all around the subject's body (2 to 4 inches away). If the alarm source is isolated, the metal object must be determined, preferably with the passenger's assistance. Good judgment must be exercised. The screener can readily ascertain that a large belt buckle or artificial limb is not used to hide a weapon.

PREBOARD SCREENING—Airport security officer observes passenger walking throgh magnetometer checkpoint.

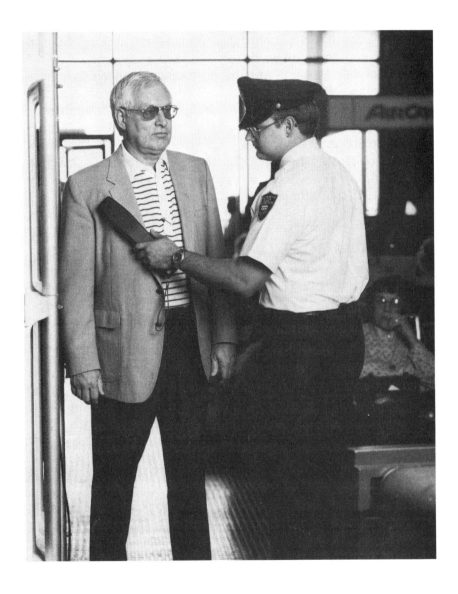

DETECTION WAND—Security officer passes hand-held metal detector all around flight passenger's clothing. This step is necessary when passenger continues to activate walk-through alarm after twice being asked to divest self of metal.

If an alarm cannot be resolved otherwise, a frisk is necessary. Physical patdowns should be conducted by the most experienced personnel. The checkpoint security supervisor or LEO should be summoned.

Step 4: The frisk should be the least offensive to the passenger, while assuring positive identification of the metal. The CSS and passenger should be the same sex.

The CSS should say, "I'm going to touch your body. Do I have your permission?"

If the cause of the alarm is not an unlawful object, an airline employee is so informed. The carrier representative may then grant permission to board.

If a weapon, explosive, incendiary device or other contraband is discovered, the CSS will take custody of it and immediately notify a law enforcement officer.

SEARCH AND SEIZURE

There have been numerous court rulings dealing with aviation security. An issue often challenged in the 1970s was the legality of searching air travelers and seizing unlawful items in their possession.

Central to this dispute is the Fourth Amendment to the U.S. Constitution:

"The right of the people to be secure in their persons, houses, papers and effects, against reasonable searches and seizures, shall not be violated, and no warrants shall issue, but upon probable cause, supported by oath or affirmation, and particularly describing the place to be searched and the persons or things to be seized."

Key words in that law are *reasonable searches* and seizures for *probable cause*. Legal bickering on those two points has long been a headache for peace officers and private protectors.

In recent years, federal courts have consistently ruled that public safety justifies searches of passengers and their luggage by airport police and security officers. With few exceptions, the courts have held that contraband seized as a result of airport screening is admissible evidence in a criminal trial. However, there's a fine line between legal and illegal inspection procedures.

The landmark case that set the standard for search and seizure reasonableness was *Terry vs Ohio (1968)*. A police detective questioned three men who appeared to be casing a store. Unsatisfied with their answers, he patted them down and found a weapon on one of them. Terry argued that the plainclothesman had neither a search warrant nor probable cause.

The U.S. Supreme Court upheld an Ohio court conviction. The high court ruled that a policeman may, on less than probable cause, stop and frisk a suspect for weapons if the officer believes that criminal activity is afoot or that the suspect is armed and dangerous.

The first federal court case involving airport security was *United States vs Lopez (1970)*. Narcotics were seized after preboard screening. That was two years before 100 percent screening went into effect. Lopez was convicted, then appealed. The appellate court overturned his conviction.

At issue was the question of consent. The court said that posting signs advising passengers that they and their baggage would be searched didn't amount to "implied consent."

A later case exemplifies the fickle nature of court findings. In *United States vs Davis (1973)*, a search of Davis's carry-on luggage was challenged. The federal circuit court held that consent-in-fact can be inferred. The court stated:

"We have held that as a matter of constitutional law a prospective passenger has a choice: he may submit to a search of his person and immediate possessions as a condition of boarding; or he may turn around and leave. If he chooses to proceed, that choice, whether viewed as a relinquishment of an option to leave or an election to submit to the search is essentially a 'consent,' granting the government a license to do what it would otherwise be barred from doing by the Fourth Amendment."

In *United States vs Lindsey (1971)*, a suspect was detained at an airport because he appeared extremely anxious and had a conspicuous bulge in his coat pocket. A frisk revealed two packets of heroin in Lindsey's jacket. A federal circuit court ruled that the drug was admissible since it was packed hard enough to have been mistaken for a weapon.

A slightly different incident produced a different verdict in *United States vs Kroll (1973)*. Metal hinges and locks on Kroll's briefcase activated a metal detector alarm. The screening security officer asked the passenger to open his attache case. A police officer on the scene became suspicious when the defendant didn't open the file section in the upper part of the case. An envelope hidden in this compartment contained amphetamines and marijuana.

A U.S. district court granted a motion to suppress the evidence on grounds that while it was reasonable to search the briefcase, it was unreasonable to inspect the contents of the envelope. The appellate court affirmed the trial court.

United States vs Epperson (1972) upheld the validity of a search based on the fact that the passenger activated a magnetometer alarm. Epperson touched off the buzzer on his first walk-through. A policeman asked him if he was carrying a large amount of metal. The defendant produced several metal objects, but the detector continued to sound. The officer then found a .22 caliber pistol in a jacket Epperson was carrying.

The defendant was tried and convicted of attempting to carry a weapon aboard an aircraft. An appellate court affirmed the original conviction. The court reasoned that a frisk of Epperson was justified by a positive magnetometer reading the second time he was screened. The court further ruled that this search and seizure didn't violate the Fourth Amendment.

United States vs Albarado (1974) proved that a too-hasty apprehension of a passenger can backfire. A policeman frisked Albarado as soon as he activated a metal detector alarm. The search turned up counterfeit currency, although that wasn't the source of the alarm. Albarado was tried and convicted, but the appellate court reversed the decision.

The court said that failure to clear the metal detector didn't justify the immediate patdown of the passenger. The proper procedure, according to the court, is to permit a passenger to remove all metal and then pass through the magnetometer again. If the buzzer is initiated a second time, an authorized officer can frisk the passenger as a last resort.

You can see from these legal precedents that your role as a security officer in preboard screening is like walking a tightrope. Your best course of action is to follow FAA procedures to the letter.

PUBLIC RELATIONS ROLE

Your dealings with huge segments of the general public require a personal approach. Since passengers are airline customers, good relations with them have an important impact on business success. Goodwill must be developed. Resentment must be avoided.

Building goodwill at a busy airport is paradoxical for a security officer. You're a symbol of authority. Many passengers view your work negatively. They think you're spying on them. They may not understand that you're there to ensure the safety and welfare of all air travelers. It's natural for people to oppose things they don't understand.

You can foster better understanding by first putting them at ease. In your initial contact, you make a friend or enemy of a passenger usually in the first 30 seconds. Say something to show the person that you realize he/she is human. The individual may be tired, aggravated, or in a hurry. Don't embarrass the person in front of his/her friends. Avoid argument. Lead rather than drive. Establish reasonableness. Indicate that your job is strictly impersonal. Patiently explain that security measures are required by law for the protection of the flying public.

When you're talking to someone, look that person squarely in the eye. Display genuine politeness with frequent use of such terms as "please," "thank you," "yes, sir" and "no, sir." The salutation "ma'am" is generally acceptable, but some women resent it because it's a contraction of madam. An alternative is "lady."

TEAM ATTITUDE

You must also have good rapport with others who work at the terminal where you're assigned. These include carrier employees, airport personnel, FAA inspectors, police and your fellow officers.

Think of yourself as a team member striving for overall efficiency.

Set a positive example to your co-workers. Keep cool under trying conditions. Be friendly, but not gabby or gossipy. Show that you're on your toes as a security officer. Don't permit rules infractions just because someone considers you a crony. Treat everyone alike. Extend the same courtesy to your associates that you do to the public. Demonstrate pride in your work. Competency commands respect.

FACILITY PROTECTION

Passenger Terminal

The passenger terminal arrangement poses security problems due to the separation of public and flight operations areas, with a sterile zone between them.

You should first become acquainted with the airport security plan. Know what doors and gates are to be locked and when they're to be opened. Also learn who has access to all areas and when. Your training should include a list of screening exceptions. Lock and key control is another important aspect of the access system.

Fire prevention is critical in buildings and on ramps. Not only are lives at stake, but also expensive airplanes and equipment. Added to the risk is the volatility of aircraft fuel. Know the locations of fire extinguishers and fire doors. Inspect sprinkler risers regularly. Your post orders should spell out how you support the airport fire brigade. Review Chapter 8, Fire Prevention and Control.

Due to the vast space covered, you will probably make your patrol rounds in a motor cart. Remember, the first patrol on each shift is the most important. Be alert for anything amiss. Don't zip around too fast. Take enough time to be thorough. Your patrol duties may include checking airline offices and/or airport shops, bars and restaurants when they are closed. Watch for burglars and signs of break-ins. Targets are cash, ticket stock and merchandise. Review Chapter 5, Patrol Techniques.

Baggage Theft

Baggage theft is reduced to a minimum by stationing a security officer at the exit to a baggage retrieval area. Deplaning passengers pick up their own luggage. The officer checks the passenger's baggage claim stubs to make sure they match the tags on each bag or parcel. Permission to exit is then granted.

You must be careful not to let anyone take the wrong bags or to remove baggage without claim checks. You should *never* take a passenger's flight ticket and pull off the baggage claim stubs yourself. Instead, politely ask the person to hand you the claim checks. A passenger who requests that you separate his baggage vouchers from his ticket could be a cheat. He'll then complain to the airline that you stole his ticket and threw it away. The carrier

BAGGAGE CLAIM—Security officer removes tag from passenger's suitcase at airport exit. Claim stubs must match tags on baggage.

issues a new ticket which the culprit later turns in for a refund.

Correct procedure rarely upsets honest passengers—and your employer never has to buy a needless ticket.

Passengers who have lost their luggage or claim checks should be referred to the appropriate airline lost and found office.

Passengers disembarking from an international flight must have their baggage inspected by the U.S. Customs Service.

Cargo Security

Air transport of U.S. mail began in 1918, eight years before the first commercial passenger service.

Today both the variety and volume of air freight are gigantic and still growing. The big advantage is rapid delivery of everything from heavy machinery to such perishables as flowers and lobsters. The value of all air shipments runs into billions of dollars annually. Some air cargo—art treasures, precious metals, gems, currency and negotiable securities—is of extraordinary value. In fact, more items of exceptional value are transported by air than by any other means of carriage. Thus, the loss potential is greater.

Theft of air cargo is primarily an internal problem. Most of the stealing occurs at the freight terminal. Assets are lost through pilferage, falsified invoices and fraudulent pickups. Effective protection boils down to the most basic security techniques.

Here are cardinal physical security measures:

1. Parking lots for the public and employees should be separated from the freight terminal by a fence. No one should be able to enter the freight area without going through a control point of some sort (a receptionist, security officer or other access control measure).

2. Cargo areas should be well-lighted at night because that's when freight is the most vulnerable to theft.

3. Isolated areas should be rigged with intrusion alarms.

4. The most valuable cargo should be monitored continuously by closed-circuit television (CCTV).

Sensible security practices in the selection, training and control of personnel also will combat cargo theft. Methods include:

- Screening of new hires
- Employee motivation to discourage pilferage
- Tightly controlled entry/exit of all persons handling cargo

- Personnel surveillance by CCTV and mirrors
- Close accountability of shipments.

Fire prevention, detection and control also are vital to air cargo protection.

Review Chapter 9, Thwarting Theft; Chapter 12, Personnel Control; and Chapter 14, Physical Security.

Perimeter Protection

The FAA stipulates that perimeter barriers around major airports must be chain link fences at least 8 feet high, topped with a 3-strand barbed wire outrigger tilted outward at a 45-degree angle.

Equally important is adequate lighting of airport buildings, auto parking areas, landing strips, flight aprons and roadways.

The FAA requires that the placement and intensity of lights should not "blind or hinder air traffic control or aircraft operations."

Fencing and lighting should be planned as co-deterrents. Fences around ramp areas near the passenger terminal are the most likely to be penetrated by skyjackers and terrorists. Hence, these fences should be well-lighted.

Fences surrounding parked airplanes, service and freight areas should be amply lighted for after-dark observation of intruders bent on theft or vandalism. Lights should shine toward an intruder and away from a security post. Perimeter lights should be as vandal-proof as possible.

Perimeter intrusion alarms are desirable, if their deterrence value warrants their cost.

On your perimeter patrols, check fences and gates to assure that they're in good condition and haven't been tampered with. On your night rounds, make sure that required lights are on. Report any discrepancies.

Traffic Control

You'll be busy if you have to control auto traffic in front of an airport passenger terminal. People arrive and depart in a flurry of passenger cars, taxis and buses. You'll have to enforce "no stopping" and "no parking" restrictions when passenger loading zones are jammed. Tempers will flare. Everyone, it seems, wants to enter and leave the terminal at the most convenient curb.

Meanwhile, you have to keep traffic moving on the street along-side the terminal entrance. During peak traffic hours, you may be stationed in the street, or on an island between two-way traffic, directing the flow of both autos and pedestrians.

Another security duty linked to traffic control is protecting airport parking lots and garages. Security officers conduct roving patrols of parking areas to deter car theft, maintain safety and discover any improper or emergency situation.

Review Traffic Control Safety in Chapter 11.

CHAPTER 20

SPECIAL EVENTS SECURITY

Chapter 15 explained the difference between a crowd and a mob. A crowd is a large assembly of people without personal identity. A mob is an unruly or lawless crowd. That chapter dealt mostly with how to prevent or contain mob violence.

Special events security entails protection services to manage crowds gathered to see spectator events. Examples of such events are sports competition, entertainment by performing artists, fairs, expositions and parades. Well-planned security assures that these outdoor and indoor attractions come off safely and peacefully.

TYPICAL DUTIES

If you are a security officer at a special event, your duties typically include:

- Maintaining order among spectators
- Protecting performers/VIPs
- Facility protection, including enforcement of fire and safety rules
- Access control
- Gate checks to exclude admission of unauthorized items such as weapons, explosives and alcoholic drinks
- Credential verification
- Ushering/escorting
- Police liaison
- Emergency coordination
- Traffic/parking control.

WORLD WELCOME—Security supervisor is framed in entrance arch of Los Angeles Memorial Coliseum before opening ceremonies for 1984 Summer Olympic Games.

PROTECTING OLYMPIAD XXIII

California Plant Protection, Inc., and its associates were privileged to take part in the granddaddy of all sports meets—the 1984 Summer Olympic Games in Los Angeles.

Protecting the Olympics was an exciting, once-in-a-lifetime experience. It was also a Herculean challenge.

Grand-Scale Spectacle

The 23rd Olympiad was the biggest in history, despite the Soviet boycott. Some 7,060 athletes from 140 nations competed in 23 sports. (Americans won a record 174 medals; runners-up were West Germany with 59, Romania 53, and Canada 44.)

National enthusiasm was hyped up by having community runners carry the Olympic torch across the United States. The route from New York City to Los Angeles totalled 9,100 miles and went through 33 states. Torch bearers ran continuously for 82 days.

Events were staged in five Southern California counties: Los Angeles, Ventura, San Bernardino, Orange and San Diego. The 92,655-seat Los Angeles Memorial Coliseum was filled to capacity for the opening and closing ceremonies.

An estimated 5.5 million persons attended the 16-day sports program, July 28 through August 12. About 2.5 billion people watched the Games on television—more than half of the world's population.

Record Security Force

Two prime contractors and three subcontractors provided 13,000 private security officers for the Games. This was the largest private security force ever mustered for a temporary enterprise. These personnel supported about 5,000 police, sheriffs and agents from 50 city, county, state and federal law enforcement agencies. The combined protection force was equal in size to a small Army infantry division.

California Plant Protection in tandem with its out-of-state arm, CPP Security Service, was the principal prime contractor. The firm formed a new division to recruit and train 7,500 security officers for the Games. The CPP Olympic unit alone was the fifth largest private security organization in the United States at the time.

Main Security Goal

Elaborate security measures at the 23rd Olympiad were aimed at protecting athletes and spectators from criminal acts.

Organizers especially wanted to prevent incidents like the international terrorism that marred the Munich Games. On September 6, 1972, Arab terrorists murdered 11 Israeli Olympic athletes. In the ensuing gun battle, West German police killed 5 of the 8 terrorists.

Security preparations for the 1984 Summer Olympics really paid off. No serious offenses occurred—which was quite a feat, considering the scope of the project. Minor infractions, such as intoxication and toting suspicious objects, were nipped in the bud.

Applicant Qualifications

The following qualifications for security officers were developed jointly by the Los Angeles Olympic Organizing Committee (LAOOC) and participating security companies:

1. Must be a U.S. citizen or legal resident alien
2. Minimum age 18
3. Excellent health, no physical limitations
4. Must speak fluent English (and preferably another language)
5. Ability to write detailed reports
6. No criminal convictions other than for minor traffic violations
7. No history of narcotics or alcohol abuse
8. Must have reliable means of transportation
9. Willing to undergo up to 40 hours of special training.

CPP went a step further by giving applicants a personality evaluation. This test was designed for the Olympics by Dr. Arthur F. LeBlanc, a psychologist who is an employment consultant for CPP. These traits were assessed:

1. Would the security officer show up consistently for assignment?

2. Would the security officer take directions without raising objections?

3. Would the security officer react positively to immediate stress?

4. Would the security officer be easily distracted from duties?

5. Would the security officer be prone to misuse alcohol or drugs?

6. Would the security officer be prone to create artifical incidents?

CPP Recruitment

CPP hired a temporary staff of 25 to recruit candidates for Olympic security duty. Recruiters contacted young people at universities, colleges and clubs. Appeals were by direct presentation, rather than help-wanted advertising.

Response was overwhelming. About 11,000 applicants showed up. Youths and older people were so eager to take part in Olympic pageantry that they lined up in sweltering heat, filled out lengthy questionnaires, and permitted background checks by police.

The firm accepted over 8,000 applicants. Sixty-three percent were men, and 37 percent were women. They comprised a balanced ethnic mix.

Their success ratio turned out to be a significant surprise. Of the 7,500 security officers hired, only 10 were severely reprimanded or discharged. That translates into a good conduct rate of 99.87 percent! The management of any company with 7,500 employees would be elated with that kind of performance. It proved that careful pre-employment screening saved lots of headaches later on.

Training Program

A 20-hour training course for security officers was developed by security companies and the LAOOC. Subjects and the time devoted to them were:

Orientation to Olympic Security (1 hour)

Orientation to Accreditation Management (2 hours)

Emergency Operations Procedures (3 hours)

Bomb Orientation (1 hour)

Terrorism Awareness (1 hour)

Communications (1 hour)

Report Writing (1 hour)

Equipment and Uniform Care (1 hour)

Data Procedures Orientation (1 hour)

Powers to Arrest (4 hours)

On-site Orientation (4 hours).

In addition, CPP showed its personnel a special Olympic training film. It discussed such things as Olympic history, security tips based on corporate experience, and how to protect athletes, officials and spectators.

Each CPP trainee was given a pocket-size Olympic Security Officers Manual. It spelled out administrative policies and expanded instructions covered in the official curriculum and CPP film.

The firm employed 75 training instructors. They consisted of teachers. graduate students, military veterans and security supervisors.

Trainees were taught in groups of 50-100. Classes were held in three different public schools.

Graduates received LAOOC accreditation as security officers, then were issued uniforms.

Uniforms

The Olympic security uniform was distinctive: tan slacks, short-sleeved tan shirt, a blue beret and a matching blue web belt with a special buckle. Men and women wore the same outfit.

Foreign athletes dubbed security officers the "Blue Angels" (not to be confused with the Navy's stunt-flying team). The implication was that Olympic defenders were angels compared to beret-clad soldiers in oppressed lands.

Olympic Security Duties

CPP security officers performed a variety of duties at about 100 different Olympic locations. On-site guidance was provided by 750 field supervisors.

Assignments included:

- Crowd control at competition sites, called venues
- Monitoring dormitories/grounds in Olympic Villages where athletes and officials were housed
- Protecting athletic training sites
- Guarding Olympic Arts Festival events
- Armed posts at places where cash, tickets and payroll checks were issued or kept

ALL'S WELL—Olympic security officer radios report at one of venues during 23rd Olympiad held in five Southern California counties.

- Access control
- Badge control
- Warehouse protection
- Perimeter patrols
- Vehicle inspection
- Parking control.

Security officers used metal detectors and x-ray devices to screen pedestrians at facility entrances. Some areas were monitored by closed-circuit television.

Sports competition took place at 25 separate facilities. Some of these were large complexes or vast outdoor areas. Temporary installations included 47 miles of chain-link fence, 65,000 bleacher seats, 3,000 tents, 95 turnstiles and computer terminals at every Olympic site.

Olympic Villages were located at three universities: UCLA, USC and UC Santa Barbara.

The Olympic Arts Festival was an 18-nation cultural exchange, featuring foreign and American art, music, dancing, drama and visual exhibits. These shows were held at 48 sites in the Los Angeles area such as the Music Center, Los Angeles County Museum of Art, and Pasadena Civic Auditorium. The festival ran from June 1 through August 12.

Communications

CPP set up a five-man, 24-hour command center to coordinate Olympic security operations. The command center was linked directly to field personnel by telephone, radio and computer.

On-site people communicated with each other on walkie-talkie radios.

Troubleshooters were on hand at each event, venue and village. Thus, security officers had immediate help to cope with any kind of flap that developed.

The security communication system for the Olympic Games was designed and built by Motorola, Inc. This network enabled rapid coordination among private security personnel, police, medics and firemen. Fortunately, few emergencies occurred.

Protecting TV Crews

The American Broadcasting Company (ABC) televised the Olympic Games to the world—a huge undertaking in terms of people and equipment. Besides protecting the Games, CPP provided security for ABC's crews and their equipment wherever they roved throughout five counties.

Fiscal Triumph

Mindful of the $1.16 billion debt Montreal incurred in the 1976 Games, Los Angeles voters forbade the use of public funds to host the 1984 Games. This break with tradition posed challenges never faced by Olympic organizers.

The LAOOC proved to the world that the Olympics can be sponsored without taxpayers' help. American enterprise reshaped the way the Games formerly were financed. The success of this venture will be very hard to match in the future.

Sales of tickets, souvenir coins and television rights produced record income. Advertisers gladly paid to call their wares "official" Olympic products. Use of excellent athletic facilities in and around Los Angeles greatly reduced costs. Few new facilities were needed, and some were donated by more than 30 corporations that shared Olympic sponsorship. Fifty thousand people served as unpaid volunteers. Contracting private security services to augment law enforcement also trimmed expenses.

To everyone's amazement, the 1984 Summer Games generated a handsome profit. It had grown to $250 million by mid-1985. The surplus was earning interest at the rate of $5 million a month. At first, Olympic officials were in a quandary on how to apportion this unexpected windfall.

Reflections

The 13,000 people who served as security officers in the 23rd Olympiad were a credit to themselves and to the private security sector. All can take pride in contributing to the most successful Olympics to date.

They learned first-hand what it means to be guardians of the peace. Their increased awareness of law and order will benefit society and the security industry for years to come.

Hopefully, some of these fine officers may later seek careers in the security field. The majority will pursue other vocations. One prediction seems fairly safe. Those who become corporate executives will take more interest in business security because of their Olympic experience.

SPECTATOR EVENTS SPECIALISTS

A Los Angeles firm, Contemporary Services Corporation, specializes in ushering/protecting large spectator events such as Super Bowl football games, Los Angeles Lakers basketball games and the Ice Capades. Damon Zumwalt is president and Peter Kranske is vice president of the company.

Their philosophy and methods—gained in many years of experience—offer practical tips in crowd management to security officers everywhere.

Crowd Control Basics

The primary aims of crowd control at a spectator event are to maintain order and safety.

Security measures vary according to the size and nature of the gathering. For example, a rock festival usually presents more problems than a symphony concert. The throng packed into a football stadium isn't spread out as loosely as the general public at a parade. Regardless of the type of event, however, the same principles apply to keeping peace among onlookers.

"Effective crowd control is 80 percent good public relations," Zumwalt said. "When you talk with a spectator, that person's mind-set depends on how you approach him or her. Your best asset is politeness. Being a good listener to a patron's problems is an important first step.

"Often a patient explanation will resolve a complaint. If the reason for a stadium rule is explained to a sports fan, the average person usually accepts it.

"At other times, you simply have to say, 'I'm sorry, these are the rules and we can't make any exceptions.' Be diplomatic but firm, especially regarding safety.

"Crowds are much easier to manage if you use the soft approach, rather than coming on like a steamroller."

Security Duties

Typical security duties at a stadium during a sports event include:

- Preserving order among spectators
- Access control at gates, doors and ramps
- Checking tickets and directing seating
- Protecting teams and their equipment

- Facility protection, including fire prevention
- Barring unauthorized access to athletes' locker rooms, reserved seats and press boxes
- Parking control
- Perimeter control.

Good Planning Essential

Proper planning is absolutely necessary to ensure that an event comes off smoothly and trouble-free. The first consideration is making sure that the protection force is adequate to handle the crowd. Laying out duty stations on a grid-by-grid basis assures maximal coverage.

Security officers should be placed where they can control the crowd most effectively. The plan should be broken down into specific duties for each officer. Planners should try to anticipate every contingency. It may be advisable to place an officer the size of a fullback at a certain location. What stations need two officers to ward off any challenge?

Facility protection should be an integral part of the plan. Rules laid down by the property owner, as well as local safety ordinances, must be obeyed to prevent accidents and facility damage.

Briefings Vital

Security officers should be thoroughly briefed before each event. Given enough information—what to do in every conceivable situation—an officer is less likely to be in over his head if a problem arises. Samples of key instructions follow.

You must constantly be alert for disturbances in a crowd. In fact, central to your job is protecting spectators from each other. If you encounter two or more people arguing, here are some pointers:

1. Stay calm.

2. Don't get into the squabble yourself. Try to cool down the antagonists. Find out what the argument is about and, if possible, arbitrate a peaceful settlement.

3. If your persuasion fails, call your supervisor on your radio and ask for police backup. A skillful supervisor may be able to pacify hasslers without police help. A law enforcement officer should be brought into the act only as a last resort. That will have the ultimate chilling effect on hostility. A surly person who is telling you "no" will say "yes" to a policeman.

When a dispute erupts into a fight, call the police immediately. Let them deal with all violent offenders. Never use physical force against a spectator unless your life is endangered. Your actions are severely limited by the liability insurance carried by the stadium (and your employer, if you're a contract officer).

People attending an event often forget where they parked. Talk them back through their arrival. Ask for any landmarks they remember. If you recognize the bearings, give specific directions: "Your car is probably in Section C or D." You really have to know the facility well.

To keep an aisle clear, you must know the seating arrangement on both sides of it. Direct people to their seats in an efficient manner. Politely, but firmly, move dawdlers along to prevent aisle blockage.

If you're guarding the athletes' locker room, you must have a system to exclude curious bystanders, yet permit access to those who are authorized to enter. You must know who's who. Use finesse, but don't bend the rules. If you have any questions, ask your supervisor.

Note: Pinkerton's Inc. also has a long and proud record of special events security. Some examples include: The 1980 Winter Olympic Games at Lake Placid, N.Y., The World's Fair in N.Y. City, 1964, The New York Racing Association (all N.Y. Race Tracks) since 1890!! — And many others, such as the Master's Golf Tournament (since 1932).

CHAPTER 21

NUCLEAR SECURITY

TOUGH REQUIREMENTS

Nuclear security is probably the strictest, most demanding specialty in the security field.

To be assigned to a nuclear facility, your character and physical fitness must be excellent. You must first undergo a thorough background check similar to that required for a national defense security clearance. Screening includes personality tests. Then you must complete an exhaustive federal training program. You are retrained often to keep your certification as a nuclear security officer up-to-date.

Your on-site performance must be precise, with little or no tolerance for error.

If this challenge sounds far more difficult than the average security post, it's exactly that. Of course, the pay is above average, too.

TYPICAL DUTIES

Here are some of the main things you are expected to do well as a nuclear security officer:

- Write accurate log entries and reports
- Maintain ultra-safety in a radioactive environment
- Prevent plant sabotage and theft of fissionable material
- Control access to high-security areas, including search of persons, vehicles and packages
- Escort visitors and vehicles
- React to emergencies such as injuries, fires and bomb threats
- Control civil disturbances
- Surveillance

- Patrols
- Lock and key control
- Operate communications equipment
- Test and maintain security devices
- Respond to intrusion alarms
- Liaison with law enforcement agencies
- Traffic and parking control
- Special duties during construction and maintenance or refueling shutdowns.

FEDERAL REGULATIONS

Rigid protection of nuclear power plants and research labs is mandated by the U.S. Department of Energy. The U.S. Nuclear Regulatory Commission (NRC) licenses and supervises all privately held nuclear facilities. Those that are government-owned are regulated directly by the Department of Energy.

Security provisions for these sites are set forth in Title 10, "Energy," of the Code of Federal Regulations (CFR). This title, abbreviated 10 CFR, has 199 parts. Part 73, Appendix B, details training requirements for security personnel.

Actual lessons fill volumes. For security's sake, much of the instructional matter is not public information.

Thus, 10 CFR is the nuclear security "bible." The NRC is the "watchdog." That commission enforces nuclear regulations.

However, there is much more. The 10 CFR is revised frequently. Regulatory amendments, notices and guides are published regularly. The security department of a nuclear facility must constantly be alert for changes to avoid penalties for non-compliance.

DANGEROUS MATERIALS

Why all the stringency? To answer that question, you must understand the dangers involved in radioactive materials, and there are several kinds. A special nuclear material (SNM) commonly used at nuclear power plants is enriched uranium. Another is plutonium. Enriched uranium fuels the nuclear reactors in such power-generating stations as San Onofre in California and Indian Point in New York. There are about 90 nuclear power plants nationwide.

RADIATION GAUGE—Visitor clips a dosimeter to clothing while touring a nuclear facility. At exit security officer checks instrument to see if person was exposed to excessive radiation.

Major Security Aspects

The three most vital protection concerns for a nuclear facility are:

1. Safety of people
2. Prevention of sabotage
3. Removal of atomic fuel.

Need for Safety

Nuclear fuel must be ridigly controlled. In its pure or near-pure state, it emits radiation harmful to plant and animal life. In fact, high-intensity radiation is lethal. It can kill or seriously damage human tissue and vital organs.

Therefore, extreme care must be exercised in nuclear facilities to ensure the safety of all personnel—especially those closely associated with SNM. People (including security officers) who work in "hot" labs and nuclear storage areas are particularly vulnerable. They must be checked for excessive radiation each time they exit an area containing SNM. The same is true of workers who repair reactors.

So, the need for strict safety precautions is self-evident. One of a security officer's key functions is to enforce safety regulations. He or she sees to it that dosimeters are worn and checked, that protective clothing is donned in certain areas, and that such garb is inspected and properly stored. A dosimeter is a small vial-shaped device that measures radiation. The instrument usually is clipped to a shirt or coat pocket. Visitors must wear dosimeters while in a radiation area or on plant tour. When visitors leave, a security officer checks all dosimeters to see if anyone was exposed to excessive radiation.

Actually, a nuclear facility poses very little danger to visitors or employees. This fact is borne out by many years of safe handling of nuclear materials. But that's no excuse to relax the rules. Thanks to NRC stringency, radiation dosage is held far below any amount that could even begin to harm a person. Coupled with plant integrity is a strong safety-awareness among the workforce. Adherence to effective regulations has chalked up an impressive safety record. Security officers strive to keep it that way.

Sabotage Scenarios

Sabotaging a nuclear power plant is chilling to imagine. Crucial aims would be to damage or destroy the reactor or storage area. Serious damage could release intense radioactive particles into the atmosphere. These emissions could inflict widespread harm. An entire city might be imperiled. That's one reason nuclear facilities are built distant from large population centers.

Who would be so senseless as to attempt havoc on a nuclear plant? It must be assumed that there are villains at large who would deliberately commit sabotage. Some are criminally insane. Others have a pathological need to achieve fame through highly visible deeds. Presidential assassins often fall into that category. Hateful militants may use demolition as a protest against authority or society. Then, too, foreign enemy sabotage is possible. The assumption of a mythical enemy is necessary because all threats to radiation leakage must be considered—and secured.

Therein lies one of the greatest challenges to nuclear protection. The problem is to anticipate every possible way a saboteur could breach physical security. An ideal security system blocks both anticipated and unanticipated penetration.

For example, assume a mythical enemy. Assume that enemy sends a squad-size combat team of highly-trained, suicidal commandos to commit sabotage. Also assume a decoy operation to divert attention. Let's say a small plane is crashed at one on-site location and a vehicle is wrecked at another. These diversions are intended to split the plant security force and keep it occupied while the main attack force breaches physical barriers. The raiders need little time to achieve a well-planned mission.

This is a worst-case situation. Would the protection force be able to ward off the attack while being decoyed in two separate areas? Could this scenario even occur? It hasn't yet, but nuclear security officers are trained to handle just such a crisis. They're fully equipped to repel a small-scale assault until reinforcements arrive. Anti-invasion tools at each site include gas masks, riot helmets, batons, sidearms, shotguns, semiautomatic rifles and other weapons.

The NRC insists on security measures to meet any contingency. That explains the never-ending revision of 10 CFR. It's also why on-site security personnel are continually retrained and inspected.

What if a security officer decides to commit sabotage? That contingency also is covered. Nuclear security personnel are under constant surveillance to detect changes in behavior, attitude and off-site habit patterns. These officers must have a high degree of dedication. They actually take pride in being closely watched. They're often subjected to surprise urine tests to determine if drug use is evident. That's how *personal* nuclear security can be.

Security Against Sabotage

Tight screening cuts down a saboteur's odds to gain access to a sensitive area or take hostages. Visitors and employees alike are put "through the paces" before entering the protected area of a nuclear facility. The contents of pockets are emptied into a container. All hand-carried objects (such as briefcases, purses and packages) are closely inspected, including x-ray examination. Bomb-sniffing equipment also is used. All persons are identified by a closely controlled badge system. Everyone walks through a magnetometer, a metal detector similar to those at airports. Then a more sensitive metal-detecting wand is passed all around a person's body.

Such a thorough search of people and objects they carry is sure to turn up any concealed weapon, explosive or incendiary device. Furthermore, no one can go anywhere in the protected area without an escort—even to the restroom.

Accidental Reactor Damage

An accident, such as an airplane crash, could cause a serious radioactive leak. Reactor cooling towers are built to withstand the force of a plane smashup. The parabolic shape of many of these towers is designed partly to resist a severe impact.

Earthquakes and other natural disasters also could cause damage resulting in a nuclear leak. Here again, NRC stringency comes into play. Advance planning tries to anticipate every eventuality. NRC personnel inspect each phase of construction, step by step, to ensure the highest possible engineering standards. An operating license will be granted only when the NRC is satisfied that the building meets specifications.

Continual caution is exercised to assure plant stability. Some nuclear plants have been shut down when it was discovered that they were built too close to an earthquake fault. The NRC has shut down others because of operational weaknesses in the reactor systems.

Removal of Special Nuclear Materials

The other major concern of a nuclear security force is removal of SNM. By regulation, attempts to steal SNM must be prevented — even at the cost of a security officer's life. That's real commitment!

Most power-generating stations have less worry about SNM removal than certain research centers. The enriched uranium fuel rods used at power plants are 14 feet long. It would be hard to walk off with one. Besides, the technolgoy to extract the uranium from the rod is available only at highly specialized labs. Still, the possibility is a security consideration.

Some nuclear R&D labs work with a variety of radioactive materials which may include uranium and plutonium in "pure" form, unattached to fuel rods. Again, removal of this material must be prevented. Could someone steal enough SNM to make a bomb? Probably not, but the NRC mandates special security measures at sites that keep "strategic quantities" of SNM.

The problem of removing SNM is complicated by the fact that the material is intensely radioactive and would certainly overdose the carrier. Experts avoid human contact with this stuff. It's handled by a remote manipulator in a sealed compartment. Despite the obvious risk, the possibility of a suicidal person concealing an SNM container in a body cavity must be guarded against.

What could be done with a vial of plutonium? Pollute a water system, or at least make the local populace believe it's polluted? Threaten a city or an institution by announcing possession and intent to harm? One guess is as good as another. Whatever the motivation, the fact remains that highly dangerous material would be out of responsible control. That in itself is reason enough to be concerned about removal of SNM.

Proprietary Techniques

Special techniques to prevent breaches of nuclear security are beyond the scope of this book. All of this information is proprietary. There's no such thing as a typical security plan for a nuclear power plant. Each licensee has a different protection plan. Security and contingency plans are safeguarded information — not for public disclosure.

Assignment to the protected area of a nuclear facility carries a high level of trust. It's similar to qualifying for a Department of Defense (DOD) security clearance. However, the NRC doesn't use such DOD classification terms as "secret" and "top secret." If a security officer works in a nuclear operation at a defense facility, he or she will have the appropriate DOD clearance.

Background checks and precise training are mandatory for all security personnel who work within a protected nuclear area. The NRC also requires that security officers' emotional stability is certified by a professional psychologist.

Reliability Stressed

The core requirement for a nuclear security officer is superior reliability.

He or she is always a team member. What may happen to others or to the facility rests heavily on each officer's dependability—to the maximal degree. There is absolutely no margin for error. For example, if a nuclear security officer leaves his post for even part of a minute, that post is open and vulnerable. Moreover, the open-post period must be logged for NRC inspection. That single breach of security regulations can cost the offender's employer a stiff fine. In nuclear security, the performers report their violations, thereby exposing themselves to penalty.

NRC officials are exacting in their inspections. Only alert, proper performance is approved. Relaxation in the form of an improper patdown or inaccurate log entry is not tolerated.

Naturally, such emphasis on exactness requires tight supervision. Many utility companies employ their own security supervisors at nuclear sites to ensure continuity. The belief is that separating proprietary supervision from contract personnel helps to prevent breach coverups by security officers.

In some nuclear facilities the high-security tasks—such as armed duty and response to emergencies—are performed only by proprietary security officers. In those situations, contract personnel function more like watchmen or perimeter guards.

There are several variations the security organization of a nuclear plant might adopt. But the objective is always the same: 100 percent reliability on the part of every security team member.

ELIGIBILITY REQUIREMENTS

A nuclear security officer's pay is well above that of the average security officer. The reason is that candidates must meet exceptional requirements. Eligibility essentials are:

- U.S. citizen
- High school graduate
- No physical defects (determined by medical examination)
- Sharp physical fitness
- Capable of obtaining a national security clearance
- Psychologically sound (determined by licensed psychologist)
- No record of drug or alcohol abuse
- no felony convictions
- No adverse background problems

All requirements for employment are verified by background investigation.

INTENSIVE TRAINING

Once accepted for employment, the candidate must successfully complete a battery of training courses and tests to qualify for nuclear assignment. Training length varies from site to site, but 80 hours is common. At some facilities, combined off-site and on-site training can run from 4 to 6 weeks.

Off-Site Courses

Off-site training usually covers such topics as:

- Powers to Arrest
- Rules of Evidence
- Patrol Procedures
- Communications
- Self-defense
- Report Writing
- Arrest Techniques
- Search and Seizure
- Response to Crimes in Progress
- First Aid.

On-Site Courses

In recent years, the NRC has increasingly emphasized the need for on-site training. Site-specific instruction typically includes subjects such as:

- Radiological Safety

- Threat Situations
- Routine Procedures
- Emergency Procedures
- Facility Alarms
- Firefighting.

In addition, range qualification is a must for armed security officers. The range course may include night firing and stipulations for accurate firing after a period of heavy exercise, such as running.

NRC Certification

To be certified as a nuclear security officer, the candidate must pass written tests on all required training courses. A medical doctor must certify physical fitness for assigned duties. A professional psychologist must certify that an officer is emotionally stable for assignment to a protected nuclear area.

Physical endurance qualification varies, but when imposed, can be very taxing. It requires the security officer to be in excellent physical shape.

Psychological evaluation involves a multi-phase assessment of an officer's behavioral makeup.

Perpetual Process

Training is a never-ending process. Requalification in certain general and site-specific topics is at least an annual requirement. For example, firearms requalification is necessary at least once a year and often every 3 to 6 months.

Each site has a training officer. Many sites have more than one. These officers circulate among the security force daily to correct improper performance. Shift supervisors also act as training officers. They're responsible for consistently high-quality vigilance on their shifts.

ELITE GROUP

This chapter should convince you that nuclear security is a serious business. How serious is demonstrated by the strictness of NRC requirements for the selection, training and performance of security officers. The extremely personal nature of this duty further attests to its gravity.

The end result is a pride-filled team. Nuclear security officers are an elite group, dedicated and reliable.

Without doubt, the nuclear industry has done much to upgrade the status of security officers. Following the NRC's lead, other governmental agencies are turning to the private sector to fill their security needs.

CHAPTER 22

LITTLE THINGS COUNT BIG

ATTITUDE IS CRUCIAL

If you've read this far, hopefully you have gleaned some instructional nuggets that will help you to be a better security officer.

But the final determiner is YOU.

Your proficiency hinges on your attitude. You must take pride in your company and its employees, your work, and your association with fellow officers.

How you perform the so-called "little" things in your daily duties measures your competence as a security officer. Superior protection service is a multitude of little things done well. Think of yourself and your work as important. The protection of assets is truly a BIG factor in the success of any business.

OUTSTANDING TRAITS

To refresh your memory, here's a brief summary of qualities that count big in your performance. If you develop even modest ability in the following traits, you will be considered an outstanding protection officer.

Know Your Functions. You protect business assets. These assets consist of people, property and information.

Adequate Reporting. Report everything that happens while you're on duty, even happenings that seem trivial to you. You needn't worry about your lack of writing skill. What you report is more important than how you report it.

Reliability. Reliability is your greatest long-term asset as a security officer. If people can rely on you, they will respect you.

Promptness. Attend to your responsibilities quickly. Be at your post on time.

Neatness. Neat appearance and military bearing are "musts" for anyone in uniform. These attributes dovetail with courtesy.

Courtesy. Maintain disciplined politeness in all of your working relationships. Courtesy will pay dividends for you and the company you protect.

Tact. Be considerate of other people. Guard against words or actions that upset persons you contact in your work. You can be firm, but still tactful.

Curiosity. Develop inquisitiveness. Habitually question things you see, hear or smell which don't seem quite right. Also question anyone you suspect is violating a security rule.

Discretion. Guard your own tongue. Keep privileged information "in the family."

Tolerance. Cultivate the ability to endure abuse and frustration without exploding. Be patient with annoying persons unfamiliar with your responsibilities.

Vigilance. Be alert at all times while you're on duty.

Firearm Safety. Remember, your weapon is only for self-defense. Your gun can kill. Never fire your revolver in line of duty unless it's imperative to save your own life or that of another.

FULFILL YOUR PURPOSE

A student once asked Plato, hoping to trip up the Greek thinker, "What is the purpose of an acorn?"

The philosopher answered without hesitation, "The purpose of an acorn is to become a full-grown oak tree."

The moral to everyone is clear:

Be the best of which you are capable. That's all Mother Nature expects of any living organism.

INDEX

DOD Industrial Security Manual, 7, 124
domino effect (of theft), 104
drug abuse, 152

E

earthquakes, 214-217
economic crime, 102
embezzlement, 99
emergencies (basic duties), 13
emergencies (bomb), 199
emergencies (fire), 91
emergencies (life threatening), 73
emergency control center, 200
emergency transportation, 89
employee relations, 21
employee theft, 99
employee walkout, 148
elevator emergencies, 134
evacuation, 200
expense account cheating, 103
explosions, 212
extinguishers (fire), 96

F

facility layout, 226
facility safety, 131-139, 149
Federal Aviation Act, 244
Federal Aviation Administration, 239-244
Federal Communications Commission, 176
federal regulations, 272
fences, 162
films (training), 19
Financial Industry Security Council, 187
finger sweep (breathing), 77
fingerprints, 184
fire alarms, 93, 174
fire classes, 95
fire extinguishers, 96
fire hazards, 52, 92, 234
fire prevention, 91-98
fire stages, 173
firearms, 59-69, 149
firearm policies (CPP), 61
firearm regulations (state), 60
firefighting, 94
first aid, 71-89
flammable liquids, 195
force, 229

G

gambling, 151
gases (hazardous), 133
general orders, 9
general policies, 7
general procedures, 148
Guest, Edgar A., 3
gun safety, 63

H

habits (good security), 6
hackers (computer), 121
Hallcrest Systems, Inc., 1, 101
hardware (military), 125
hazards (fire), 52, 92
hazards (safety), 36, 54, 132
Heimlich Maneuver, 76
honesty, 17
horseplay, 132
hunches, 34
hurricanes, 213

I

identification, 186
illegal procedures (first aid), 73
image (public), 21
impartiality, 21
incident (defined), 38
incident report, 41
information (protecting), 123-130
injuries (disabling), 137
injuries (disabling by industry), 138
injury (to officer), 8
insecure access, 143
inspections (post), 20
intercoms, 31
inventory shortages (retail), 116

K

key control (office), 106
key stations, 45
keys, 9
kickbacks, 103
kidnapping, 233, 245-246

L

language (foul), 9
life support ABCs, 74
lighting, 166
links (information), 32
liquids (hazardous), 133